I.R. Dujon is a British writer of St Vincent and Irish descent who after many years of therapy, healing and self-reflection have written and documented the devastating true accounts of child abuse she suffered throughout her childhood and adolescent years.

Dujon was born in Hackney, in 1973 to parents, Bernadette McGuire and Joel Nehemiah Adams. Her mother, Bernadette, born into a convent in Dublin Ireland, in her early teens fled to the United Kingdom seeking a better life. Her father, Joel, born in the Caribbean Island of St Vincent migrated to London where he too settled and met Bernadette.

Dujon is one of eight children on her father's side, this biography details her truth, finding her way through a lifetime of exploitation and abuse, and becoming the beacon of hope she is today. The accounts and stories in the book are told from the ages of 6–13 covering the child abuse that she and her siblings were subjected to. It is graphic and hard-hitting, difficult to read but even harder to put down.

All persons mentioned in this book has had their names changed to protect anonymity and confidentiality. With her mother, Bernadette, being deceased and her father, Joel, having a criminal conviction that has been published in the public sphere, these names have not been changed from their original form.

Dujon's mission in life has always been to have children of her own and provide them with the love and security every child deserves. Today she is a proud mother of five and with all of them being adults, her next goal is to share her story and inspire any and everyone who has ever been subject to any form of abuse. Dujon seeks to educate a wider audience of people who may not be familiar with child abuse and creates a detailed picture of how people who are external to an abusive environment can still do so much to prevent or change a situation.

Dujon is proud to release this book with potential sequels in mind to provide education and closure on a series of dark and life-changing events.

To my baby brother Andrew may you Rest in Peace.
22/07/1987 – 21/11/1987

I.R. Dujon

I WILL PROTECT HER

For the protection of oneself is key to
survival after all

AUSTIN MACAULEY PUBLISHERS™

LONDON · CAMBRIDGE · NEW YORK · SHARJAH

A CIP catalogue record for this title is available from the British Library.

ISBN 9781035818488 (Paperback)
ISBN 9781035818495 (Hardback)
ISBN 9781035818518 (ePub e-book)
ISBN 9781035818501 (Audiobook)

www.austinmacauley.com

First Published 2023
Austin Macauley Publishers Ltd®
1 Canada Square
Canary Wharf
London
E14 5AA

20231115

I would like to thank D.C Tony Weed for taking on our case and allowing us to obtain justice, without him, none of this would have been possible. His belief in us gave us a voice. Thank you, Tony.

Thank you, Sheila Burchell (Psychologist) who helped me to unravel some of my most painful memories.

Thank you to all my brothers and sisters, I am so proud of you and I love you all deeply. To my big sister Sammie, what can I say to thank you just doesn't seem enough, for all the times you protected me from dangers I couldn't see, even though you had no one there for you. I pray that I see you again one day. To my big brother Valentine, we all have our demons that we face on a daily basis, you are strong and brave, a true survivor, and I am so proud of you. To Lorrinda, my amazing little sister a true warrior at heart, stay as you are always.

Thank you to my foster parents (Robert and Veronica Etienne) who taught me what real love was, thank you for caring and trying to undo the damage within me, I know it took a lot.

Thanks to Marie Kay, for putting up with my endless telephone calls, when I was at breaking point.

At the time I started to write my story, I was in tremendous pain. As time has gone on, I appreciate that everyone around my father were groomed and made to feel terror by what he was capable of. Unfortunately, abuse can ruin generations within a family. To all my friends who suffered at the hand of my father, I send you love and pray you are all safe and well.

To my children, Jordan, Brandon, Montana, Lawrence and Nevada, never give up on yourself. You are my heart and my world. XXX

Table of Contents

If you could see the child in me, you will see that I am fragile, resilient and agile. To deal with the hurt within, I recoil to heal and tell the child in me that I can deal. As I am strong and no longer alone, walk with me and you will see that you have the strength to set yourself free.

— **I.R. Dujon**

Chapter One:
My Story

Audley House E5
22nd May 1980

"Ingy, Ingy love, wake up." Mum's scent of perfume was overpowering, that was the smell that greeted me in the mornings. Tugging at my blankets she continued to tell me to get up, "Come on, my big brown eyes, it's your seventh birthday today." As I looked up Mum was peering down at me, a big smile on her face, she leaned down and kissed my head, the smell of stale alcohol overpowered her cheap perfume.

"Where's Sam, Mum?" I asked her while looking over at Sam's empty bed. Sam is my eldest sister; she is three years older than me. Mum was searching impatiently through my underwear drawer.

"Where are your knee-length socks I got you?" she questioned me. The bedroom door opened; there was Sam in her towel, her long-wet hair dripping down her back; the length almost touched her bottom. I smiled; it was just like her to be up before me. "Oh Lord, what did you do with your socks, Ingy? Your dad will be here in an hour, you have to be ready!" she shouted, her face was red and flustered. Sam and I looked at each other with huge grins on our faces. Without saying it to each other, I know we felt the same thing, Dad's coming! Dad's coming! Life was great when Dad was around, Mum would be in a good mood until he left again to be with his new wife, whom we both adored. It was difficult for all of us at times. Mum and Dionne were two different people; Mum smoked and drank every day, whereas Dionne did neither. Dionne was one of those ladies you would feel protected by. You would have to do your homework and wouldn't be allowed out after a certain time. But most importantly to us, we would have clean clothes every day and dinner ready when we got home from school.

"Mum, we set our clothes out from last night. Remember you told us to get our things ready when you came home from Kim's house," Sam told her while unwrapping the towel from her head and sounding slightly disappointed.

I never really understood why Sam always had an attitude toward Mum. Maybe it was because when Mum was out on her drink binges, Sam was left with me. "Don't get fucking smart with me, Sammie," Mum snapped back.

"I ain't I was just saying," Sam said back in her defence. My heart filled with dread because I felt so sorry for Sam, Mum always snapped at her. If it weren't her, it would be Val she would be gunning for. Val is our eldest brother; he didn't live with us as he lived in a children's home. We never knew why. He would come and visit us now and again. Mum walked out of the room, slamming the door behind her. We could hear her cursing under her breath, from the other side of the door. We didn't care because Dad was coming; as long as Dad was coming, we were untouchable. Mum had to be on her best behaviour. "Before you put your clothes on, Sam, come let me trim the end of your hair quickly," Mum ordered Sam. "Come on, Sammie, bring the scissors from the kitchen and come sit!" Mum shouted impatiently from her bedroom. Ah, the feeling of a new vest and knickers which Mum got from Marks and Spencer's felt great. I walked into Mum's room to show her how it looked. "Ingrid, why ain't you dressed yet?" Mum asked me whilst snipping away at Sam's hair.

Sam looked up at me and laughed. "What you doing, Inx? You can't stay like that," Sam told me.

"Why not?" I answered whilst jumping around on Mum's bed.

"For fuck sake, Ingrid, I'm trying to cut Sammie's hair. Keep still."

"Ouch! Mum," Sam said. Mum had no patience when doing our hair, she would rip sections apart when it knotted. Forced to keep still, I sat down on Mum's bed and started to play with the clumps of hair Mum cut or ripped out of Sam's head. Without a second thought, I stuck the hair on top of my knickers, so I looked like Mummy. I stood up to have a better look at myself.

"Look, Sammie." Sam looked around and burst out laughing. With that Mum hit her on the head in order for her to keep still.

"Agh Mum, look what she's doing, God!" Sam snapped.

Mum wasn't amused. "That's disgusting, what the hell are you doing, Ingrid?" Lashing out, she struck me with the brush across my leg. "Now go put your bloody clothes on, you dirty girl!" Mum screamed. The sting in my leg lingered for ages.

"We'd better tidy our room, Inx," Sam told me. If there was anything Dad wouldn't let us get away with, it was untidiness. We rushed around grabbing our clothes and toys from the floor and stuffed them in the wardrobe.

"Quick girls, Daddy just pulled up downstairs!" Mum shouted out from the middle room. The middle room was Mum's room. We weren't allowed in the middle room. Everything was green. 'Green for the Irish' Mum would say. "And don't tell him I was out last night," she threatened. "You know what he's like, he'll go berserk." If there was anything you could be sure of, it was that Dad would kill her if he knew that she went out. We could hear his footsteps coming nearer to the door. Sam and I leapt off the sofa and fought our way to the door. As predicted Sam got there first. As she opened the door, his strong cologne 'Old Spice' breezed through; well-groomed he stood there dressed in black and wearing sunglasses. We both threw our arms around him, squeezing tightly. This was Daddy, who everyone knew as Joey. No one messed with our dad. The ladies loved him, children adored him, and men feared him.

"Hello, my princesses," was the first words from his mouth. "Let me look at you, Daddy missed you so much," he said, stepping back and taking a look at us. "Where's your mum?" he asked while taking off his sunglasses and tucking them away in his outer jacket pocket.

"Inside, getting ready," I answered, following him into the flat. Sam looked at me strangely and then put her head down, following us in.

"Getting ready for what?" he asked. "Bernie, what you doing? Going somewhere?" Well, that was it, his tone changed. As he opened her bedroom door, we could see her sitting on her bed putting her finishing touches on her face. "Girls go and sit in the living room, I want to talk to your mum, I won't be long," he told us. Whilst we waited patiently, we could hear them arguing.

"Maybe it's because she's going out, or it could be he knows she was out last night," Sam suggested. I felt scared because I could hear Mum was crying. "Oh, what you getting upset for Inx?" Sam asked. "God, you're always crying."

"It's not my fault, I hope Mummy's okay, do you, Sam?" I asked hoping she felt the same.

"Of course, she's okay, and anyway maybe he should know she went out," Sam responded very firmly.

"Yeah, well what you nagging me for? It's you who fucked off with Dionne that bitch!" Mum yelled. We heard a thud, and then there was silence. I ran across the living room to sit with Sam. Mum was crying.

"You fucking slag!" Dad shouted at her. Slamming her bedroom door behind him, "Come on you two, let's go," he told us. We leapt off the sofa and followed him. There wasn't time to kiss Mum goodbye. Her cries were echoing down the corridor. My heart was pounding, Sam's eyes were streaming, wiping them quickly so that Dad did not see. As Dad unlocked the car, he peered over at us and asked, "Who's going to sit with Daddy?"

"Me," I answered before Sam got a chance.

"Nah let Sam sit with Dad okay, Ingrid, she is older than you, it's safer."

"Yes Dad," I replied. *Why was she always in the front?* I thought to myself. When she's not there I'm allowed to sit in the front. It's not fair. There was a moment of silence when we got in the car. Sam glanced back at me, her eyes were sad, and then cutting her eye at me she turned to face the front. As we pulled away, my thoughts were with Mum. If only Mum would stay home and not go out ever, if only she had no friends to influence her to drink and smoke, if only she dressed like Dionne and was a good woman, I'm sure Dad would stay with us, then we could all be happy together. Dad looked at me in the rear-view mirror.

"You okay, Ingrid?" he asked me.

"Yes Dad," I replied. But I wasn't, Mum is really upset. I hoped Dad hadn't hurt her. Dad reached across and placed his hand on Sam's lap. "Are you alright, Fanny?" he asked her. I couldn't see her face; I just saw her move her leg away towards the door.

"Yes," she said, not looking at him, just staring out the window. Neither of us liked it when he called us 'Fanny'.

Wyllen Close E2

The drive to Dad's didn't take long, as we drove into Wyllen Close, the sound of Jim Reeves was bellowing out of Dad's open front door. This usually meant he had a house full. As Dad parked up the car, Dionne came to meet us at the front door. Immediately, I ran over and gave Dionne a kiss on the cheek. Sam and Dad got our bags out of the boot of the car. "Hello Sam," Dionne said while taking the bags from her hands.

"Hi Dionne," Sam replied with a big smile on her face. As we stepped inside, we could hear many different voices, the smell of stew chicken filled the air, going straight to our room, well the spare room. We put our clothes away, couldn't throw anything under beds here, Dionne kept the house spotless. The smell of mothballs filled every drawer and wardrobe. I could hear Dad's voice very loudly announcing to everyone that we were there and that he had to sort Mum out before we left.

"That woman I tell you, she is one slag. Every fucking night she's out. She just goes and leaves the girls home."

"You know what Bernie's like, Joey, don't know what you bother for, she'll never change," Dionne interrupted.

"Don't fucking tell me, Dionne, just get my dinner so I can finish my game of dominoes with Charlie!" Dad snapped at her.

Poor Mum, yeah she would go out almost every night, but we were okay weren't we? Just wished Dad didn't talk about her the way he did. But that was Dad, and that's how everyone knew him. After a long day of eating heaps, and playing out around the flats, Dionne called us in.

"Ingrid and Sammie, it's eight o'clock, time to come in!" she shouted out across the whole estate. We went into the living room to say goodnight to everyone, Dad's eyes were red, he stank of drink. Him and the guys were shouting and swearing at each other; you wouldn't have thought they were playing a game, slamming their Domino's down on the table.

"Come kiss your dad goodnight, my beautiful girls," he said holding his arms out. "You see my daughters, Charlie, if anyone troubles my girls, I will break their fucking legs," Dad told him.

Charlie just sat there looking at his next hand, glancing up at us he smiled, and said, "Goodnight, Ingrid and Sam." Charlie was a nice man, very quiet; he looked up to my dad, but then all of his friends did. Dionne was at the other side of the living room singing along to the tunes she selected. It was nice to see she was enjoying herself.

"Samanta!" Dad shouted, he always called her Samanta when he had a lot to drink. "You see your dad, I will chop up anyone for you and Ingrid, you hear me?"

"Yes Dad," we both replied.

"Oh Joey, let the girls get to bed," Dionne told him.

"Okay Dionne, listen you two," Dad said just as we were leaving the room.

"Yes, Dad."

"Make sure you don't sleep in your knickers, it's not hygienic. You've been playing all day, and you're all sweaty." God, it was so embarrassing, but he was right, I guess. His face was so serious, I actually felt scared. Even if we wanted to wear them, we wouldn't have dared said no. I had a restless night; it was hot and stuffy and being an asthma sufferer, it was impossible to sleep. I noticed Sam tossing and turning. The sound of loud voices and music coming from the living room didn't help. I heard Dionne say goodnight to the guys ages ago, eventually, I finally started to drift away into the land of nod, when suddenly, I was woken by the sound of our bedroom door opening. The streetlamps outside the window lit the door to our room. A tall silhouette stood at the doorway; it was Dad. He quietly crept in. "Night Dad," I whispered, turning over to get back to sleep.

"Night, my angel," was the last thing I remember him saying. It didn't seem like I had been sleeping long before the sound of sobbing woke me, Sammie was crying. I rubbed my eyes in a desperate attempt to focus to see what was wrong with Sammie. Before I could ask what's wrong, I heard Dad's voice. "Shut up Sammie, don't you love Daddy?"

I heard her muffled voice say, "Yes Dad."

"Good well open your legs then, I wouldn't hurt you, so don't hurt me by pushing me away." I was in shock, still not sure what to make of it. I just lay there, hoping Sammie would not be sad. I pulled my blankets in a desperate attempt for Dad not to see me. "Don't you tell Dionne or anyone else, or I will be really angry with you." That was the last thing I heard him say before he left the room. I didn't say anything to Sam; although I could still hear her crying.

The next morning was bright and sunny. "Wakey-wakey, girls." Dionne was bright and refreshed. "Come on, up you get, your breakfast is ready." *Ah breakfast*, I thought. We didn't have breakfast at home. I jumped up to put my dressing gown on. All these comforts! I didn't give Sam a second look; I left the room and made my way to the living room. Hot porridge and toast. Sammie slowly made her way to the table to join me. I didn't think about last night at all, it was only as Sam sat with me and we made eye contact that it crossed my mind. What did he do to her to make her cry? Just as quickly as I remembered it, I dismissed it and continued with my breakfast.

"What are we doing today, Di?" Sam asked Dionne. Dionne was busy dusting the furniture; she had Randy Crawford playing in the background. The smell of today's dinner was coming from the kitchen, which led on to the living room.

"It's a rainy night in Georgia. I feel that it's raining all over the world," Dionne sang out at the top of her voice. "Eileen, Lorrinda and Tina are coming up today, so as soon as you're finished, you'd better get washed and dressed," she answered Sam. Dionne continued her singing whilst making her way into the kitchen. "Ingrid, come and take this coffee into Dad for me, and Sam you come and take Daddy's breakfast for him!" Dionne shouted from the kitchen. We both got up immediately and made our way to the kitchen.

"Open the door then Ingrid!" Sam snapped at me, as we stood at Dad's bedroom door. With a hot cup of coffee in my hand, I found it difficult to open the door without spilling it.

"Alright!" I snapped back. "You've only got a plate," I continued.

"Oh move out the way I'll do it." Sam nudged me aside.

"Pig," I mumbled under my breath, hoping she didn't hear me. Dad was already awake, sitting up in bed.

"Ah look what my angels have brought their daddy," he said with a huge smile on his face. As soon as I placed the cup on the side table, I jumped on the bed to give him a kiss and cuddle. "Where's my kiss then, Sammie?" Dad asked Sam. Sam sat reserved at the end of his bed. "What don't you want to kiss your dad anymore?" his face was serious.

"Of course, I do." Sam leant forward and kissed him reluctantly.

"That's my girl, now go and get yourselves ready," he ordered.

Chapter Two:
The Fountain

"Dionne! Lorrinda and Eileen are here!" I shouted into our front door which was always left open. Sam slammed her scooter down and ran towards Eileen's car. Eileen was another so-called stepmother; she was the mum of my sister Lorrinda who is one year younger than I am, that makes her six years old. Sam got on very well with Eileen, we both did. She was the fighter out of all my dad's women. We saw her as a woman of strength. We cherished all visits from Lorrinda, for reasons unknown to us; Lorrinda lived with her nan, in Harrow. She was known as 'Little Nanny'. Eileen parked up with a pleasant smile on her face; we could vaguely see Lorrinda's head pop up through the window at the back of the car. Sam and I waited patiently for the car to come to a stop. Lorrinda stepped out, well-groomed. Her hair was in two pigtails, with ribbons tied at the end of them. She had a long knee-length Mac on and knee-length socks. Lorrinda was always dressed nicely. Unlike us, we would sometimes have to get our clothes out of the dirty wash basket, to wear again and again because Mum couldn't be bothered to wash them. Excitedly, we rushed Lorrinda in to say hi to Dad. We were very keen to get her outside with us to play.

"Hello, Fanny," Dad said to Lorrinda. "Did you miss your dad?" he asked.

"Oi Joey!" Eileen snapped. "Don't call her fanny." Lorrinda sat on his lap; we could tell she was in no hurry to leave him to play. Dionne remained in the kitchen and briefly popped her head out the door to say hello to everyone. It was clear that Dionne did not like Eileen; I think maybe she was scared of her. Sam and I waited patiently at the front room door for Lorrinda to join us.

"Come on, Inx, let's go and play," Sam suggested. Eventually, Lorrinda came out, we asked her if she wanted to come to Bethnal Green Park, and she said yes. We spent hours playing on the swings, chasing each other in a game of tag. Then we came up with a plan to keep Lorrinda from going home that day, we desperately wanted her to stay with us. Lorrinda had a sense of purity about her that we somehow found comforting. On the route home, there is a fountain that sits outside the local shops, we decided to push Lorrinda in so that her mum has no option but to let her stay because she had no clothes.

We laughed all the way back to Dad's. Poor Lorrinda was dripping wet but it was all for a good cause; if it meant we got to spend more time together then it was well worth it. As we approached Dad's door, we could hear loud music and raised voices. Reluctantly we stepped inside. Dionne was passing the hallway and spotted us first. "What on earth have you done?" she shouted at us. Taking Lorrinda by the hand and leading her into the living room.

"For fuck sake, Lorrinda," Eileen said slamming her glass on the table, Dad wasn't really interested. He sat in his chair with his eyes closed, listening to his music.

"Well, we were on our way home and I fell in the fountain," Lorrinda explained.

"I bet this was you're doing, wasn't it, Sam?" Dionne asked her. Don't know why Sam got the blame.

"No it wasn't my idea, we just wanted Lorrinda to stay." Sam had tears in her eyes.

"Yeah, well she can't stay, you lot should know better!" Dionne shouted. It was obvious that it was Eileen that Dionne did not want to stay, as she sometimes would. Lorrinda staying over meant Eileen would leave later.

"Joey! Joey wake up, look at what the girls have done!" Eileen nudged him to get his attention. Dad sat up when he realised what had happened, he laughed. What a relief, for a moment I thought we would be in serious trouble.

"Ah let Lorrinda stay," he told Eileen, still laughing. Without much thought, Eileen agreed. Dionne walked out into the kitchen and started banging dishes around. We knew she was angry, but we didn't care. Lorrinda was staying and we were happy. We sat and spoke for hours that night; well, it seemed like hours, until we fell asleep.

Sunday morning, I heard the front door slam. It could only have been Dionne. She went ritualistically to the Sunday market in Brick Lane. "Wake up Sam, wake up Lorrinda," I whispered. Lorrinda started to stir.

"What?" she asked me, yawning as she spoke.

"Dionne has gone out, come on, let's go watch telly," I suggested. I picked up my pillow and signalled to Lorrinda that I wanted to hit Sam with it because she wouldn't wake. Quietly we laughed; I swung the pillow through the air and hit Sam on her head. I've never run so fast as I did at that moment. I left Lorrinda standing by Sam and made a quick getaway into the living room. Lorrinda wasn't far behind. She jumped on the sofa next to me where we sat huddled up waiting for Sam to chase us.

"Oi you two, what you doing?" she screamed from the bedroom. At the sound of the bedroom door slamming, I buried my face in the pillow. She was coming to get us.

"Ingrid and Lorrinda what are you doing?" it was Daddy, not Sam.

"Sorry Dad," we both said.

"We forgot you were here," I told him. Sam appeared behind him.

"Dad, I was sleeping, and they hit me with a pillow," Sam complained. Sure, that we were going to get smacked.

Dad said, "Why don't you lot come sit in my room, and we'll watch TV?" he surprisingly suggested.

"Yeah!" Lorrinda and I shouted. Throwing my cushion aside I jumped up and followed Dad into the bedroom. Lorrinda grabbed her stash of sweets and brought them into the room with us. All three of us lay huddled up on Dad's bed watching TV. Dionne would never let us doss like this. The minute your eyes were open you had to get washed and dressed immediately, that's why being with Dad was so cool.

"Ingrid, what did I tell you about sleeping with knickers on?" Dad asked me. He brushed his hand over my pyjama bottoms feeling for the outline of my knickers, I put my head down feeling slightly embarrassed. "Didn't I tell you it was only dirty women who sleep in their underwear?" he continued. I couldn't look at him. How could I forget to take my knickers off? "Look at me when I speak to you." My eyes welled up with water, I could feel Sam and Lorrinda looking at me as though I was dirty.

"Shall I go and take them off now, Dad?" I asked. Desperately hoping that would make it okay.

"Yes, go on, and hurry up," he said. As I went to leave the room to change in the bathroom, he said, "Where are you going, I'm your dad change here." Feeling very embarrassed I did what he asked. While removing my bottoms, Dad in turn felt Sammie's bottom and asked Lorrinda if they had their knickers on too. All of us did, which was a relief for me; I wasn't the only dirty one. One by one we removed our bottoms. "Now take your tops off," he demanded. We stood there feeling very silly; we looked at each other and laughed at the sight of each other's bodies.

"Dad, I don't want to be like this, can I put my clothes back on now?" Sam asked.

"No, you can't, Samanta, now come and sit by me, all of you," Dad said. *What was going on?* I thought. Lorrinda looked at me curiously, I felt dreadfully uncomfortable. Dad had not asked this of us before, and Dionne will be home soon. God, I didn't want Dionne to see me like this. Dad picked up Lorrinda's sherbet that was on the side table next to the bed, holding it in one hand he undone his dressing gown with the other. He was completely naked; I couldn't look at him. Sam began to cry and Lorrinda just looked at me, Dad's willy looked huge. He poured the sherbet over his nipples and told Lorrinda and I to lick it off.

"Daddy, please don't," Sam said.

"Shut up and do as you're fucking told," he warned her. My heart was racing.

"Why do you want us to lick it off, Daddy?" Lorrinda asked him.

"Just do it." Pushing Lorrinda's head down towards his chest. This was not the Dad that I knew, maybe all Dads did this. I know he loves us. Yeah, that's it, we're doing this because we love him, and he loves us. Dad was stroking his willy up and down. Err, I thought. Sam continued to cry.

"Kiss it, Ingrid," Dad told me. I didn't want to, Dad's voice was changing, he sounded more desperate and angrier. "Go on, just think of it as a snake," he said. I kept waiting for the door to open. Where was Dionne now? I needed her to come home. Lorrinda stopped licking Dad's nipples and watched me. "Open your mouth," he ordered me in a soft tone. I was gagging and Dad was making strange noises. It wasn't long before white stuff came out of his Willy. I jumped. "It's okay," he said to all of us. "You have just shown me how much you love me," he said. "But it has to be our secret, Dionne won't want you to love me like this she will get jealous," he said. "And if Dionne gets jealous you won't have a Dad anymore, they will take me away from you," he continued.

"Who will, Dad?" Lorrinda asked.

"The police," he replied. We didn't question him; we didn't want anyone to take him away. From this day forward, I was never able to look Dad in the eye, without feeling strange. I had a dark secret that no one must know. I loved my dad, we all did. No one was going to take him away from us.

"Joey, Bernie is on the phone," Dionne shouted from the living room. Dad looked as though he couldn't be bothered to talk to her.

"Ingrid, tell your mum I will call her back," Dad told me.

"Hello, Mummy." I clutched the phone tightly to my ear trying hard to hear over the loud gunfire from the TV, which was deafening, westerns were Dad's favourite.

"Ingy love, it's Mum," she said, her soft Irish accent was comforting. Mum sounded pleased to hear my voice.

"Hi Mum," I replied.

"How is Sammie?" she continued.

"Fine, are you coming to get us, Mum?" I asked her hoping she would say no. We had plans to go and make a camp after dinner; Eileen will probably come and get Lorrinda soon too. The sound of the TV was too much, I couldn't hear a word Mum said, her money had run out, I could hear beeping noises then silence. "Dad, the phone has gone silent, Mum isn't there anymore." I turned to him to see what he would say, but he said nothing.

Yorkshire puddings, roast potatoes, roast chicken, carrots, and peas smothered with gravy. Mmm. Dad wasn't amused; he wanted West Indian. We didn't complain, this was a luxury compared to what we had at home. Well apart from the vegetables. I never liked vegetables.

"I've finished, Dionne, can I get a drink please?" Sam asked her, tucking her chair neatly back under the table.

"Yes Sam, make sure you wash your plate up," Dionne told her. Lorrinda and I looked at each other's plates to see who would finish first. Lorrinda was far ahead of me, not surprising though she liked vegetables. "You'd better make sure you eat all your veg, Ingrid, because you ain't leaving the table unless you do," Dionne threatened. Everyone had now finished and I was left behind; I could hear Lorrinda and Sam playing outside. Dad had fallen asleep in his chair; Dionne was straightening up the house and getting our belongings together ready for when our mums came to take us. "For fuck sake, Ingrid, you have been there for two bloody hours and you still aren't finished," Dionne said. I could see the disappointment on her face, I truly wanted to eat it, but I couldn't. I felt sick. There was a loud knock at the door and Dad woke up immediately.

"Dionne. Dionne!" he shouted.

"What Joey?" she snapped back.

"Woman can't you hear the door?" he shouted, whilst fixing his dressing gown. Dad often wore his dressing gown on top of his trousers when he was home. Dionne opened the door, it was Eileen. I knew it; we weren't going to get to play at all. Dad looked over at me still sitting at the table; my eyes welled up straight away. He leant over and pulled the slipper from his foot, throwing his slipper with force, hitting me in the head. "Backside, Ingrid, you still there eating!" he shouted. Dad was angry with me. My heart was racing, I began to cry. With food still in my mouth, I tried not to choke. "What you bloody crying for? Eat your food. You have ten minutes to finish or you'll see the wrong side of me, you hear?" Dad wasn't joking and I knew it. I quickly tried to fix myself before Eileen entered the room, wiping my eyes with my sleeve and swallowing my mouthful of food.

"Hello Ingrid," Eileen said. Eileen was always well-dressed and very pretty. She hadn't noticed I had been crying. She went straight over to Dad and sat on his lap. Dionne wasn't amused; she left the room and went to the kitchen to put the kettle on. Dad started laughing; Eileen started to wiggle on him. "How you been, you miserable git!" Eileen asked him.

"Eileen, do you mind, you are squashing my wotsits?" he said, they both began to laugh. Dionne brought Eileen her tea then sat down in the armchair. Eileen glanced around the room then stopped on me.

"You all right, Ingrid?" she asked, while taking a sip from her tea.

"Ingrid," Dad said, then kissing his teeth he continued "Dionne cooked her food, and she's still there. All she wants to do is go and play," he interrupted before I could speak. I put my head down and started crying again. I didn't want to cry, it just kept coming out. The more I cried the more I dribbled, and the more I wound Dad up.

"Joey, you know Ingrid don't like vegetables, don't know how you can give the kids that rubbish anyway, Di," Eileen told Dionne in my defence. Eileen always spoke her mind; I didn't dare look up. Eileen got up from Dad's lap and came over to me. She took the fork from my hand and ate some of the carrots with gravy. "It ain't even got seasoning in it, Ingrid, go and play," she told me. Whilst taking me by the hand to get me out of my seat.

"No," I said, looking at Dad. Waiting for him to snap.

"What you looking at him for, Dionne doesn't mind do you, Di?" Eileen wasn't really asking her – she was telling her.

"Why should I mind? I just cook for fucking nothing in this house?" she said sarcastically. I stood there waiting for Dad's approval.

"Go on," he said. I couldn't believe it! I only wished Eileen had come sooner. As I picked up my plate, I was desperate to ask Dionne for a drink, but I didn't dare to. She was angry. I wasn't sure if it was me, she was angry with or if it was Eileen who went straight back to sit on Dad's lap. We didn't have long to play, maybe an hour at most, and then Eileen came outside to us and told Lorrinda to get her things as they were leaving. Lorrinda came out with her bag and walked to her mum's car. Eileen explained to us that she had to go now because she was going out and that Lorrinda's nanny was waiting for her in Harrow.

As we watched Lorrinda waving goodbye, Sam said, "It will probably be ages now before we see her again." I knew Sam felt as sad as I did; we only had to look at each other to know how we felt, without saying a word.

Audley House E5

We reached back home to No.5 Audley House. Dad knocked on the door, there was no answer. Sam and I were laughing about the weekend's events and the fun we had with Lorrinda.

Dad knocked again, no answer. "Sammie, do you know where Mum would be now?" he asked.

"Umm, she'll probably be at Phyllis's," Sam suggested. Dad looked at his watch, and then kissed his teeth.

"Come on you two." We ran down the stairs to keep up with him. He was fuming; he put his sunglasses on and got in the car. Phyllis only lived a few blocks away from us. She was an old lady with a disabled daughter. Phyllis also drank a lot. She was a kind woman. It was Sam and me who met her first, whenever we used to go to the shops, Phyllis would see us from her window. She told Mum that she used to see these two beautiful brown girls, well-dressed with ringlets in their hair, walking or playing outside. One day, she asked us to go to the shop for her; she explained that she couldn't leave her daughter alone. So it went from there, we would often go to the shop for Phyllis. Then Mum eventually befriended her, and now Mum is there most nights. Phyllis looked as though she was about 50 years old to me. She would sit there all day with her legs crossed, swinging the top leg constantly, whilst twisting and pulling her hair with one hand and dragging it across her mouth. Dad was driving fast, he pulled up abruptly. "Wait there," he told us. He slammed the door behind him. Sam and I looked at each other.

"God, do you think Mummy's drunk Inx?" Sam asked me.

"Hope she ain't," I replied. I was worried for Mum again. We sat there silently, hoping to hear something. We could hear Dad laughing. It didn't make sense. Maybe he wasn't angry. Shortly after the door opened out came Mum and Dad. Dad led the way. Now I was really confused, his face was furious. Mum followed behind him. She spotted us in the back and smiled. She looked pretty. She must have had new clothes on. I hadn't seen her in that blue knee-length pencil skirt and black top. Although she smiled, she looked worried. It was then I knew things weren't alright. Mum only asked us once in the car if we were okay, then there was silence all the way home. Those few minutes' drive felt like forever.

Sam and I went straight to our room and sat on our beds. Mum went into the green room with Dad. Mum screamed, "No Joey, don't beat me." Sam and I began to scream. There was nothing we could do but sit there. Mum continued to scream and Dad continued to shout.

"You fucking slag, you're just a fucking whore!" he shouted. As I looked over at Sam, I noticed water running down her leg and into her socks. She had wet herself again. I noticed on a few occasions that Sam would wet herself when there were fights. The banging I heard wasn't furniture, it was more like thuds. Mum would beg him to stop but he never did. Finally, silence. Silence was good because it meant he had stopped. But then it was bad because we didn't know what state Mum was in. We could hear Mum's door open; we jumped off our beds and peered through the crack of our door. It was Mum. She was walking towards the bathroom. I was overwhelmed with fear, pain and sadness. The emotions were unreal to me. Mum's back was covered with blood, I wiped my eyes to clear my vision, was I seeing right? Mum's back looked like it had been torn open, I let out a gasp. It was the strangest noise. Mum couldn't walk properly; Sam began to scream really loud.

"Mummy!" she shouted. We were out of control, both of us screaming. I couldn't breathe. I was having an asthma attack. She didn't look back; she kept walking. Dad came out of the room and straight into ours. We were standing behind the door.

"Ingrid and Sam," he said in a calm voice. Taking us by the hand, he sat us on our bed. "Shush," he said.

Sam was pointing to the door. "I want Mummy, what have you done, Dad?" she asked him frantically.

Dad was holding me on his lap, trying to calm my breathing. "Mummy's okay," he said. "I had to hit Mum because of you two. She's always out and it's not right. What if something happened to you? I have to make sure Mummy puts you two first. She's out there every night with bad people, what about you two?" he explained. Dad was trying to keep us safe, I guess. He wanted Mum to love us like he did. Sam heard movement behind the door; she leapt to the door and opened it. Sam screamed as the door flung open. It was Mum. Or was it? It didn't look like her, she was unrecognisable. We both began to cry uncontrollably again. Mum's eyes were purple and bulging, her eyebrow cut and bleeding. Her lip on one side was hanging. How did he do this? His hands couldn't have, she looked like she had been hit by a bus.

Mum started to cry. "It's okay," she mumbled to us. She couldn't speak properly. She tried to kneel down to comfort us but she couldn't.

Dad held her and said, "Tell them, Bernie, it's because I love you all that I done this." Mum couldn't speak, she just nodded in agreement. Dad assured us that it was over, and that he had to make up with Mum now. He told us to get into bed. Sam didn't say that she had wet herself and I didn't tell. Still sobbing we climbed into bed reluctantly. We wanted to be with Mum. Mum left the room and went to her bedroom. Dad followed, leaving both the doors open. Our door was directly opposite Mums. A few moments later I could hear noises.

"Sam, do you think he's hurting her again?" I asked.

"No Ingrid, they're having sex, you know what Daddy does to us," she answered.

"Oh," I said and turned over to sleep.

Chapter Three:
Home Alone

It took weeks before Mum's face went back to normal, Mum was soon back at work. She had a packing job in a football factory, packing scarves and ornaments for different teams. She would always bring us back something. Sam was waiting for me by the school gates, Southwold primary school. Her eyes were red as though she had been crying. She took me by the hand and led me out the gates. "You fucking half-breed!" a voice shouted. Sammie started to walk faster, pulling me to keep up. Occasionally, Sam looked over her shoulder.

"What's wrong, Sam?" I asked her.

"Them girls again," she replied. What had they done now? We made our exit through the flats. As soon as we were out of sight, Sam told me to run. It wasn't until we got home that I realised what they had done to her. Sam was stabbed in the face with a pencil and chewing gum put in her hair.

"Why did they do this to you, Sam?" She opened up the kitchen drawer and took out the scissors. "Don't cut it, Sam, Mum will go mad," I told her.

"How else will I get it out," she replied. Holding the scissors in one hand and hair in the other, she began to cut. Sam's hair was very long, falling in loose curls. She could sit on her own hair it was that long. I stood and watched her snip away the chewing gum. Her cheek looked very sore, where they had stabbed her with a pencil. We often had bad names shouted at us; half-breed, half-cast, and caramac. Even Mum would get called names at times. Girls would call her a black man's whore when we would go to the shops. Sometimes she even got stones thrown at her. As Sam cut away the last bits of gum, she explained to me that the black girls picked on her more because she was slightly lighter than me. My hair was of tighter texture than hers. The black and white girls would ask me what I was. It was obvious that Sam was mixed race, and not as obvious for me as I looked blacker.

Strangely enough, there was one girl who was worse than all of them and her name was also Ingrid. On a regular basis, she would start on me, Sam and Mum, whatever chance she got. Eventually, she backed off. Mum told Dad what Ingrid would do when we went to the shops. Dad was angry. He took us both with him and he knocked on Ingrid's door. Her dad opened it.

My dad told him what she was doing to us. She was called to the door where we stood, I couldn't believe it! Dad slapped her across the face really hard. She fell to the floor. Her dad didn't do anything, He just picked her up and told my dad it wouldn't happen again.

Some hours went by, Mum wasn't home yet. My stomach was rumbling. "I'm hungry," I told Sam.

Sam was sitting on Mum's bed with her dolls. Putting them down she said, "so am I." And she wandered off to the kitchen. I followed her. There was a pot already on the cooker, Sam lifted the lid. "Err," she said, placing the lid back quickly. It was soup, that Mum had cooked a few days ago the soup had now fermented. Sam opened the big cupboard, there wasn't much choice; bags of half-full rice, potatoes with legs, and seasonings, along with half a loaf of bread, which was blue. And heaps of plastic bags and laundry bags on the floor. Sam shut the cupboard. "What are we gonna eat?" she said out loud. I just stood there.

"We can't eat the soup, it smells funny," I replied.

"Let's go and play, Mum will be back soon." Darkness soon came, Mum's room felt cold. Neither of us knew how to use the heaters. My stomach was cramping and I felt sick. Sam and I went back to the kitchen, in the hope there would be something there to eat that we didn't see before. After searching the cupboards again, and found nothing, Sam looked at the pot on the cooker. "We'll have to eat some, Inx," she told me. "Maybe when it's warm it won't taste as bad," she said unconvincingly. Sam took the matches from the sideboard and lit the cooker. We waited patiently until it started to bubble. I took my seat at the table and waited. "There you go, Inx," Sam said, placing my bowl of soup in front of me. Sam was right, it didn't taste as bad as I expected, although it definitely did not taste the same as when Mum first made it. The evening dragged on. We had no idea as to what time it was, because neither of us could tell the time. Outside was pitch black, and the flat got really cold. Every so often we could hear footsteps outside the door; we would listen excitedly for Mum's key to go in the door. The footsteps we could hear grew fainter.

"When's Mum coming back?" I asked Sam. I needed Mum. As it got later, I got more scared; the flat was too quiet.

"Come let's go in Mum's bed, until she comes home, Inx," Sam suggested. Brilliant idea, Mum's bed was the biggest, warmest, and the safest. Eager to get warm, we curled up in Mum's bed. Sam fell asleep first. I lay there watching the bedroom door. I couldn't help watching the silhouette behind Mum's bedroom door. I'm sure it was Mum's clothes, but tonight it looked like a person. I squeezed my eyes tight then opened them, in the hope it would change. It still resembled a person.

"Sam," I said, nudging her.

"What Inx? Go back to sleep," she moaned.

"I'm scared, Sam," I replied, pulling the duvet over my face, and moving closer to her.

"Oh move over Inx and go to sleep, you're being silly." My heart was pounding; I couldn't help thinking it was going to move any moment.

"Inx, wake up." Sam was nudging me. I couldn't see Mum but I could hear her voice, she sounded giggly. "Get up, Ingrid," Sam demanded. Sam took my hand and led me around the bed towards the door. Before leaving the room, I looked back. Mum was home, but she wasn't alone. It definitely wasn't Daddy. His voice was strange. I couldn't see any more, Sam pulled me into our room.

The next morning, we got up before Mum. I opened Mum's door curiously to see who was with her. It was a white man with ginger hair. The room smelt of stale alcohol. This guy had a huge belly; it was bulging from under the duvet. His moustache was thick; it curled up at each end. I left the room quickly to tell Sam. "Sam, come and see this man, he's got a massive moustache."

"No, I don't want to see him," Sam replied.

"Oh, go on, you've got to see it Sam it curls up at each end." My persuasion didn't work. Sam wouldn't move.

"Anyway, Inx you'd better wake Mum 'cause there's nothing there to eat," Sam told me. Slowly and quietly, I pushed open Mum's door and crept to her side of the bed. The ginger man started to move; quickly I knelt down beside Mum's head.

"Mum, Mum, wake up," I whispered in her ear. The ginger man was awake and he was staring at me. I shook Mum as hard as I could.

"What!" she shouted. "Ah, my Ingy! Come to Mummy!" She reached out to me to take her hand, but I didn't want to.

"Bernie," the ginger man said with a strange accent. Mum sat up quickly as though she didn't realise someone else was there. "Is this your daughter, Bernie?" he asked Mum. He began to stroke his moustache in an outward direction, then curling it at the end.

"Yes this is my Ingy, my big brown eyes," Mum replied. She grabbed my hand and pulled me to the bed. Uneasily I sat down next to her. "Ingy love, this is Smudge, my friend," she introduced him.

"Smudge," I repeated and laughed. "Is your name really Smudge?" I asked him.

"Yes, I am a friend of your mum's."

Mum pulled me close and kissed my cheek, she didn't smell nice. It was kind of stale and her hands smelt frowsy. It wasn't the smell that I was used to with Mum. I had to pull away. "Mum, we're hungry, there's nothing there to eat," I told her.

"Where's Sammie, that cheeky girl," Mum asked with a smile on her face. Smudge lit up a cigarette and reached for his trousers. The smoke was choking me. It was even worse when Mum lit one too.

"Sam's in the living room, Mum," I replied, getting ready to make my exit.

"What's your lass's name, Bernie?" Smudge asked Mum, while pulling out a handful of pound notes.

"This is Ingrid, my baby, and the other one is Sammie. She's the cheeky one," Mum answered dotting out her fag in a beer can next to the bed.

"Why don't you and your sister go and get what you want from the shops?" Smudge said reaching out to me with a wad of notes in his hand. I looked at Mum before grabbing it. She didn't say no so I took it.

"Sam, Sam, look what Smudge gave us! We can go shops and get what we want," Sam took the money and began to count it.

"What did you say his name was? Smooch?" Sam burst out laughing.

"No, I said Smudge." We couldn't help but laugh.

"Come on, Inx, let's go," Sam said. We didn't even get dressed, we put our coats on top of our pyjamas. No one would see us at this time of the morning.

"Sam, can I get a Mars Bar?" I asked. My mouth began to water just by the name Mars Bar!

"Is that all you can think about, Inx, chocolate, chocolate, chocolate. You're so greedy!" Sam snapped. My eyes began to water. I desperately wanted a Mars.

"Mum would let me get one if she was here," I told her. I began to drag my feet; I wanted to go home.

"Yeah, that's because you're spoiled," Sam let go of my hand and began to walk in front. My eyes welled up with tears; it was as though my life depended on it. *Wait till I tell Mum*, I thought to myself.

"And I ain't spoilt!" I yelled at Sam.

"Yes, you are, Mummy gives you everything. You put on the waterworks, and Mum gets it. What do me and Val ever get?" Sam shouted back. I couldn't understand why Sam felt that way, but then I didn't quite know what spoilt meant. By the time we reached home, I was hoping Mum would be up so I could tell on Sam. But there was no movement in the flat. I could hear moaning noises coming from Mum's room.

"I'm telling on you!" I made a dash for Mum's room. Sam had caught up with me and grabbed me by my collar.

"Don't go in there," she whispered.

"Why not? I want to see Mummy," I demanded. Sam shoved me into the living room.

"You're so stupid, Mum won't want you in there she's probably getting dressed." I sat on the sofa sulking. I hated her. Just because I wanted to tell Mum what she did, she didn't want me to go in. Sam left me alone for a moment and went to the kitchen. This was my chance! I made a dash to Mum's room but the door was locked.

"Who is it?" Mum shouted.

"Me Mum, it's Ingrid," I said as quietly as I could before Sam came back.

"You can't come in yet babes, I'll see you in a minute!" Mum shouted back. Why couldn't she see me now? If I leave it, I won't get to tell her. Quietly I snuck into my bedroom and grabbed a chair. The adrenalin of getting caught by Sam gave me extra strength; I placed the chair down in front of Mum's door and climbed on it. I wasn't tall enough to see through the window above the door. Tiptoeing, I was just about able to see Mum to get her attention. I saw her alright; I nearly fell off the chair. Smudge's bum was in the air, his body was pale white. I couldn't see Mum. To my horror, I jumped off the chair and ran to Sam in the kitchen.

"Sammie! Sammie! Smudge is on top of Mummy." My heart was racing.

"How do you know? What have you done, Inx?" Sam grabbed me by the hand and pulled me into the hallway. "Oh Inx," she said, shaking her head. I looked up at her face and she was laughing. I didn't know what to think. I too began to laugh. Sam did the unexpected. I thought she was going to move the chair, but instead, she climbed on it. Sam peered through the window. There was a moment's silence, then Sam burst out laughing as she jumped down. "Err that's nasty," she said running into the living room. Mum must have heard.

"For fuck sake!" she shouted from the bedroom. She overheard what Sam had said. I ran to Sam in the living room, Mum's bedroom door flung open, there was Mum in a towel. "You fucking bitch!" she yelled at Sam, slapping her around the head. Sam kept her head tucked into her lap covering her face with her hands.

"It was Ingrid who done it first!" Sam shouted, her voice was muffled and buried in her lap.

"Don't blame Ingrid she's younger than you, you're fucking disgusting," Mum continued to slap Sam with each word.

"Mum. Mum, it was me," I said hoping she would stop. I felt dreadful; it was only a laugh. Sam was sent to her room for most of the day, which also meant Sam wasn't talking to me.

"I'll see you later then, Bernie, at Phyllis's," I heard Smudge tell Mum. This means she won't be here again tonight.

"Yes, babes," Mum told him. Her voice was really softly spoken. It didn't seem like her. She always put on a voice when she was talking to a man friend. Mum shut the door behind him; I heard her stomping down the corridor. Our bedroom door swung open. "You two have got no fucking manners!" she was so furious spit came from her mouth as she yelled. I wanted to say sorry, but I thought if I speak now, I would make things worse. "Get yourselves dressed, your bloody brother will be here soon. Another one to give me fucking stress," she said slamming the door behind her. There's three years between all three of us. Val was 13 years old, Sam 10 and I, of course, 7. Mum never hid how she felt about Val, she always moaned about the pain she went through giving birth to him. She said the labour lasted a whole week, and that he weighed 11 pounds at birth. None of this made sense to me; she would then go on to complain about the nuns in Ireland who delivered him. I would feel sad when she would tell us how they used to beat her, and that she never knew her parents. She never said why she put him into care when he was five years old. Mum always spoke about it when she drank.

"Ingrid, come quick Val's here." Sam was standing on her bed looking out onto the fields, which were behind our house. Val spotted us from the window; he was waving with excitement. We were jumping and waving back. Val was wearing jeans, a navy-blue V-neck jumper with a white t-shirt underneath. The excitement was too much; we rushed out the front door, completely forgetting about Mum. We left the front door wide open as we made our way down the stairs.

"Hi Inx, hi Sam," he said with a huge smile on his face.

"Hi Val!" we shouted.

"Where's Mummy?" he asked. "Has she got any black eyes yet?" I bit my bottom lip, didn't know what to say. Sam laughed. Don't know why they found it funny. It wasn't funny, that was just Val's sense of humour. He always said what people thought but never had the guts to say. "Has she brought any men home yet?" He asked. We all laughed. Val was brilliant. We never laughed with anyone like we laughed with Val. Sam tried to fill him in before we got upstairs to Mum. She told him what I had done and that she got the blame for it. "That's not surprising is it, Inx, it's not your fault." He smiled. "Mum needs someone to blame." Mum and Val had a strange relationship, Val loved her desperately, but I don't think Mum loved him the same as us. That we all knew, but we loved him heaps. "I've only got until eight o'clock with you, so we'll have to make the most of it," he told us just before we stepped indoors. Already we had to watch the clock when he had just arrived.

"Hello Mum," Val said to Mum as he placed his sports bag on the floor. Mum was standing next to the sideboard in the kitchen smoking.

"Alright Valley," Mum replied, that was the only greeting he got from Mum. There was a moment's silence. "Why don't you lot go and play and make the most of your day?" Mum suggested. Turning her back facing the sink, as if she was washing up.

"Can we have money for some chips, Mum?" Sam asked her. Mum quickly went to her bag hanging on the door and gave us 30 pence each.

"If I'm not here when you get back, I might be at Phyllis's, and Val make sure you leave at eight o'clock," Mum told him. Val's face dropped to the floor, he looked sad. I think it was because he wanted to spend some time with her.

"Come on let's go over the marshes," Sam suggested.

"Yeah, we can go to that factory," I said.

"What factory?" Val asked us.

"Oh, there's a factory that makes plastic bags, and they have huge containers with tiny bits of plastic in them. Me and Ingrid jump in them—" Sam explained.

"Yeah, it's wicked fun, Val," I interrupted. We walked over the bridge that crossed the River Lea. I left Sam and Val talking behind me and raced on in front. The ground beneath me felt squishy, my feet started to sink. I would have sunk if I stood still for too long. The amount of mud fights we had here and late walks down the river. We would occupy ourselves for hours when we were locked out of Mum's. Finally, the factory was in my view. "There it is, Val!" I shouted, still yards ahead of them. I sighted one of the factory workers and stopped in my tracks. I crouched down behind some boxes out of his sight, waving to Sam and Val to crouch down too. We hid for a moment until it was clear then we made a dash for it. We were in. Crouching down, we crawled around on our knees in the hope of not being seen. The smell of plastic was pungent. Giant canisters were filled to the top with shreds of plastic. It was all clear; Val gave me a push-up into one of the containers. It felt lovely. I wiggled around until I was almost buried in it. Sam crawled into one next to me. I could just see her head peeping over the top. "Val! Val! Get in then," I whispered. Val had other ideas.

"I'll be back in the minute, Inx," he said heading off in a different direction. I was scared we were gonna get caught.

"Sam, where's Val going?" I asked her, peering over the top of my container.

"Oh no, he's going to the forklift," she said covering her mouth in shock. We scrambled out of the containers. Taking most of the plastic with us. I couldn't believe it, Val actually got in and started it. The fear of getting caught was too much.

"Sammie! Tell him to stop, we're gonna get into trouble." It was pointless, Sam was laughing.

"Oh, shut up, Inx, it's fun," she snapped. Val didn't have a clue; he was driving recklessly back and forth, crashing into the stacked bags.

"Oi you, what you doing?" an angry voice shouted. A tall white man with a cigarette hanging from his mouth dressed in an overall and boots came dashing towards us. My heart was in my mouth, I was shitting myself.

"Sammie, Ingrid, run!" Val screamed. Val was way ahead and Sam wasn't far behind him. I was miles away. My chest felt tight and my breathing was heavy. My legs just weren't going fast enough. My asthma had crippled me. I had to stop; I could still hear the man's footsteps behind me.

"Sammie!" I screamed. I couldn't say anymore, my hands on my knees and breathing frantically I broke down crying. I could just about see Sam and Val in the distance, but they didn't turn back.

"Oi you, what do you think you're playing at?" The man was not amused. He grabbed me by the arm and held me tight. Still, I couldn't speak. "I should call the police," he threatened.

"Pl…Pl…Please don't. I didn't want to do it, they made me." This was the only thing I could think of to save myself from getting arrested.

The man still kept hold of me and said, "Who are they?"

Pointing to Sam and Val in the distance. "That's my brother and sister," I replied.

"That's bloody nice isn't it running off and leaving you like that," he said, his grip got looser. It was clear I wasn't going anywhere. I was wheezing. "Are you alright?" he asked me with a concerned look on his face.

"You leave my sister alone!" Val yelled from the distance.

"Ingrid, come on!" Sam screamed at me. What did she want me to do just run away? And make things worse. I couldn't even if I tried. I just wanted them to come and get me.

"Your bloody brother's a coward leaving you like this, go on get out of here and don't let me see you lot here again," he said, letting go of my arm. For some reason, I cried even more. I think it was the fear that I could hardly breathe, mixed with anger that they had left me all alone.

"What did he say, Inx?" Val asked.

"He said that if we come back again he will call the police," I told him.

"It's always you who gets caught," Sam said, walking off in front.

"It's not my fault, Sam, I couldn't breathe," I replied, still crying.

"Oh, don't tell me, it's your asthma again." Sam was mocking me; she often did when I had an attack. She would exaggerate my breathing loudly and make faces. Sam and Val left me walking behind; they were laughing and giggling about Val driving the forklift. I desperately needed my pump. I wanted Mum.

"Let's go and get some chips," Sam suggested.

"I don't want to go, I want Mummy," I told them.

"You're a spoilsport, Inx, Mummy's not even home, she's at Phyllis's. We ain't going there yet. Anyway, she's probably drunk," Sam replied, looking at Val for backup.

Again I started to cry even more. "I don't care I don't want to be with you two I want Mummy." They had no idea how badly I needed my pump.

"Let her go then, we'll drop her then go and get our own chips, Sam," Val said. I felt as though they hated me. I often felt invisible around them two. If I ever suggested anything I would be ignored; if either one of them suggested something it would be brilliant. "We're not coming in. Inx, you go in, tell Mum we've gone to the shop," Val said, leaving me at the door. I could hear loud voices and music coming from inside. It sounded as though Phyllis had a house full. I watched Sam and Val walk off up the street before knocking.

"Just a minute," a familiar voice said through the door. It was Kim. Kim was a Scottish, skinny looking white woman with quite a large head. She was supposed to be Mum's best friend, but as soon as they had drinks, they would fight. Sam didn't like her at all, she said Kim was spiteful but Kim was nice to me. Always fussed over me. She would say I reminded her of her daughter she left in Scotland. "Hello, darling." Kim stepped out and gave me a big squeeze. She stunk of cigarettes.

"Hello Kim," I replied. I was distracted by Mum's voice coming from the room.

"When the Irish eyes are smiling." Mum was definitely drunk. She always sang when she drank.

"Come in, darling, Mummy's in Phyllis's room." I walked through the dark dingy hallway, as I entered the bedroom Phyllis was sitting on her bed with a room full of people. Twisting her hair and then dragging it across her mouth. She had always done this but no one knew why, I was certain she was swallowing her hair. Next to her was her boyfriend, Jonnie, Jonnie was a fat white man with large warts on his face. He spent most of his time doing long-distance lorry driving. When he was home it was a bit like 'Willy Wonka and the Chocolate Factory'. They never left the bed. Mum was sitting in an armchair behind the bedroom door.

"Oh Ingy, my baby." Mum reached out for me. As soon as she took my hand she began to cry. *What?* I thought I had done something to her. I didn't want to get too close because Smudge was sitting at her feet. Mum pulled me onto her lap and started kissing my cheeks. Her mouth was wet, her tears were rolling down my face.

"Mum stop," I asked her. Her breath smelt like a brewery.

"You're my baby, Ingrid, I love you." With those words, she started to cry uncontrollably. Now I wished I had gone with Sam and Val.

"Bernie, don't start, you'll upset Ingrid," Kim told Mum. Big mistake. Mum switched.

"Don't fucking tell me what to do, Kim, she's, my baby. Oh God, I love you so much, Ingy. I didn't know my mum," Mum said. She was crying like a baby, I felt so sorry for her.

"Oh, we're all fucking fed up of hearing it, Bernie. Come, Ingrid, come sit with me," Kim interrupted loudly. No way! I didn't like Kim for saying that to Mum; now Mum was crying even more.

"Yeah, you're just fucking jealous, Kim, because I've got my Ingy, where's your daughter? You fucked off and left her." Mum's body was trembling with rage. She was literally foaming at the mouth with fury.

"Mum, please don't cry," I asked her, cuddling her, hoping she would stop.

"Wasn't your wee lass with her brother?" Smudge asked Mum. The room went silent. Mum picked up her can of Tenants beer and took a large swing.

"Ingrid, where's Sam? I didn't think to ask you when I opened the door," Kim said.

"I wanted to come and meet Mum, because I needed my pump. It's okay I told them to go on without me," I replied, I could sense where this was going. I didn't want Sam or Val to get into trouble. "They will be back in a minute, they've just gone for chips," I continued. Mum slammed her tin down and pushed me off her lap.

"You see that fucking big head, Val, it's his fault. Nah they should have come with you!" Why was she taking it out on him? Kim didn't help the matter, she was agreeing with all that Mum said. "That dunce, wait till he gets back," Mum went on and on.

"Bernie, Bernie, the important thing is Ingrid is okay. I'm sure they'll be back in a minute," Phyllis said, still chewing her hair. I dared not ask Mum for my pump now; she will never leave it alone if I told her I needed it. They would get the blame for that too. Mum continued to drink more and more. The number of times I had to take a fag out of her hand and dab it out because she had fell asleep, nearly burning the chair. It was uncountable. Dribble poured from her mouth; her legs sprawled apart. Kim would sit there telling Smudge what a good girl I was and that I weren't like Sam or Val. I started to dislike myself. I was sick of it. It got darker and darker, and Sam and Val still weren't back. By this point, Mum had partially sobered up a little and was ready for round two. Smudge had already gone to get a bottle of Bell's Whisky. It was way past Val's home time; the ten o'clock news had been and gone. I couldn't tell the time so that was the only way I knew how late it was without asking one of them and risking starting them off again. My chest was bad the smoke was killing me. I left the bedroom and sat in Phyllis' unused living room. It was cold and unlived in. The fake brown leatherette sofa was cracked, with green crochet cushions. I laid down trying my hardest to stay awake for when Sam and Val came back. My sleep was disturbed by Val's voice. It was like a wailing. Was I dreaming? No, it was real. There were screams coming from outside the living room. I jumped up, tripping over the coffee table as I scrambled through the dark room. Everyone was in the hallway. Val was curled up in the corner by the front door with his hands protecting his face. Mum was beating him. I couldn't take anymore. What had happened? Why didn't I hear them when they came in? Maybe I could have warned them. Kim had Sam by the hair pulling her into the bedroom.

"No Kim, leave my sister! Mum tell her!" I yelled. Mum couldn't hear me. She was punching Val, continuously.

"Mum stop!" Val was screaming.

"You ugly big head, you're a fucka, Val, get out and don't come back." Mum opened the door and demanded he left. Val looked at me straight in the eye. I was torn. I didn't want him to go. My heart was breaking. How would he get home? No one cared. Mum slammed the door behind him. He was screaming, kicking at the door.

"Mum please," were his last words. Mum pushed me into the room where Kim had Sammie. I hated Kim now. I wished I was bigger so I could stop her. I was hoping Mum would tell her off, but she didn't. Sam cried for at least half an hour, neither of us knew how Val was, or if he had got home okay. That night Mum made Sam take me home and put me to bed; it was at least a thirty-minute walk and gone midnight. Dad never would have allowed this; he would have kept us safe. I wish we were with him right now.

"Ingrid, wake up." Sam was shaking me. "For God's sake wake up, Inx."

"What?" Still half asleep, rubbing my eyes I could see Sam sitting at the bottom of my bed and her face was worried. I sat up immediately. "What is it, Sam?" I asked her with concern in my voice.

"Mummy's not in her bed, that means she couldn't have come home last night." Sam put her head down. I could see the tears falling onto her lap. Still not awake properly I couldn't understand why she was so upset.

"Maybe she did come home," I said naively.

"Don't be silly, Inx, she hasn't slept in her bed. What if something has happened to her?" Sam kept sobbing. I had Sam to look after me so it wasn't that important if Mum came home.

I thought selfishly to myself. Sam stood up and left the room. "You just don't get it, Inx." She slammed the door behind her. I was too tired to go after her. I just laid there reflecting on last night's events. Then it dawned on me, what about Val? Eventually, I got up and went to the green room. Sam was curled up in Mum's green Ida down.

"Can I have something to eat, Sam?" My belly was rumbling.

"See what I mean it's alright for you, Inx, but who looks after me?" she snapped so quickly I jumped. There was silence for a moment. I stood there thinking about what Sam said.

"Shall I make you a coffee?" I asked her.

Sam began to laugh. "You! You can't make coffee." At least she was laughing.

"Yes I can, I'll show you." I took a pot from the kitchen cupboard, and tipped the jar of coffee into it, with some water. Striking a match, I lit the cooker. The cooker was too high and the coffee started to burn. "Ingrid, what are you doing?" Sam could smell the smoke. I stood back, and just watched it. Sam came charging in and turned it off. "What you doing you idiot, I told you, you couldn't make coffee. You don't cook it, you have to boil the kettle, you twit." This was the start of many days and nights Mum didn't come home. She practically lived at Phyllis's. "We still have to go to school, Ingrid, come on we'll see if Mum's at Phyllis's on the way." Searching through the dirty laundry basket, I pulled out a pair of socks I had worn from last week, as I pulled them out, I noticed they were in a permanent shape, dried damp from the wet towels moulded them into a ball. There weren't any other clean socks so I had to wear them.

"I hope Kim isn't still there," I said to Sam. It was freezing outside. I could tell Sammie was worried about knocking. I felt her hold my hand tighter as we reached the front door. Sam knocked at least three times there was no answer.

"Come on, Inx, let's go. We'll try again after school," suggested Sam. The walk-up Southwold Road seemed endless. I wanted to be with Sam always, I often wished I could be in her class just for a day. "See you, Inx, wait for me here when you finish school."

"Okay Sam," I replied. Today was a long dark dreary day. The images and sounds from last night made it hard for me to concentrate. I felt exhausted, putting my head on the table and pretending to write was the only way to get through the morning. It wasn't until after lunch I kind of came to life. I knew home time wasn't far off. Routinely our last lesson would be spent in the library watching Look, Listen and Read. Wordy was my favourite character. For a moment, I would lose myself in the magical world of space men, and knights whilst drinking our daily miniature bottle of silver top milk.

Chapter Four:
He's in the Closet

As we reached the top of Southwold Road, Sam spotted Dad's car turning into our flats. "Ingrid, it's Daddy! Daddy's here," Sam shouted, pointing down the street. I just managed to see the tail of his green Jaguar pulling into the flats. "Come on let's run," Sam suggested. I couldn't wait to see him, I wanted to tell him what Mum and Kim had done last night. *Maybe he already knows, that's why he's here*, I thought. Dad will sort it out; he always does. Outside the front door, Sam and I stood there for a moment in the hope to hear what was going on inside. It was quiet; the only sound was from the people walking past our flats. I knocked on the door; I could hear Mum laughing as she walked towards the front door. The door opened and there was Mum; hair well done, wearing a white three-quarter length sleeve top, and a pale green knee-length skirt. Her shoulder-length curly hair was immaculate. Mum never looked like this after a night of heavy drinking. I was baffled. "Ingy, Sammie," Mum had a massive smile on her face. She took us both by the hand and pulled us towards her. "Joey, your angels are back!" she hollered down the corridor.

"Is that my girls?" Dad replied. I was overjoyed. I pulled away from Mum's grasp and ran to the living room.

"Daddy!" I ran into his arms; Sammie wasn't far behind. We didn't give him time to stand up; he just sat forward and cuddled us.

"Ah Bernie, look at how big and beautiful my girls are." Dad took us both by the hand while standing to his feet he twirled us around. Mum stood at the door looking proud, her arms folded and smiling. "How was your day at school?" he asked Sam.

"Fine," Sam replied.

"No problems then?" he asked her again.

"No Dad, it was fine," Sam answered. I had forgotten all I wanted to tell him.

"Are you staying for a bit, Dad?" I asked. Still holding on to his arm, I inhaled his scent, Old Spice. Dad was once again well groomed.

Still standing he replied, "Of course I am, my princess." Mum walked over to take his jacket. Dad was wearing a black polar neck with black trousers and black shoes. His face was flawless, clean shaven and he stood tall. No wonder no one messed with my dad.

Bet he could beat up the world if he had to, I often wondered. I glanced around the living room, then realised it was spotless. I followed Mum into the kitchen and noticed that too was spotless. The pot I had burnt coffee in was clean. The wooden sideboard was clear of clutter. The greasy worktops were greaseless. Wow, Mum had worked hard today. "Sammie love, come to Mum for a minute," Mum called from the kitchen. Mum took the lid of a pot on the cooker and began to stir.

"What is it, Mum?" I asked, my mouth began to water. I was hungry, and whatever it was it smelt good.

"It's chicken curry love," she replied. What was with all the niceness, I definitely wasn't going to ask in case she switched. Sam appeared at the kitchen door, "Yes Mum?" she asked.

"Listen, love, I don't want you two to tell Dad what happened last night. You know what will happen. We will fight and he'll go back to Dionne, then God knows when you'll see him again," Mum told us. There was silence for a few seconds.

"Yes Mum, but where were you last night? We were scared this morning," Sam asked her.

"Shut up," Mum whispered, "we'll talk later."

"Mum, can I have my dinner if it's ready?" Taking my seat at the table.

"Yes babes," Mum replied. Sam sat down with me. The dinner was nice, I can't remember the last time we had West Indian. Mum left us to eat and joined Dad in the living room.

"Listen to her laughing, what's happened to her?" Sam asked me. Mum's laughter grew louder and louder. I didn't care what was up with her; I was so pleased they were getting on.

"Maybe they're gonna get back together," I suggested to Sam.

"Don't be silly. He wouldn't leave Dionne for Mummy, Inx," Sam told me.

"I think Dad still loves Mummy. Don't you?" I asked her.

Placing her plate on the side, she replied, "I don't know and don't care, it's better Dad's with Dionne. At least we get to stay away from here every now and again." Sam left the kitchen. I could still hear Mum laughing in the front room; curiosity got the better of me. What was so funny? I took one more spoonful of rice and went to see what was going on. Mum was sitting on Dad's lap; they both looked around at me looking in from the living room door. It wasn't like Dad was tickling her or anything, so I went back to finish my food. With my belly full I was now ready to go and watch TV. "Mum, can I put the TV on?" I asked her.

"Of course, love," she replied, still laughing. It started to annoy me. I took my place on the floor and began tuning the TV in search of my favourite programmes. Sam came and joined me on the floor.

"Oh, what's so funny, Mum?" Sam asked, sounding just as fed up as I was. Mum didn't answer. She just turned and looked at Dad. As if she wanted him to tell.

"Nothing, Samanta, I'm just playing with Mum," Dad answered.

"Yeah, but you've been playing for ages," I said. "Ah Worzel Gummidge!" I shouted. I was excited, my favourite. I took my place in the armchair. I tried my hardest to block out the laughter but couldn't.

"What's that in your hand Dad?" Sam asked curiously. I looked around to see.

"What?" Dad said. "I ain't got anything," he continued. Sam stood up and sat at Mum's feet. I saw something red, Dad obviously wanted me to see it because he opened and shut his hand quickly. He did have something, maybe it was for me. "You see how smart our girls are, Bernie." He looked at Mum with a smile on his face.

"Oh, I want to play." I got up and joined Sam on the floor. Dad was holding Mum tightly around her waist. I tried my hardest to pry his hand open. It was no use.

"Okay I give up," Dad said. Surrendering to our constant nagging. Sam and I sat up eagerly, waiting to see what was so interesting. Dad opened his hand. The excitement turned to disappointment.

"What is it?" I asked.

"It's a sausage," Sam answered. We looked at each other with a blank expression.

"It's a toy sausage key ring," Dad explained. *What was so funny about that,* I thought. I've just missed Worzel Gummidge for a sausage. The expression on Mum's face was strange. She looked like a kid who's been caught with sweets, that she shouldn't have.

"Lift up, Bernie," Dad told her. Dad's hand disappeared under Mum's bottom.

"Come on, Inx," Sam told me.

"Where you going?" Dad asked. The laughter stopped; the atmosphere changed. I felt uncomfortable. Dad's face was serious.

"Nowhere, Dad, we're just gonna watch TV," Sam replied, taking our places back in the armchairs. I wasn't sure what was going on, but I knew I no longer wanted to play.

"Come on you two, time for bed," Mum called from the next room. Already? I'd just set up my Sindy Dolls.

"Oh, Mum, can't we have just a little bit longer?" I called back. The bedroom door opened. It was Mum. She stood at the door in her green satin nightie.

"No. Come on, bed." Mum wasn't amused. We didn't normally go to bed at this time. In fact, we didn't have a bedtime at all. Dad appeared behind her.

"Ah look at our angels, Bernie," he said.

"Night Dad, night Mum," I said, pulling my covers over me. I was hoping they wouldn't spot the Sindy doll I was hiding underneath. Mum came over and kissed us on the head, then left the room. "Do you think we'll get bitten tonight, Sam?" I asked her. Scratching my belly at the thought of it.

"Why do you ask such silly questions, Inx? We get bit every night," Sam replied.

"Yeah, but I think that when Dad stays, we don't get bit. They don't come out for some reason," I continued.

"Maybe it's because he always smells nice," Sam explained to me. "Now go to sleep." Throughout the night I tossed and turned, I was literally tearing at my skin. I began to cry.

"Sam? Sam, wake up," I called. Sam wouldn't wake. I was scared of the dark, but I needed to put on the light. I counted to ten then attempted to make a dash for the light switch. My body wouldn't move. Counted to ten again and this time I made it. I opened the bedroom door and called for Mum.

"Oh, for fuck sake, what is it, Ingrid?" Mum shouted, pulling her door open violently.

"Mum, something hurts my arm, it's sore," I told her. Mum grabbed me by the arm and pulled me into the bathroom.

"Shut up, Ingrid. I don't want your dad to hear," she yelled in my face. "Now lift up your arms and let me take your top off. Jesus," Mum said as she pulled my top over my head. As I looked down and raised my arm to see what it was that hurt so badly, there it was. A huge flat-looking bug was squashed under my arm, in my blood. I cried. I started jumping around frantically; I just wanted it off my skin. "Don't you tell your dad about this Ingrid," she whispered. Her face was serious.

"But what is it, Mum? Maybe Dad can get rid of them?" I asked.

"No, it's only a little bug, you're okay," she told me.

"But Mum I think this is what bites us every night," I suggested. Mum wasn't having it. She wiped me down and sent me back to bed. It was worse now that I had seen them; my imagination was telling me that they were all over my bed. I waited until I thought Mum had gone to sleep, to put the light on and I left it on all night. By the time we woke Dad had already left. "Mum, can you wake up?" I asked her. The room was dark and smelt stale.

"What is it, Ingrid?" She asked, rolling over, squinting her eyes as she tried to focus on me. "What time is it anyway?" she continued.

"I don't know," I replied, confused by her question, Mum knew I still couldn't tell the time.

"Where's Sammie?" Mum asked, dragging herself out of bed.

"In the bedroom," I answered, watching Mum putting her bra on, with her back to me.

"We are going to your dad's today. Go and see if there's any letters, I'm waiting for my Giro," she told me. "Sammie come!" she shouted, I handed her the letters and sat down next to her on the bed. Sam came in and sat at the end of the bed. Mum handed Sam the letters, she opened them one by one.

"Here's one from Val's social worker," Sam read.

"Hurry up then. What's he done now?" she asked impatiently. Mum often got impatient when Sam read, Sam said it was because Mum couldn't read or write. That the nuns who brought her up in Ireland didn't teach her to read, just how to clean and would beat her when she did something wrong. Sam continued to read, "It's a date set for us to go and see Val next week with his social worker, because their planning on moving him to a borstal called Ditton Place, in Surrey," Sam explained.

"Fucking dunce," she snapped, lighting up a fag. Mum reached over and snatched the letter out of Sam's hand, and placed it in her top drawer next to the bed. "See if my Giro is there," she told Sam.

Sam went through the letters. "I think this is it," Sam said holding up a brown envelope. "Can we go and see him, Mum, before he leaves?" Sam asked, whilst tearing open the envelope.

"Mmm, we will see," she replied. Paying more attention to what was in the envelope. She smiled, "Lovely, right go and get dressed, we're going to Wriggly Market," she told us. She took the Giro off Sam and left the room.

"I hope we get to see him, Inx," Sam said to me. Her face was sad.

"Me too, I wonder what it will be like there," I responded.

"Bet it's better than here," Sam said, leaving the room. I followed Sam into our room and looked at my reflection in the mirror.

"I hate my hair," I said, pulling at my pig tales.

"Why? Because you've got hair like Brillo Pad?" Sam laughed.

"Why is my hair tighter than yours?" Mine was shoulder length but much tighter in texture.

"I don't know, we've got the same Mum and Dad, maybe you're meant to have a picky head," Sam said laughing even more.

"Shut up, Sam!" I told her, feeling hurt by what she said.

"No, you shut up, stupid," Sam snapped.

"Why should I, pig?" I yelled back. Sam flew across the room and punched me in the back. I cried instantly, after a few seconds there was no sound coming out, I couldn't breathe, I felt as though I was being suffocated. Sam stood there mimicking me and laughing. I was having an asthma attack. Thank god Mum came into the room.

"What you done, Sammie?" Mum screamed. She grabbed Sam by the hair and slapped her in the face. "You wicked girl!" Sam began to cry. Mum took me in her arms and calmed me down. "Do you want her to go back to the hospital, Sammie?" Mum asked her.

"No," Sam replied, still holding her face. My hospital trips were frequent. "Spoilt brat," Sam whispered as Mum left the room. I didn't say anything. "Mum would never hit you like that, it's always me and Val," Sam said.

We spent most of the day following Mum around the market, being knocked around and squashed amongst the herds of people. When Mum had finished, she suggested we go into the Kings Head Pub. Just for a quick one, she would say.

Sam and I still weren't speaking to each other. I felt bad, as though it was my fault she got hit. *Maybe I am horrible Val would say the same thing,* I thought. The pub was full of smoke, and ladies drunkenly trying to dance. All of them knew Mum. The men all knew her too. "Go sit over there." Mum signalled to us to sit at a table in the corner. Mum walked over to a tall black man standing at the bar. He was well dressed; he wore a long cashmere coat and a matching hat with a feather on one side. As she walked over, he put out his arms, she walked straight into them. He squeezed her bottom and kissed her on the cheek.

"Here we go, we will be here all night now," that was the first thing Sam had said to me since we left home. I was pleased we were friends again. The man whispered into Mum's ear, she pointed in our direction. As he looked over, he smiled and walked over to us.

"Hello girls, I'm your mum's friend, my name is Sparky." He put his hand out for a handshake, I reached over the table and shook his hand. Sam looked at him for a moment then reluctantly shook his hand. "Can I get you a drink and some crisps?" he asked.

"Yes please," we answered. He walked away and joined Mum back at the bar. Mum picked up her drink and our crisps and walked over to us.

"Mum are we gonna be here long?" I asked her.

"No, I'm just gonna have a few then I'll take you to your dad's." It seemed like we were there for ages. Mum brought all her friends over.

"Bernie, your daughters are beautiful!" They would say, stroking our heads and kissing our cheeks. Mum was getting drunk. Sparky leant over and nudged Mum to follow him. Mum got up and followed him to the far side of the pub where they stood there talking, glancing over at us every so often. Mum staggered back over and said, "Come on girls, Sparky is gonna take us home." Taking the final swing from her glass, slamming it down on the table.

"But Mum, we're meant to be going to Dionne's," Sam said.

"Fuck Dionne. That bitch, she ruined my life that goodie-goodie. We're going home." Mum pulled Sam up by the arm.

"Come on, Inx," Sam told me. I got up and followed. Sparky stood holding the pub door open for us, dangling his keys in one hand. We followed him to a green car parked around the back streets. It was silent in the car most of the way. The tears rolled down my face, trying my hardest to not let out a sound. Thank God I was sitting behind Mum so she couldn't see me. I glanced over at Sam; she was sad but not crying. I looked across at Sparky. I noticed on the side of his face he had a scar from the corner of his eye down to his chin. I poked Sam on her hand and gestured to her what I had seen. Not realising Sparky saw me in the rear-view mirror.

"Is there something wrong little lady?" he asked me.

"No," I replied looking out the window.

"If you're wondering how I got this scar, I will tell you. I got it from a man many years ago that thought he would take my woman from me, but he came out far worse," he explained. Sam and I just looked at each other. We pulled into the drive of our flats, Sam and I got out.

Mum looked at Sparky and said, "I will be a minute."

Sparky opened his window and said, "Just cool, girls. I will bring your mum home soon." Sam gave him a dirty look and took me by the hand leading me upstairs. We stood by the front door waiting for Mum to come and open it.

"What did he mean, Mum?" Sam asked her.

"I'm just popping out for a while, make sure you be quiet in here," Mum told us.

"But—" Sam interrupted.

"But nothing, Sammie. I'm gonna lock the door, just behave yourselves." I didn't get to say bye. Mum slammed the door shut and locked it from the outside. The sound of her footsteps grew faint as she walked away.

"See I'm left with you again," Sam said.

"Where's Mummy gone?" I asked her.

"Where do you think? Off to get drunk again," she said. Once inside, we made ourselves a jam sandwich and set up our Sindy dolls. Eventually, we fell asleep. I woke to hear the sound of banging and tapping on the window. I sat up to see Sam sitting on the edge of her bed listening.

"What is it, Sam?" I asked her. I was scared; I could hear my heart pounding.

"I don't know, Inx," she whispered. Sam got up and sat next to me. "How can someone be outside the window, we're on the second floor?" she asked me. Then we heard a familiar voice.

"Samanta!" the voice shouted. Sam got up and went to the window.

"It's Daddy Inx," she told me happily. Sam opened the window; Dad had been throwing stones at the window to wake us.

"Where's Mummy?" he shouted up.

"Not here, Dad," Sam told him.

"Open the door," Dad requested.

"I can't, Dad, Mum's locked the door," Sam told him.

"What?" he shouted. Dad was mad.

"Ingrid, come see what Daddy's doing!" Sam told me. I looked down to see Dad was climbing up the drainpipe. He climbed over onto the balcony. I don't know if I was scared or excited. Dad knew the balcony door would be open; Mum often forgot to lock it, normally when she had finished sunbathing. Dad gave us a hug, and asked us how long she had been gone, and who she was with. We told him.

"Okay listen, when your Mum comes I want you to stay in bed, I'm gonna hide in your wardrobe for her," he told us.

"Why Daddy?" Sam asked.

I started to cry, "Are you gonna hit Mummy, Dad?" I asked him. Watching him take off his thick yellow leather belt and placing it around his neck. Dad calmed us and told us it was for us. He was going to teach Mum and Sparky a lesson, if he was stupid enough to come home with her. There was no way I could get back to sleep. Every time I wanted to speak; Dad would tell me to shut up. He wanted to hear exactly when Mum got home. He sat down on the floor outside the wardrobe. He was still, and quiet. His eyes were red. *Poor Mummy,* I thought. Suddenly, Dad jumped up and scrambled into the wardrobe, we could hear footsteps outside on the landing. Sam began to cry.

"Shut up, Sammie, please. For me," Dad told her, trying to stay calm. I could hear Mum laughing outside the door. As she opened the door, I could hear sounds as though Sparky was kissing her. She said goodbye to him and shut the door. Mum did not come to our room she went to the toilet. I was waiting for Dad to burst out of the wardrobe at any moment. My door opened.

"Ingy, Sammie, are you awake?" she whispered. As I looked up Mum smiled. Dad flew out of the wardrobe and Mum screamed. Dad took his belt and lashed Mum across the face with the buckle. Her face opened up instantly. Sam was huddled up in the corner of her bed screaming. The sounds were unforgettable. She screamed and pleaded for him to stop, she begged for her life. With each blow and kick, he called her names. His face was in a rage; he didn't look like Daddy. I shut my eyes, opening them every so often. I looked for Sam in the commotion, she was jumping around frantically on her bed, screaming. She looked like a wild animal trapped in a corner with nowhere to go. Spurts of blood were around the room and on my covers. I shut my eyes again. Eventually, there was silence. I wanted to open my eyes but couldn't.

"You see what you made me do, Bernie!" Dad shouted. Sam let out a loud scream. I opened my eyes, Mum wasn't awake. She lay there huddled up in a heap covered in blood against the dresser drawer.

"Daddy, Daddy, is Mummy dead? What you done?" Sam screamed. I was speechless.

"Shut up, Sammie, you want the neighbours to call the police?" he shouted at her. I wanted to go to Mum but was too scared. Sam made the first move; she jumped off her bed and pulled at Mum's hand.

"Mummy? Mummy, wake up!" she cried. Dad sat there; he didn't look afraid at all. It seemed like ages until eventually, Mum flinched. Blood poured out of her mouth and onto the carpet. "What did you do to Mummy, Dad?" Sam screamed again. She must have not been thinking; she turned to Dad and began slapping him uncontrollably. Dad grabbed her hands tightly.

"Stop it, Samanta," he said.

"Sammie, Ingy," Mum moaned from the floor. I could not move. Dad pushed Sam onto my bed, and then knelt down by Mum's side. He started to cry. He picked up her head and put it in his arms, he was sobbing.

"Why Bernie? Why did you make me do this?" he asked her. Mum couldn't speak. Mum never got to go to the hospital. Dad didn't go home; he stayed with Mum, because he loved her. Sam and I slept the rest of the night together. Mum didn't leave the house for a few weeks. Once Dad left, we didn't see him again for a long time. Even whilst Mum was healing, she still sat awake at night crying for Daddy. I think if she was physically able to, she would have gone out to look for him. Mum would send us with a note to go to the off-licence and get her a bottle of Old English medium wine, every night. When the off-licence was sold out of her favourite wine, we would get a bottle of Bells Whisky. Mum would say that she needed it and that Dad had broken her heart. Mum was drinking every night, sometimes we would be sent to get her drink after 10 pm. Everything just felt hopeless. Mum couldn't stop crying for Dad and would keep us up telling us her life stories. How she came to England from Ireland at the age of 17. She said she ran away because the nuns would beat her. And stories of Val's dad; how he was a handsome soldier who was in Ireland serving from America. He was a tall, fair-skinned, Afro-Caribbean man, and very kind. His name was Valentine. She said she had lost touch with him when he returned back to the States. Mum spoke very fondly of him, often saying she wished she had gone with him. It wasn't until sometime after Val's birth, that Mum somehow reached out to Val's dad to tell him.

"When you told Val's dad that you had his baby, what happened, Mum?" Sam asked. Mum sat slumped against the headboard on her bed, clutching to her half-filled glass of wine. Mum looked like she was in a daze, just staring out of the bedroom window.

"Well, he came back," Mum replied vaguely.

"What do you mean, Mum?" Sam continued.

"He came back to meet me because we had to travel together to collect Val from the convent, 'cos Val was born in Ireland," Mum explained. Wow, I did not know this. Sam and I looked at each other in disbelief. Mum seemed keen to get it off her chest, she continued to explain. "The nuns wouldn't let me take him when I wanted to leave, but I had to go. I couldn't take anymore. It was Val's dad who contacted them to make the arrangements." Mum looked as though she was starting to feel uncomfortable.

"So then what, Mum?" Sam continued to dig for information.

"We had to pretend that we were going to get married, that was the only way I would have got him back." Mum started to wiggle and change position in the bed, she didn't like the questioning.

"That's enough now, Sammie, you don't need to know anymore. All men are bastards, just remember that." So many thoughts went through my mind, so we never would have known Val if his dad had taken him. The thought saddened me.

"So, when you got him, Mum, didn't his dad want him?" Sam kept pressing for information. Mum took a large gulp of wine followed by lighting another cigarette.

"Yes, he did want him, he wanted to take him back with him to America, but I told him no."

"Why would you say no Mum, he could have been with his dad!" Sam snapped back. I could see Mum was getting wound up.

"He probably had another woman and wanted to take Val to her. Anyway, he's naughty that's why he's not with us," Mum snapped. I knew she didn't want to talk anymore.

"Yeah, but you keep saying Val's naughty but what has he actually done, Mum?" Sam asked back in Val's defence. Mum slammed her glass down and began to raise her voice. "He's a lazy fucker. Anyway, your dad wasn't any better, Sammie."

The atmosphere began to change. Sam stood up and said, "What do you mean my dad, you mean our dad, Mum."

Mum sat up straight, looking Sammie in the eye and said, "No! Joey isn't your real dad. George is." Mum had a strange grin on her face a look of satisfaction. For the first time, I think Sam was lost for words.

"Mum, what do you mean?" I asked.

Mum didn't want to talk anymore. "Now get out both of you." Sam ran to the living room. I could hear her sobbing, I followed and sat next to her. Not knowing what to say, I sat quietly with my head down, maybe Mum was joking? After a few minutes, Mum came to the living room to join us. Holding a shoebox in one hand and her wine in the other, Mum sat on the floor in front of us and began to look through a bunch of photos we'd never seen before. There was silence as Sam watched her. "This is your real dad, Sammie," Mum said, holding up a black and white photo. Sam reached out and took the photo; I huddled up closer to see the person standing in this black and white photograph. Sam stared at it; it was an old photo but you could clearly see the image of the man displayed on the front.

"Oh my God, Mum is this my dad?" Sam asked, looking at Mum in disbelief.

"Yes Sammie, he's a Jamaican coolie man," Mum responded.

"Where is he, Mum?" Sam asked, looking desperate.

"I think he went back to Jamaica. As far as I know, when I had you, he wanted to take us both back to Jamaica, but the black landlady who we lived with was jealous and told him that we weren't there…but we were there. She lied to him. So, he left me a letter," Mum explained. Sam just cried. I felt lost for a moment, I wouldn't have had Sammie either if he had taken her, the thought made me cry.

"So, I might have other brothers and sisters," Sammie stated. I didn't like what I was hearing, a feeling of jealousy came over me, *I hope she hasn't got other brothers and sisters*, I thought. I was left with a feeling of loss, even though Sammie was sitting right next to me. Mum finally had enough. She got up and left the room, leaving Sammie clutching at her dad's photo. Mum slammed her door shut. Sammie looked at me helplessly. "I want my Dad, Inx," she said, and then broke down in tears. "I could have a whole other family out there, Inx. I do love you but I might have had a better life with him," Sam said sounding muffled, wiping away her tears. "This is why Mum is nice to you, Inx, 'cos your Dad is still around," she continued. Her words made no sense to me, why would she love me more? I just couldn't understand. As the days went on, I felt as though Sammie was slipping away, we didn't feel as close. Whenever Sam would argue with Mum she would always shout out, "I wish my dad would come and get me." This made Mum furious and resulted in Sammie getting beaten.

"Right you two, up you get up," Mum told us from our bedroom door.

"Why Mum? It's Saturday," I asked loudly as Mum disappeared from the door.

"Valley's social worker told me yesterday that we can see Val one more time before he goes to that place," Mum announced from another room. Sam and I looked at each other with huge smiles on our faces.

"Yes!" Sammie said in response. "Why didn't she tell us this yesterday, Inx? I bloody hate her," Sammie said, cutting her eye at me as she spoke.

"I can't wait to see him, Sam! What we gonna do?" I asked.

"I don't know, but I can't wait to tell Val all of what's happened, and that I've got my own Dad like him!" she answered. There it was again, that feeling of loss. It was like they were in a special club, which I wasn't a part of. My mood dipped; I couldn't help but feel left out. "Quick let's tidy up a bit," Sammie instructed. Grabbing as much of the left-out clothes as I could, I opened up the wardrobe and threw them inside. It didn't take long I had mastered how to hide things. Suddenly, without warning, I heard the front door slam. "I bet she's gone out again," Sam predicted. "Let me see," she said, running to the front door. "Mum, where you going? I thought you said Val's coming?" Sam shouted out. I ran to the door and spotted Sam leaning over the balcony, running over I looked down to see Mum walking away.

Mum didn't look back, she just shouted, "I'll see you later."

"She's such a fucking bitch, I can't stand her, Inx," Sam said as we walked back through the flat. Finally, the front door knocked loudly; it seemed like we were waiting for hours for Val. We both jumped up and rushed to the door. There Valley was, he had a big smile on his face, his dimples deep in his cheeks.

"Hi Val!" we both said in sync.

"Hiya!" Val replied as he stepped inside. Stepping aside, we allowed Val to walk ahead, and we followed him into the kitchen. "Where's Mummy?" he asked.

"I don't know, but she said she wouldn't be long," Sam told him. "So Val, you're going away," Sammie said while pulling out one of the dining chairs to sit on.

"Yes, it's really nice! My social worker took me there a little while ago," Val replied. I took my seat at the table to join in on the conversation.

"I don't want you to go, Val," I interrupted.

"Neither do I, Val. We're gonna be left here with her," Sam said abruptly.

Val gazed at us for a moment. "I know Sam, but it's got to be better than this," Val said, he broke his gaze and stared at the floor.

"Will we get to see you?" Sam continued to question.

"Of course, you will, my social worker said she will give Mummy travel money so you can all visit."

"Maybe we can stay with you," I mentioned.

"You can't, Inx. It's a Borstal for boys only," Val said with a sad look on his face. "It will be okay! We will still see each other! Val reassured us. Anyway, what's been happening here?" Val asked raising his eyebrows.

Sam jumped in to answer, "Oh my God Val, guess what! Daddy isn't really my dad. I mean Joey isn't my real dad."

Val looked confused. "What? What do you mean?" Val started to laugh, jumping out of his chair; Val put his hands to either side of his face and kept shaking his head.

"Yes, Val! Mum told me not so long ago that my dad is called George, she thinks he lives in Jamaica!" Sam answered. "Come, Val, I'll show you his picture." Sam beckoned him to follow her. They ran to our room. I stayed where I was, I could hear them laughing, Val kept saying,

"I can't believe it, Sam, I really thought Joey was your dad!" Once Val got over the shock, they both returned to me in the kitchen. "So Ingrid, it's only your dad left, it's only your dad who beats Mummy," Val said, rushing over to me and putting his hands on my shoulders. I felt so bad inside. "I'm only joking, Inx, it's not your fault Joey is a woman beater." Sam burst out laughing and then so did Val. I couldn't help it I began to laugh too. It was how we dealt with awkward situations. Sam filled Val in on the details of when Dad hid in the wardrobe and beat Mum. His eyes welled up with tears. I could see he was holding them back as he spoke, "I know what Mum's like but it does hurt me when Joey hits Mum. I just wish she could get away from him." He seemed genuinely concerned. "How is Mum now?" Val asked.

"Yeah, she's back to normal, I think, still wicked," Sam answered, and we all laughed.

"Come on enough now, let's go and do something," Val suggested. We decided to play downstairs; Val sighted a huge wardrobe, which had been dumped by the bins. "Look, Sam," Val called out while unlocking the wardrobe door with a tiny vintage key. Sam and I ran over. It was a tall solid wood wardrobe with very little damage. "Get in Sammie!" Val told Sam. Without question, Sam stepped inside, with a huge grin of excitement on her face.

"I'm not getting in there," I stated. Val looked at me and smiled. Closing the door behind her, he locked it with the little key.

"I can't see anything, Val," Sam shouted out from inside. Val laughed and began to tip the wardrobe from side to side, Sam screamed with what sounded like excitement from inside. Val was beside himself with laughter. I watched on in amazement, all the while thinking I know he's gonna ask me to get in. The longer Sam stays in there the better. Val ran around the wardrobe banging it's panels violently, Sammie screamed with both fear and excitement from inside. "Right enough now. Val, you get in!" Sam ordered from inside. Val unlocked the door freeing Sammie from inside. Sam squinted up at us trying hard to adjust her eyes to the light. "That was so cool Val, oh my god I was so scared!" she said still laughing.

"I'm not gonna get in 'cause I'll be too heavy for you to tilt, you get in instead, Ingrid," Val suggested. I knew it, I wanted to not be here right now, but there was no getting away. "Come on, don't be a spoilsport," he said. Hesitantly I stepped inside; fear of the dark took over as Val closed and locked the door behind me. It no longer felt like a game. Thoughts of Dracula jumping out at me was all I could think about, he was my most feared blood-sucking being that haunted my dreams.

"I want to get out," I shouted, I could hear Val and Sam laughing heartedly.

Without hesitation or warning the wardrobe hurled to a crash and my body hurled to the other side. Sam and Val screamed out with laughter. "I want to get out, open the door," I screamed again.

"I...I...It's okay, Inx, just pretend you're on a fair ride." Val tried his hardest to get his words out through his laughter. Once again, my body was hurled in the other direction. I didn't know which way was up. I began to scream at the top of my voice. Eventually, I could hear the lock turning, and within a split second, I could see light. I looked up, still sitting inside the wardrobe, to see Sam and Val's face. They both looked unsure of what they would see inside. Val kept his hand over his mouth and muffled, "Are you okay, Inx? It was only a laugh." I was okay; the feeling of relief and adrenalin ran through me. Wiping the tears from my eyes, I stepped outside and laughed with them.

"I hate you two," I said with a smile on my face.

"What shall we do now?" Sam asked.

"I want to go upstairs now," I replied.

Val had another idea. "It's too soon, let's go to Clapton! It will be a nice walk, then we will come back I promise," he suggested. After what seemed like a few hours' walk in the heat, we eventually reached Clapton pond.

"Now what? I'm tired," I complained.

"Okay let's sit on one of the benches and rest for a bit," Val said, looking over at me and smiling.

"But I'm thirsty and hungry," I moaned.

"Val, shall we go and nick some sweets?" Sam suggested.

"Yeah, good idea," Val agreed.

"No, I don't want to!" I snapped. I was so hungry, I wanted sweets so badly, but the fear of getting caught was too much.

"Look Inx. You want it, but you don't want to help us get it," Val replied.

"Well, let's get some and not give her any," Sammie responded. I knew Sam meant it. I was adamant.

"I know! You two stay here, I'll go," Val said, walking away from us. "The shop is just there. Do not move." Val crossed the main road leaving us to sit on the bench in Clapton Pond.

It seemed like he had been gone for ages when Sam turned to me and said, "Oh my god what if he's been caught." Her face was worried. Then, at that very moment, Val appeared from the shop with a huge grin on his face. As he got closer to the park gate, he emptied his pocket to reveal what he had inside. My eyes grew wide.

"Wow, look how much he's got Sam," I told her. Val placed the sweet treats down on the bench.

"How did you do this?" Sam asked him whilst sieving through the large pile of sweets.

"It's easy Sam," he replied. Val didn't look worried. I knew he would come back with something; I just didn't expect there to be so much. My mouth began to water once I caught sight of a Mars bar. We sat there in the heat watching the ducks floating on the pond with our sweet picnic. *What a great day*, I thought. "Come, I think we should head back now," Val suggested. "I only have three hours left then I have to go," he continued.

"I don't want you to go, Val," Sam said. Life was great when Val was around. Val put the remaining sweets in his pocket.

"Come on let's go," he said. As we walked past the edge of the pond, suddenly I felt suspicious, something did not feel right. Then, without warning, I found myself scrambling through water – dirty smelly water. Panic took over I was drowning. I wasn't a good swimmer but managed to swim to the top where I took a huge breath of air. I was terrified. My clothes began to weigh me down; the cold almost paralysed my body. I could see Val and Sam in the distance, laughing uncontrollably. Can they not see I am drowning? I waved my hand in the air and screamed for them to get me out. "Swim to us, Inx!" Val shouted. Following his voice, I swam a doggy paddle until my feet reached the bottom. But I was still so far away. The water was dark green and foul-smelling. I was exhausted; every time I tried to stand, I slipped back in. The sloped edge was thick with green Algae. I couldn't stand, it was pointless. With each attempt I just went under; Sam and Val were no longer laughing.

"Grab this," came an unfamiliar voice. As I bobbed back up, there was a branch in front of me being held out by a male stranger. Finally, I managed to grab the branch and he pulled me back to the edge, then pulled me out. "Are you two bloody stupid?" the stranger screamed at them, "she could have fucking drowned. I saw what you done, you wicked girl." The man continued to scream in Sam's face. I was freezing and embarrassed. I could feel all eyes on us by people staring from the bus stop near the park gates.

"Well, we didn't mean it," Val said in Sam's defence. Val didn't seem to have much to say as he stood there, looking embarrassed.

"Get home, love, I hope you will be okay," the stranger said while tapping me on the shoulder then walking away. The walk home was long and cold.

"I'm really sorry, Inx," Sam repeated over and over. It was okay; at least I managed to make them laugh for a moment. When we reached home it was clear that Mum was home. I could hear her banging around in the kitchen. "Oh, Inx please don't tell Mum, me and Val will be in so much trouble." I didn't want them to get into trouble, and maybe this way they'll be nicer to me. Val rushed me straight through to the bathroom without Mum noticing. Trying to be as quick as I could, I undressed and washed while Sam and Val kept Mum distracted in the kitchen. Mum sounded pleased to see Val; she was sober and made some conversation. The only thing I found difficult to disguise was the smell coming from my pond-drenched plaited pigtails. I couldn't take my hair out; it was too long and too thick for me to manage alone. Besides, there was no shampoo. I placed each braid under the cold running water from the tap and squeezed it tightly to get rid of the excess water. Finally, I was able to join them in the kitchen. Mum didn't bat an eyelid; she was too focused on whatever it was she was cooking on the stove. This felt nice all of us together.

"Sammie, get out some spoons," Mum told Sam. We took our places at the table while Mum dished up her Irish stew. Mum placed mine and Sam's plates down in front of us. Then placed the third bowl down away from Val, we looked at each other confused. Mum turned away to fill the fourth bowl, looking back at the sound of Val dragging the third bowl across the table and placing it in front of him. "That's not yours, Val, this is yours," Mum snapped. Her tone changed.

"Oh, sorry Mum," Val responded, laughing nervously. Mum placed the fourth bowl on the side next to the sink. Sam, Val and I glanced at each other with the same confused look on our faces. Mum sat at the table with us, leaving Val's bowl on the other side of the kitchen. Mum began to eat not looking up. "Thanks, Mum," Val said, whilst getting up to grab his bowl. Picking it up, Val turned back to take his seat at the table.

"No. You eat there," Mum told Val with a stern cold look on her face. Val looked deflated and confused but did as he was told. He turned his back and began to eat standing up by the sink.

"Why has Val got to eat there?" Sammie asked, her eyes filling with tears.

"Because I fucking said so, he's too naughty, he's not sitting with us," Mum shouted, almost spitting her food out. I couldn't help but wonder what was it that he had done. Mum didn't know what had happened today, it made no sense.

"It's okay," Val said quietly. He seemed used to this. I felt deeply sad. Val was eating, but I could hear he was crying. Not loudly, it was like a whimpering. The sounds of his cries began to agitate Mum.

"What you fucking crying for you dunce!" Mum screamed, jumping out of her seat and hurling her bowl in Val's direction. The bowl smashed as it hit the wall in front of Val, who quickly moved his arms to cover his face. Mum ran over and began punching and slapping Val around the head and body. Sam and I both ran into the front room, and the sound of plates and cups smashing echoed around the flat. "You fucking bastard, I hate you!" Mum screamed out. Val's cries were deafening. Mum dragged Val's helpless body up the corridor by his curly black hair, continuing to punch him in the face. Throwing him into what we call the back room. The back room was supposed to be Val's room, but we used it more for storage. Mum slammed the door shut. There was no door handle on this door, so when we would get put in there, we were locked in. Mum would have to get pliers to open it. Val cried for ages. I was distracted by our cat, Ginger, hiding under the sofa. Ginger never came home. I would see him once every few weeks; he would appear out of nowhere sleeping on the balcony or scratching the front door.

"Aww look, Sam, Ginger is home," I told Sam, pulling him out from under the chair for a cuddle. Mum hated Ginger. I found him when he was a kitten down by the wood factory. He was left in a box with his brothers and sisters; the man who worked there said they had been abandoned. So, I brought him home.

"Mum, I need to go to the toilet," Val called from the back room. Mum stormed past the front room door with a bucket in hand, opened the back-room door and threw it into Val, I could hear it bounce off whatever surface it hit. Then the door slammed shut again. Val cried for a while and then there was silence, maybe he was sleeping.

"I hate it here, Inx, I wish I knew my dad," Sam said to me, she looked like she was in deep thought. Mum returned from her bedroom with her cigarette in her hand.

"You okay, Ingy?" Mum asked me.

"Yes Mum," I replied. "What you doing holding that filthy thing?" Mum asked, referring to Ginger. Before I could answer, Mum walked off, returning to the back room. Within seconds, Val began to scream again, Sam and I rushed to the hallway just managing to catch sight of Val. He was huddled in the corner dripping with urine and faeces. Mum had thrown the bucket of waste over him, still screaming and shouting. "Mum!" Sam bellowed out. Mum turned to see us both watching from the hallway. Val didn't look up. Mum rushed towards me snatching Ginger out of my hands, and hurling my cat at Val, in panic Ginger had clawed Val's back in fear. Mum pushed us out of the way in her quick exit and slammed the door locked closed again. Ginger was locked in the room with Val; I could hear Val crying for ages.

Eventually, Mum let Val out. The only words she said were, "Go clean yourself you disgusting boy and go home."

Sam and I cried endlessly for Val. With Mum's words, Val let out a different-sounding cry. I think Mum's words had hurt him more than the beatings. Val was late in getting back to the children's home. It was so painful, watching him walking alone across the fields from our balcony. I wished so hard that Sam and I could have gone with him.

Mum started going out as before, almost every night. She had got new friends over in Lewisham in South London. We spent most nights just the two of us and as usual Sam took care of me. "We're going to spend the day with Phyllis, there's someone I want you to meet. A good friend of mine," Mum told us.

"But it's boring there. Can we play out when we get there?" Sam asked Mum. Mum was in a good mood.

"Of course, you can," Mum said, putting the final touches of makeup on.

"We'll go with Mum, get some money then go over the marshes, Inx," Sam suggested.

"Yeah, that will be fun," I agreed. As we approached Phyllis's, I could hear the sound of Gregory Isaacs, and many voices singing along to Night Nurse.

"How long do we have to stay for Mum?" Sam asked. Mum held onto our hands tightly as we walked up the street.

"Shush cheeky," Mum said, laughing. "I love you two," Mum continued her words were comforting, it's been ages since Mum's been like this. Her mood made it worth going and spending a boring day at Phyllis's. Mum didn't bother knocking, we just walked in. Everyone seemed mellow and merry. I went over and kissed Phyllis on the cheek, then looked around at all the unfamiliar faces. Kim was sitting in the armchair by the window; I didn't say hello to her neither did Sam. "Ingy, Sam. Where's your manners?" Say hello to Kim. Mum demanded.

"Hi Kim," I said reluctantly.

"Come give your Aunty Kim a kiss," she said pointing to her cheek. We moved closer and kissed her on the cheek.

"Hello Bernie," a deep voice said, coming from the bedroom door. In stepped a tall, built, black man, smartly dressed carrying a briefcase. Mum's face lit up, this was another side I hadn't seen for so long. Mum walked over and kissed him on the mouth.

"Hello Carl," she said as she wrapped her arms around him. "Ingrid and Sammie, come say hello," she said.

"Who's this?" Sam asked.

"Is it your boyfriend Mum?" I asked. Mum laughed.

"Hello," Sam said. Carl walked over, shook her hand then kissed her on the cheek.

"So, you must be curly," he said to Sam with a huge grin on his face. "And you must be who Mum calls Big Brown Eyes," he continued looking at me.

"Can we go out now?" Sammie asked Mum.

"Go on, let the girls go have some fun, Bernie," Carl said, taking out his wallet.

"Go on then, don't go far," Mum said. Carl pulled a pound note out of his wallet and gave it to Sam.

"Thank you," she said. We quickly left the flat, making our way to the shops. We got a good supply of sweets and chocolates, then we made our way to the marshes. The sky became a bit cloudy; it looked as though it was going to rain, which never stopped us. "What do you think of Carl?" Sam asked me.

"He seems nice, what do you think?" I asked her.

"I'm not sure," she replied. We reached the marshes and began to explore. We played tag and we rolled around in the dirt. We really didn't care; it was so much fun. Occasionally, we stopped for a rest and a few more sweets. "I wish Val was here, we would have so much more fun," Sam mentioned.

"Who's that?" I asked pointing to a figure through the trees not too far away.

"I don't know, come let's see," Sam said, stuffing the sweets back in the bag. We walked together through the trees. As we approached it was clear that we weren't the only ones who liked the marshes. There stood a young white man with his back to us but looking over his shoulder, in our direction. "Hello," he said, still keeping his back to us and smiling.

"Hello," I said. Sam tugged on my arm. I think to tell me to shush.

"What you doing?" Sam asked him.

"Nothing, just looking at some pictures of my family," he said smiling. "Do you want to see it? Come you can see my daughter, she's about your age," he said, nodding to me. We slowly took a step forward. As we got closer Sam suggested he hold them up. Holding my hand tight we took another step closer. "Take it, go on. I ain't going to do anything," he said. He reached his arm out behind him and passed Sam a photo. To our shock it wasn't a photo, it was a playing card like Dad has with naked women on it. We screamed, dropped the card and ran. I looked back to see he wasn't following, he wasn't. The man stood there with his willy hanging out of his trousers.

"Sam!" I yelled.

"I know, Inx, come on let's keep going," she told me. I couldn't keep up; my asthma had started. My chest got tighter and tighter and I started to wheeze. "For God, sake, Inx, come on!" Sam shouted, trying to pull me on further.

"I can't," I cried out. Sam had to stop I couldn't go on. We took a slow walk back to Phyllis's. Sam tried explaining to Mum what had happened. To my shock, Carl jumped up and began swearing.

"Who fucking scared you like that? I'll kill him," he shouted out.

He seemed genuinely upset by what happened. Mum was already tipsy, and Kim too. In fact, they all were. "Come here, girls, as you know I'm Mum's boyfriend now, and I want you to know I will protect you. I've heard lots about your dad, but even he can't do nothing to me." He looked us straight in the eye. His breath stank of drink and cigarettes. Sam nudged me in the side when he spoke about Daddy. I couldn't help it, I started to laugh. "You think I'm joking?" he asked us. "Tell them, Kim, tell the girls what I'm like. There will be no more beatings from him to your mum," he explained. *Wow, he must be stronger than Dad,* I thought. Mum eventually passed out on Phyllis's bed. I could see Carl was getting on Sam's nerves. All night he kept asking, "Are you okay?" and each time Sam would say yes.

"Carl, can you wake Mum now, we're tired," I asked him.

"Of course, precious," he said. He didn't wake her, he just pulled her up, and carried her out the door and to his car parked outside. Carl put Mum to bed. She was groaning.

"Ingy, Sam, come kiss me goodnight!" she yelled.

"Don't worry about your mum, you two get to bed," Carl told us. It was late and we were tired.

"Night Carl!" I shouted.

"Night," he replied. Sam didn't say a word. She just stood by the light switch, waiting for me to get into bed.

"Come on, Inx," she moaned.

"Alright, Sam," I said as I climbed into bed.

"What do you think of him now, Inx?" She asked me, trying to feel her way into bed.

"I think he's nice, what about you?"

"Not sure yet," she replied. A few weeks later, Mum sat us down and told us that we would be moving to a place called Lewisham in South London. I didn't mind. Anywhere would have been better than living here with these things that bit us every night. Sam didn't mind too much either, at least those girls wouldn't be able to get her. Carl seemed nice; he always gave us money and gifts, even luncheon vouchers.

Chapter Five:
The Move

Aged eight. We didn't take much furniture with us. Mum said we would come back for it at a later date. She said that we would be staying with a friend of hers called Irene. We had never met Irene, but Mum said she was nice and that we would get on with her. It took ages to get there. Val crossed my mind; I wondered how he would find us. It was then I felt overwhelmed with dread and sadness. By the next week, we were moving house. Carl's car was stuffed to the brim with our belongings. As we drove along our road I looked back, this was all we knew. I wasn't sure how I felt. I knew I would miss my school friends and our walks over the marshes but knew I felt at least a little excited. The drive was long, hot and stuffy. Finally, Carl turned and said, "We're here girls." I peered out of the window to see a huge estate with built-up flats all around me.

"Is this it?" Sam questioned.

"It's a new start for us all," Mum turned around and said, dabbing her fag out in the ashtray. As we took our bags out of the car, I looked around hoping to see any sight of other children. There were none. Our flat was on the fifth floor, overlooking a small swing park. The sound of reggae music bellowed out of doors as we made our way up the stairs with our bags. Our front door was yellow; number 42 was our new home. Once inside the flat, I threw my bags on the floor and made a dash around the flat. It was clean and smelt nice.

"Is this our room Mum?" I asked her. Standing in the doorway.

"Yes love, you and Sammie will share that room," she replied. Her face was red and flustered. "I could do with a beer, Carl," she said wiping her forehead with her arm.

Sam followed me into the bedroom. "Feels weird, doesn't it Inx?" she asked me, pulling open the wardrobe door.

"Come, let's go see the rest," I told her, rushing out of the room. Next to our room was Mum's room – it looked cramped. I'm sure her other room was bigger.

Mum is gonna have to paint it green again, I thought. There's no way Mum will leave her room white. As I followed Sam into the living room, I was surprised to see a large woman sitting in the armchair.

Mum stepped out of the kitchen which led onto the living room, and said, "Ingrid, Sammie, this is Aunty Irene." We had never seen her before.

"Hello darlings, I'm Irene. You will be staying with me until Mum finds somewhere for you to live," she told us, trying to edge her heavy frame forwards, off of the seat, which looked impossible. She was the width of the chair she sat in. Sam and I looked at each other and laughed.

"But I thought this was our house?" Sam asked.

"I didn't say that did I, Sam? Don't worry, you will see. It won't be long before we get our own place," Mum reassured Sam, putting her arm around her. I wasn't bothered; I stood there, fascinated with Irene. She looked strange. She had a pretty face with jet-black hair and was wearing red lipstick. Her hands were small but her arms big. I continued to stare.

"You must be Ingrid," she said, reaching out to me with one hand. "And you Samantha," she continued. We both stepped towards her; she leant forward and kissed us on the cheek. Her lips were cold, and her face sweaty. I turned away and wiped my cheek, hoping she wouldn't see me. Sam didn't care; she wiped her face while Irene was still looking at her.

"Right Bernie, I'm off. I will pass by tomorrow and see how you are settling in," Carl said, stepping into the living room, and placing our last case on the sofa.

"Say thank you and goodbye to Carl, girls," Mum told us as she followed him to the door.

"Bye Carl," we said in sequence.

We settled in well. Mum got me into a school just across the road from our estate. Sam hadn't got a place yet, it seemed to be more difficult because she was just going into her first year of secondary school. I made friends easily, although sometimes I felt really alone. There were a handful of girls who used to start on me occasionally because they found out my mum was white. They would say that I was a diluted black girl. That used to hurt because I saw myself as black just like them. "Right girls, Mummy is going out with Aunty Irene and Carl in a minute," Mum told us whilst putting on her makeup.

"But we're gonna be scared, Mum," Sam told her. Sam and I sat fascinated on Mum's bed, watching her get ready. "I thought we were all gonna go out when I saw you getting ready, Mum," Sam continued.

"Don't be silly, you will be fine. I won't be long, and I promise I'll bring you a treat back," Mum said, looking at Sam in the mirror.

"God it's only been a few weeks and you're leaving us already!" Sam yelled, slamming Mum's bedroom door behind her.

"I don't want us to stay on our own, Mum, can't we come with you?" I asked her, slowly making my way towards the bedroom door.

"No, you can't. Don't you start now, you can go out if you want. You can go downstairs to the park." Mum picked up her bag. A car was tooting continuously downstairs. "Irene, Carl is here, come on let's go," Mum yelled, shoving me out of her way. Mum never said goodbye, she just left. Suddenly the flat felt empty and larger than I thought it was. Sam was sitting on her bed crying.

"See, she's gonna do this all the time now," Sam said, wiping her eyes. "You watch, I bet Carl takes her away from us." *Carl won't do that, he's a nice guy*, I thought. It was all about to happen all over again. Mum was never home and the only good thing was that Irene always made sure we were fed. Whenever Mum was home, she would send Sam to come and get me out of school early, the teachers would come to my class telling me that there had been an emergency at home and that I had to go home early. Mum never came to get me. I would get home to find there was no emergency; Mum would be drunk along with her friends. Sam would be left to do nothing, just sit and watch.

One day after being collected early, Sam and I went straight to the swing park and spent a few hours there before going home. As we walked through the estate, we noticed Carl's car wasn't there. We climbed the stairs and Sam said, "Carl can't be home, I hope Mummy is." Sam knocked on the door a few times. No one answered. Sam opened the letterbox and called out Mum and Irene's names. "Err!" Sam yelled, slamming the letterbox shut.

"What is it, Sam?" I asked her, trying to push her aside so I could see. Directly opposite the front door was the toilet. Big fat Irene sat there, drunk, feeling herself down below whilst she was doing a wee. She didn't even know we were there. We could not stop laughing.

"I can't wait for Mum to come to tell her," Sam said. It seemed like she had been sitting there for ages.

We had to wait for her to finish, checking occasionally, before we called her again. What started as funny wasn't funny anymore. We were tired and hungry. Eventually, she let us in.

"For fuck sake, Carl," I could hear Mum's voice in my sleep; was Mum back? I rubbed my eyes and crept to our bedroom door.

"Sammie, Sammie, I think Mum's back. Come see." Sam joined me by the bedroom door. Carl started to shout, and then we heard cries. "I'm scared, Sam, do you think Mum's gonna get hit again?" I asked her.

"No, it sounds like Irene crying Inx," Sam replied, opening the bedroom door some more. I had never seen Carl like this before. He was being really mean. He began screaming in Irene's face. She sat there crying. Why doesn't Mum help? Sam opened the door fully and crept to the living room door. I ran behind her and looked over her shoulder. Carl spat in Irene's face.

"You fucking cunt, I'll kill you. You think you can mess with me?" he screamed. He grabbed hold of my black dolly, which was lying on the arm of the chair, and smashed it across her face. I couldn't believe it.

Sam yelled out, "No, Mummy don't let him hit her!" Carl wasn't at all bothered that we were there, he continued to hit her. After he finished hitting her with the doll, he used his fist. Mum tried to get us out, but not once was she bothered about Irene. "I hate you, Carl!" Sam shouted to him, whilst Mum dragged her up the corridor. My heart skipped a beat; I could hear Carl run up behind us. Mum threw us into our bedroom but it was too late. Carl dragged Mum out of the way and began to yell in Sam's face.

"You hate me, you ungrateful bitch! I told you your dad couldn't help you, where is he now?" he screamed.

"My dad will get you for this. You wait and see!" Sam shouted back. She flinched and covered her face. Carl raised his hand to hit her.

"No don't!" I shouted. I just wanted Daddy.

"Oh Sammie, why don't you shut your mouth? Your dad doesn't give a shit about you and you know it!" Mum screamed, standing by the bedroom door. Sam ran over to me and put her arms around me. I wished Sam would stay quiet. I didn't want Carl to hit her. I realised that Mum wouldn't have stopped him. Carl left the room swearing and slamming doors.

"Go to your fucking dad then, you little bastards!" he shouted, as he paced from one room to the next. Mum left the room, running after him trying to comfort him. Sam scrambled under the bed and pulled out our suitcase.

"What you doing Sammie?" I asked her.

"We're leaving, Inx, we will run away when Mum goes to sleep, we'll go and live with Daddy." Before I could say a word, the bedroom door flew open. It was Carl.

"Get your fucking bags, go on. I'll tie you both to the back of my car and drag you down to your dad's!" Grabbing the case out of Sam's hands, he began stuffing our clothes in the case.

"Mummy! Mummy!" I shouted. Mum came into the room and started crying.

"Don't leave me, Sammie, why?" Mum asked her. "You're not taking my Ingy with you!" she demanded.

"Let them go, Bernie, who fucking cares," Carl interrupted. Whilst Carl packed our stuff Mum paced up and down, from room to room, lighting one cigarette after another. Carl kicked our cases down the flights of stairs, still swearing and calling us bastards and warning us that we shouldn't fuck with him. Sam struggled behind, pulling along one of the bigger cases. Mum dragged me by the wrist, rushing me to the car. Carl had a scary look in his eyes, he was out of control.

"Bernie, don't do it, don't let your kids go!" Irene shouted down to Mum from the window above, overlooking the car park. As I glanced up for a moment Irene's large frame was squeezed through the window. She was crying. Mum ignored her plea. We didn't get to talk to Mum all the way down to Dad's and Mum didn't speak to us. She was agreeing with most of what Carl was saying, I couldn't believe it.

Sam looked over at me and whispered, "Don't be sad, Inx, we get to live with Dad and Dionne, fuck Carl." I wanted to laugh but was too scared to; Sam was so brave. I knew Sam would look after me. As we reached Wyllen Close, I started to feel excited. Mum began to cry but didn't say anything. Carl screeched the car to a halt outside Dad's door. He jumped out, opened Sam's door and told us to get out. He threw our cases on the floor. He got back in the car and drove away. I could see Mum looking back as the car left the estate.

We stood there looking at each other, night had just settled in. Sam looked at me and smiled. "We did it Inx," Sam said, putting her arm around me. All I could think of was Mum. We picked up our cases and walked towards Dad's door. Dionne opened the door, her face looked stunned.

"What you two doing here? Where's your mum?" She asked, looking over our shoulder, searching for Mum.

"We have come to stay with Dad," Sam replied. Dionne stood back to let us in. We followed Dionne in through to the living room. Dad wasn't there.

"Where's Dad, Di?" I asked her. The flat was quiet and, as usual, spotless. The only thing out was Dionne's crossword book on the table.

"Dad's at work, you know he does security. He's going to go mad when he finds out what's happened," Dionne told us. Sam and I looked at each other. I didn't care, I was just glad to be there. To be safe. "What is going on?" She asked.

Sam tried to explain, "Well Carl was going to hit us. He said he was gonna kill us, he even beat up Mummy's friend." Her eyes started to fill with tears, but Sam didn't cry.

"What bloody rubbish, you know Carl couldn't hurt you. Daddy would kill him!" she snapped. "You should have just waited until the morning, you know what they're like when they drink," she told us. I felt uncomfortable, as though we had done something wrong. "Well put your bags down then," she continued. It was getting late and both Sam and I were getting tired. Normally Dionne would have put us straight to bed. For some reason, she seemed hesitant. I must have just drifted off to sleep when I was woken by Dionne's voice. "Yeah, Joey, they're here now. What shall I do?" She was on the phone. I sat up and nudged Sam to wake up.

"Daddy is on the phone, Sam," I told her. Dionne slammed the phone down.

"Right, you two, Dad told me to put you to bed. I don't know what time he's coming. No pissing around alright just go to sleep," she told us. Dionne wasn't happy at all. We followed her through to the spare bedroom. "There's no point unpacking, he'll have to take you back tomorrow, you can't stay here." She told us as she left the room.

"Do you think Daddy will send us back Sam?" I asked her.

"I don't know, I hope not. I'll run away if he does," Sam curled up on the bed and closed her eyes. I dimmed the light and climbed into bed.

The next morning, I was woken by the sound of banging dishes and slammed doors. Sam woke up soon after. "What the hell's that?" Sam asked, sitting up and peering over at me.

"It must be Dionne," I answered.

"Dionne, stop that fucking noise will ya," Dad's voice hollered through the house.

"Dad's here!" Sam and I rushed to the bedroom door eager to see him. There he was. He was standing in the living room, ready for work. His carpenter's belt around his waist pencil behind his ear, sunglasses hooked over the neck of his t-shirt.

"Dad!" we shouted, running over to him. We grabbed his waist tightly, almost knocking him over.

"Ah my two angels," he said. As I looked up at him, he had a smile as broad as his face, he was so happy. The sound of banging dishes got louder. "Dionne, don't fucking piss me off, I said stop it!" He shouted at her in a firm voice.

"Well, no one fucking asks me what I think, Dionne's alright with everything. How we gonna manage?" She yelled back at him. Dad kissed his teeth.

"Dionne I'm not joking with you, just shut your noise," he shouted. There was silence.

"Dad do we have to go back?" Sam asked.

Dad looked down at us and said very calmly, "You're my daughters and I want you here. That's all that matters." He bent down and kissed us both in turn on our cheeks. "Now I have to go to work, Dionne will look after you. I will see you when I get back." Dad stood up and went into the kitchen to see Dionne. "Oi fanny, give your husband a kiss," he demanded, grabbing Dionne by the waist.

"Get off, Joey." She tried desperately to peel his tight grip from around her waist. Dionne's face looked red as though she had been crying. "I mean it Joey, get off!" Dionne ordered him to let her go.

"Fuck you then," he screamed in her face. "You see that, girls, Dionne don't love me anymore," he said. He stood back from her and gave her a long stare. Dad walked out, slamming the door behind him. The rest of the day without him felt very uncomfortable.

It didn't take long for Dad's home to feel like ours. The sheets were always clean and we also had plenty of food and drink. Although we weren't allowed to eat the same food as Dad, it didn't matter. For the first time, we had a curfew, we had to be in by 5 pm. I didn't think of Mum very much. For some reason, I believed she must be happy without us because we didn't hear from her. By mid-August, we'd had lots of sun, lots of water fights and made lots of new friends. It was great. I had just finished changing my wet clothes when I heard a car beep outside; the street door was always wide open. Finally, I got my white trousers on over my damp body. Couldn't be bothered to dry myself. I wanted to be ready for my friends when they came back to knock for me. Sammie ran into the bedroom. "Ingrid, Eileen and Tina are here," Sam told me while trying to catch her breath. Tina was Eileen's younger sister. This didn't make sense to me. Eileen was white and Tina was black like me. Before I could ask Sam if Lorrinda was with them, she left the room. I could hear Dad greeting them.

"Ah Dionne, look who it is. My beautiful, sexy and sophisticated Tina!" Dad always said things like that to women. I walked into the living room.

There was Tina, looking embarrassed. Dad turned the music up even louder. It was like we were having a party. Eileen looked as pretty as she always did. "Eileen, where's Lorrinda?" I asked her, trying to be heard over the music.

"She's not here darling, she's with her nan," Eileen told me, and then kissed me roughly on the cheek. Dionne brought in some extra glasses and coke to go with the vodka. I knew it was time to leave. I went outside to meet Sam. We played for a while in the playground, which was right outside Dad's door. I noticed Tina sitting on the doorstep. I never really knew Tina. She seemed nice, just quiet she was the opposite of Eileen. Strangely they looked alike. She was a few years older than Sam, about fourteen years old.

"Shall we ask her if she wants to play, Inx?" Sam asked me.

"Ask her, because I ain't gonna ask her," I answered. "She'll probably say no anyway," I told Sam. There was no way I was giving up my swing. I kept my eye on Jason, waiting for me to get off. Jason was one of the boys who lived on the estate. I glanced over to Dad's door; Sam was already sitting down next to Tina talking to her. I eventually couldn't bear watching Jason staring at me waiting for my swing any longer. I slowed down, dragging my feet on the ground. "You can have it now, Jase." He spat his chewing gum out and rushed towards me. I took a slow walk across the estate to Dad's. Heaps of water came out the door like a waterfall. Sam and Tina leapt up screaming. They were drenched. I couldn't believe it. *Who would do this?* I thought. They separated and stood at least 2 yards away from the house. Dad stepped out the door, laughing uncontrollably, still holding the empty bucket in his left hand. Sam kept clear. She held her hair in one hand and squeezed. Water ran down her arm. Tina pulled up the bottom of her top to wipe her eyes.

"Oh, Joey, why did you do that?" Tina asked him. She looked as though she wanted to laugh. Dad ran inside the house. "Sam, shall we get him back?" Tina asked Sam. "Yeah but he will get us at the door," Sam replied, walking over to her. As I got nearer to the door, I could hear the bathroom tap running fast. I turned and waved to Sam and Tina to go away. They immediately knew what I was saying. Together, they ran behind the flats. Eileen and Dionne came out to see what was going on. "Ingrid, where's Sam and Tina?" Eileen asked me. She took out her cigarettes and lit one. I realised the tap in the bathroom was no longer running. I walked slowly to the end of the block. Gush! By the time I looked back Dad had soaked Dionne and Eileen. It had escalated into a full-blown water fight. I couldn't stop laughing. I ran around the back to tell Sam, but they weren't there. By the time I walked back around the block, I could see Sam and Tina were in the thick of it. *They didn't pass me,* I thought. They must have gone in through the back door. "For fuck sake Joey, all my fucking fags are wet," Eileen, yelled at him. Even the neighbours came out to see what all the commotion was. Tina grabbed her water bottle and ran back inside the house, to fill it up again. Dad ran in after her. Dionne really let go; she was laughing so much that she looked like she was in pain. We heard a scream come from inside the house. It sounded hollow. I knew it came from the bathroom. "Whoops, Joey got Tina back," Dionne said. Sam and I looked at each other, it didn't sound right. I knew something was wrong, I had a feeling Dad had hurt her. Eileen and Dionne went inside the house. I followed them to the bathroom where Tina sat on the side of the bath crying. I couldn't see clearly in the bathroom, as Dionne and Eileen were too tall.

"Ingrid," Sam whispered to me. I looked around; she was beckoning me to come into our bedroom. Dad was nowhere to be seen. The atmosphere changed. I didn't like it. I followed Sam into the room and she quietly shut the door behind her. I sat on the bed, waiting for her to talk. "I think Dad done something to her, you know, like what he has done to us." I put my head down and started fiddling with my hands. "Do you hear what I'm saying, Inx?" She asked me again. The voices got louder and louder in the hallway.

"I'm scared," I told Sam.

"It's alright Inx, we'll just stay in here until it's sorted," Sam reassured me. She sat down on the floor in front of me with her back against the wardrobe. Finally, it went quiet. I could hear Dad's voice through the wall, he was talking to Eileen. It wasn't clear what they were saying; Dad was calling Tina a liar. Eileen was arguing that she wasn't. Then it seemed as though Dad won the row. Dionne came to our bedroom door and told us to come out. "Is Tina alright?" Sam asked her.

"Yeah, she's fine, they're going now," she replied. Dionne's voice was calm and caring. She wanted to make sure we were okay. Sam got off the floor and we followed Dionne out. As we passed the hall, I saw Tina walking out behind Eileen. Her head was down. She glanced back at us, her face was red and her eyes were puffy. She looked so sad. Then she was gone. We sat with Dionne in the living room. Moments later, Dad appeared. His large frame darkened the doorway. He went straight for his glass of vodka on the table. He drank the lot in one gulp.

"Can you believe that slag would make up such a thing, Dionne?" he asked Dionne, slamming his glass down on the table. That night in bed I felt uneasy and unsafe. I don't know what I was waiting for, maybe an outburst of some sort. It never came. I lay there tossing and turning; eventually feeling relaxed as I rubbed my feet together. It was comforting. I could feel myself drifting off to sleep, but was interrupted by Sam shouting, "Ingrid, stop that for God's sake I can't sleep, what's wrong with you." Immediately I stopped rubbing my feet. It seemed like hours before I drifted off. The next day Dionne got us up early at 8 am. We had no school yet so it made no sense to me to get up so early. "Come on you two up you get, and get washed," Dionne ordered us whilst opening the curtains and letting the sunlight come in. I hated when she did that. I buried my face under my pillow and Dionne snatched it out of my hand, throwing it to the foot of my bed.

"Ouch, Di!" I screeched.

"Well get up then you doser," she said, slamming the door behind her. *Mum would never wake me up like this,* I thought to myself. Sam was already up, and in the bathroom getting ready. For a moment I sat on the edge of my bed and thought of Mummy. I hope she's okay. I felt a strange feeling in my tummy, a mixed feeling of emptiness and sadness. I want her and I miss her, I realised. It was too late. Mum was with Carl now, and Carl hated us but Dionne liked us. That was the conclusion I came to. There was nothing that could be done now; she's probably forgotten about us. And so, I dismissed it from my thoughts. It was another hot day, Sam and I played outside for hours, searching the estate for a camp. Somewhere we could hide or have a picnic in. A place that was ours. It wasn't long before some of the girls from a block next to us joined in our hunt for a camp. Emma and Sheryl were their names. Emma was the same age as me and was an only child, and Sheryl was a little bigger than Sam, not sure how old she was. Sheryl had an older sister too. Sheryl suggested that we climbed onto the roof to look for a camp. It was not a high roof, just one floor high. Brilliant, we thought. One after the other, we climbed up, gripping the pipes for the guttering. Sam and Sheryl gave Emma and me a bunk up and one by one we scrambled onto the rooftop. "Is this it?" Emma asked. "There's nothing here." She looked so disappointed. I felt great! To be this high up and look down with no railings to keep us from falling, it felt good. Eventually, Sam and Sheryl made it up too.

Sam sighed, looking around her. "I know! Why don't we jump off?" Sam suggested.

Sheryl laughed. "Yeah, that sounds good," Sheryl said, undoing her hair and tying it back up again. I didn't realise how long her hair was, not as long as Sam's but definitely longer than mine.

"I'm not jumping off anything," Emma told us as she backed away from the edge.

"What about you Ingrid?" Sheryl asked me. "I dare you to jump, go on, Ingrid." I felt pressured.

"Yeah, I'll do it, it isn't that high is it?" I replied without hesitation. I walked closer to the edge and took a long look down; suddenly it didn't look like such a small drop. I could feel their eyes on me, waiting to see me jump. "I can't do it, it's too high," I told them. I felt so stupid.

"Your sister's a chicken, Sam," Sheryl told her. Sam looked at me and shook her head. Before I could say anything in my defence, Sheryl leapt and jumped off the roof. We hurried to the edge to see. I expected to see her splattered and covered in blood, but there she was brushing herself down as though nothing had happened. "Come on you lot, what you waiting for? Told you it's okay," she said, gazing up at us with a squint in one eye trying to block out the sun.

"The fact is you two, there's no other way down," Sam explained to Emma and me. It was true. I was kind of hoping Sam would get me down. I glanced over at Emma; she had a scared look on her face.

"Look, Ingrid!" Emma shouted looking over my shoulder. As I turned, Sam was nowhere to be seen. Sam had already jumped without announcing it. Now there were just the two of us. I wanted to somehow magic myself back home again. "There's no point in us waiting, Ingrid. We have to get down or they're going to leave us," Emma told me as she stepped closer to the edge. Do I jump before her, or do I wait? I wondered to myself.

"Come on Ingrid, or I'm going to have to call Dionne then she'll call Dad and you know what that means, don't you?" Sam threatened. I knew what that meant. Once again, I felt pressured. Without hesitation, Emma jumped I couldn't believe it. Why did I wait so long? How did they just do it? Sam, Sheryl and Emma began walking away, "Come on Inx, it's getting boring now. I'm going to get Dionne!" Sam shouted out, looking back at me. One…two…three…I kept counting over and over in my head expecting to jump on three, but I just kept freezing. Before I knew it, I was in the air, it was too late, no turning back. I landed on my feet; my chin hit my knee then I felt the most excruciating pain. I could hear a tear clearly in my ear. I had bit my tongue as I landed. My mouth was full of warm thick liquid. It was too painful to scream.

"Look! Ingrid jumped!" I heard a voice say, not sure who it was.

"Ingrid, Ingrid are you okay?" Sam put her arm around me to help me to my feet. Finally, I yelled out, but there was no sound. It was as though I had no voice for a split second. I was screaming with no sound, and then it came blood gargling cries roared out. "Oh my God, Inx, your mouth is full of blood. What you done?" Sam asked me. I couldn't stop crying, I was going to die. The bleeding would not stop; it just kept pumping out of my mouth. The sight of all that blood made me panic, which brought on an asthma attack. Holding my mouth, Sam walked me back home quickly. Emma and Sheryl ran on ahead to alert Dionne. By the time we reached the front door Dionne already had Dad's first aid box in her hand. "For fuck sake, Ingrid!" Dionne screamed at me. The look on her face made me even more frightened. All I thought of was Mum. I wanted Mum. I was dying and she wasn't there. Dionne tore me from Sam's grip and hurried me to the bathroom. The blood was still pumping out, just not as fast. Dionne ran the cold tap drenching a clean flannel and pressed it on my tongue, "You silly girl, you want to give me a heart attack? Do ya?" she said. Her voice began to sound calmer. "You're lucky it's not that deep, Ingrid, you'll live," she said with a smile on her face. *Maybe I'm not going to die then*, I thought. "Right. Keep a hold of that flannel on your tongue Ingrid, it seems to have stopped now," she told me. She wiped my face of all the tears and suddenly I felt better. Sam stood at the bathroom door with a worried look on her face. "She's okay, Sam. Go tell your friends that's it for tonight you're not going out again now," Dionne ordered. A few moments later, Sam returned to the bathroom.

"Do you want to play dolls, Inx?" Sam asked me.

"Yes okay," I replied. Carefully lifting off the front of the doll's house that Dad had built for Lorrinda, the smell of wood glue breezed past me. *Hmm*, I thought, with a huge smile on my face. That pleasurable moment was cut short by the pain that shot from inside my mouth to the back of my head. "Ouch!" I screeched holding my mouth.

"You alright, Inx?" Sam asked me, she looked concerned.

"Mm," I replied I dared not speak. Sam leant forward and handed me her favourite doll.

"Here Inx, you can play with this one if you want to?" I couldn't believe it, Sam handed over her favourite Sindy doll! For some strange reason, her giving it to me didn't seem as satisfying as me snatching it and running for my life but I took it anyway. We played for hours; creating beds out of flannels and hand towels, drawing black eyes on them as they ran away from their boyfriends who beat them up. Then we would get them to make up again, just like Mum and Dad did. We were interrupted by the sound of the front door slamming shut. It was Dad. I could tell because I could hear him blowing his nose into his handkerchief, getting rid of the day's dust that was built up in his nose every day after leaving the site. Dropping the dolls where we were sitting, we ran to meet him at the door.

"Ah my two little angels, how's your day been?" Dad looked down at us, my head pressed against his waist. Dust trickled off his jeans and denim jacket I felt so safe. I am reminded of how much I love my dad. Sam began to cough. "I'll come see you in the minute," Dad told us. Stepping aside, we watched him remove his brown and orange knitted hat, and then his carpenter's belt. He looked over at me and smiled, his cheekbones high on his face. I smiled back. "Go on fanny, go with Sam." That word again. Suddenly, I didn't feel so happy. I followed Sam through to the living room. Sam lay slumped in the chair with her legs swinging over the arm. It had been a long day.

"Dad, guess what? Ingrid bashed her mouth today!" Sam yelled out.

"Um excuse me, Sammie, I can tell Dad what happened," Dionne interrupted. Sam looked startled as Dionne came from the kitchen, holding a handful of wet washing.

"Sorry," Sammie responded. Sam looked over at me and rolled her eyes we both began to laugh; Dionne looked back at us and tutted.

"Oh, for fuck sake," Dionne screamed, trying impatiently to unlock the back door. Her face became red and flustered as she tried to turn the lock. "When you gonna fix this bloody lock, Joey?" she shouted out. I couldn't help it, I burst out laughing, which then made Sam laugh even more. "Fuckin' funny, is it? I know what, why don't you two come and hang out the washing?" Dionne ordered. Finally, the back door opened. Following Dionne out to the balcony, Sam took the washing from her arms. Dionne pushed past me and stormed back into the living room.

"Ingrid. Ingrid come see me, I want to have a look at your mouth," Dad called from inside. Dad was sitting in his favourite chair, in his blue satin dressing gown and brown leather slippers. I knelt down on the floor near his feet and looked up at him. "What happened?" he asked, staring at my face.

"They thought it would be funny to climb on roofs and jump off, that's what happened," Dionne interrupted, whilst taking a sip of her tea.

"Is that right? Open, let me have a look." I opened my mouth as wide as I could and Dad peered inside. "Hm…your tongue is swollen. I don't think you'll need stitches," Dad decided.

"I could have told you that," Dionne snapped again. Dad glanced over at her with a stern stare and then kissed his teeth.

"Won't do that again, will you? You bloody monkey." Dad held my chin, his hand cupped around it. His hand felt rough but firm. "You're just like your dad, a brave little soldier." I nodded and left to meet Sam on the balcony. We were hanging out of the last pillowcase when the doorbell rang. *Probably Dad's friends again,* I thought.

"Joey," the voice that came through the letterbox sounded like Mum. The faint Irish voice definitely sounded like Mum. It was Mum.

"What's she doing here, Joey?" Dionne asked him, slamming her mug on the table.

"Dionne, just go get the door will ya," Dad ordered. Sam and I waited patiently for Dionne to open the door.

"Mum!" I shouted. She looked hot and bothered. Squeezing her tightly, her smell gave me comfort, even though it was the stale smell of alcohol and cigarettes. Mum started to cry; Sam put her head on her shoulder. I just stared at her.

"What's wrong, Mum?" Sam asked.

"Bernie," Dad's voice sounded from behind us.

Mum looked up, her eyes were sad, "Alright Joey," she replied. Dad folded his arms; his posture was intimidating. Suddenly I felt overcome with fear; something wasn't right.

"Where is your bastard of a boyfriend? Is he with you?" Dad asked.

"Dad, please don't talk like that," Sam asked him quietly.

"No, I am by myself, a friend dropped me down," Mum interrupted, wiping the tears from her eyes.

"Come, we need to talk," Dad responded, walking slowly to his bedroom. Sam pulled on Mum's arm, trying to pull her back. Sam's face looked terrified.

"It's okay," Mum said as she followed Dad, "I'll be back in a minute."

"Come sit with me you two," Dionne told us.

"No. I want to sit in our room," Sam told her abruptly. I followed her; I knew Sam well. At least in our room, we can check Mum's okay as it's the closest to Dad's bedroom. Dionne came to the bedroom door.

"What you worrying for? They're just talking. Come on, sit with me," Dionne requested again. Her tone sounded as though she was losing patience.

"No Dionne, we want to stay here, Daddy's gonna hit her. I know he is," Sam told Dionne, Sam gripped my hand tightly.

"Suit yourself then," Dionne said abruptly then walked away. Dad's voice began to get louder and louder. I could feel Sam's body begin to shiver; I had an awful feeling in my stomach. Sam started to pace up and down the bedroom. I sat there watching her. Sam opened the door and shouted for Dionne. Within seconds Dionne appeared at our door. "What?" she asked.

"Dionne, please go see if Mum's okay," Sam pleaded with her.

"No, I won't, let's not forget your Mum dumping you here. What did you expect? Dad not to say anything?"

"Yeah, but, Dionne, please," Sam begged again.

At that very moment, there was a loud thud. "Joey don't beat me!" Mum's voice echoed through the walls. Sam pushed past Dionne, hurling her into the wall. I jumped up and ran to Dad's door. Dad was shouting and cursing at Mum, and Mum was screaming. The slaps and punches were easily heard through the door.

Sam held on to the door handle screaming, "Daddy stop it please!" I could feel my chest tightening. Crying uncontrollably, I tugged at Sam's top. I couldn't breathe. I was suffocating. There was pure chaos and neither Dionne nor Sammie could see I was struggling to breathe. I was terrified. Every so often Sammie's screaming and jumping around slammed my body into the doorframe. Dionne shouted at us to move, not even Dionne could move us.

"You fucking cunt!" Dad screamed at Mum. Mum's screams got fainter and fainter. I looked at Dionne for some kind of help, but even she looked helpless. Dionne's eyes began to fill with tears. The sound of Mum's body hitting the furniture was clear. There was one final bang and my heart sank. Finally, Dionne realised I couldn't breathe properly with tears pouring down my face. Dad continued to swear at Mum. Dionne rushed to the bathroom cabinet to get my inhaler. Sam collapsed to the floor still holding onto the handle making sure not to let go. The door flew open. Dad stood there; he looked like a stranger to me. It was as though he had changed, and there was no sight of Mum. "You two are crying for that? That piece of shit!" Dad yelled at us, he stepped over Sam, who stayed where she was on the floor. Rushing into the room searching for Mum, I could see her feet at the other side of the bed.

"Mum!" I screamed. Mum's body lay face down.

"Dionne, help us please!" Sam screamed at Dionne, who stood looking from the bedroom door. Her face looked drained of all colour. Dionne ran over and turned Mum over. Through my tears, I noticed what looked like a tooth embedded in Mum's hair which was matted in blood. Sam screamed and screamed, "Mum, wake up!" There was nothing. Even Dionne began to scream. There was no movement, Mum's eyes were swollen and bulging. Blood seeped out of her mouth and nose. I could hear Dad somewhere in the house, still shouting and smashing things.

"Joey, we need to get an ambulance!" Dionne shouted.

"Fuck the slag!" he yelled back. Dionne placed Mum's hand on her stomach and ran for the phone and called an ambulance. What was probably a few minutes seemed like hours, Sam still screaming at Mum's lifeless body. There was a loud bang on the front door. Police and ambulance had arrived together.

"Mum. Mum, the ambulance is here," I whispered to her. Sam held on tight to Mum's hand. The paramedics rushed over to Mum and a very kind woman took us out of the room. She led us to our bedroom. Glancing into the living room I could see two policemen put Dad in handcuffs. The chaos went on and on; not once did Dad stop shouting. They took Mum away and Dionne left for the hospital with her in the ambulance. A neighbour from the next block came to sit with us. I felt all cried out. For the first time ever, I couldn't cry anymore. Sam lay on my bed with me, eventually crying herself to sleep. I felt safe with her.

She knew what to do, she will make things okay. I laid there for a little while and watched her sleep. I felt a sense of loss. Was I ever going to see Mum again? It didn't seem as though I would. I think Dad had killed her this time. I fell asleep with that on my mind.

I woke to the sound of the hoover; it was the only sound in the silence. Sam was not in her bed. Within a split second, I remembered what had happened 'Mum' I leapt out of bed and ran to the living room. Sam was sitting down on the sofa gazing at the TV. "Dionne, where's Dad?" I asked her.

"He's not back yet," she answered whilst unplugging the hoover. There was no eye contact.

"So, have you heard about Mum, Di?"

"No, but I'm sure she's okay. Well, she was when I left her last night at the hospital," Dionne replied.

"What's going to happen to Dad, Dionne?" I asked.

"Nothing as far as I know. Your mum hasn't pressed any charges," she replied.

"Can we see her, Di?" I asked her.

Before she had time to reply, Sam interrupted, "No we can't, I already asked Dionne. She said we should wait." My heart sank and I ran out of the room, crying. Why can't we see her? I just want my mum so badly. Dad returned that evening as though nothing had happened, stinking of drink. We could hear him singing from up the street. "Inx come, let's go to our room," Sam told me.

"Why, Sam?" I asked her.

"Because he's been drinking, he might start," Sam told me. I followed her to our room.

We had not seen or heard from Mum in weeks; every now and again she would cross my mind. I wondered what she was doing. She'll never come to see us again after what happened. "Ingrid and Samanta," Dad called from the living room. Once again, Dad had interrupted our game of dolls. The house was noisy. It was clear that there was a house full of people. The music was blaring, the sound of dominoes slamming on the table and men swearing at each other.

"Come on, Inx," Sam said, dropping her doll to the floor. When we opened our bedroom door the smoke came flooding in past us. The corridor wasn't very long, but it seemed long. I never knew what mood Dad would be in. The living room was packed with extra people I hadn't seen before. Dad was sat around the table with the usual suspects: Fonso, Charlie and my godfather, Sam. Across the room was Dionne, sitting on the floor by the stereo singing. There were at least three other women who I didn't know.

"Ingrid, Sammy, come let me introduce you to these gorgeous, sexy sophisticated women!" Dad shouted. He turned in his seat and reached out to one of the women. She looked dirty; her feet were dirty and she was drunk, with drink stains on her blouse. Dad grabbed her hand firmly and pulled her aggressively to sit on his lap. With one firm tug, she landed on Dad's lap and he pulled her in close, with his arms wrapped around her waist.

"Oh, fuck arf, Joey," she screamed in a strange accent.

"Shut up, you sexy princess," he said, with a huge grin on his face. "Ingrid and Samanta, I want you to meet my future wife Christine. Isn't she gorgeous?" he continued. Sam and I looked over at each other and laughed. I dared not say what I really thought.

"Yes Dad," I replied, looking across the room at Dionne. Dionne looked around, kissing her teeth. She just carried on singing. Dad grabbed Christine's breasts with both hands and began to squeeze roughly. Christine laughed. They were drunkenly laughing and swaying over the edge of the seat.

"Joey man, stop fucking around and get on with the fucking game man," Fonso shouted at him, slamming his domino down on the table. Dad was having too much fun. He jumped up and threw Christine in the air. Grabbing her by the waist, he threw her legs around him. Her face was bright red.

"For fuck sake, Joey!" Dionne shouted at him. Dad clearly couldn't hear her. They began to sway as Dad struggled to keep hold of her. The other two ladies who were sitting on the sofa leapt out of the way just as Dad landed on top of the woman with her legs still wrapped around him. Dad began to move his bum up and down like he would do to us, the difference being they had their clothes on.

"You gonna divorce me, Dionne? So, I can marry this lovely woman," Dad said, screaming over the laughter and loud music. Sam stood there biting her lip. "You can have a fucking divorce, I'll go get me a new husband then!" Dionne yelled back. Dad pulled away from Christine, leaving her breathless on the sofa. He went straight for Dionne.

"Is that right? You can never leave me, I'll kill you and him," Dad said, pulling her up off the floor. Dad was still playing. He was laughing his head off. Dionne's face was red and flustered.

"Get off, Joey." Dionne just about managed to place her glass down beside the stereo, still being careful not to spill any. Dad held her tightly, his arm wrapped around her neck.

"Dad, let her go!" Sam shouted. Dad ignored her and continued to keep hold. Dad reached behind him to stop the record that was playing, the needle screeched as he dragged it across the record.

"Right, I have an announcement to make! Ingrid and Samanta you are going to have a little baby brother or sister. There will be another Adams coming," Dad said, still holding Dionne tight with one hand and reaching for the bottle of whisky on the table with the other, taking a huge gulp.

"Ahh that's nice, Joey!" one of the ladies shouted out. I had seen that look many times before. She wasn't happy for Dad or Dionne. I had seen that look in Mum's eyes before; when Dad announced he was going to marry Dionne, Mum smiled and wished them the best. Then, later, told us she wished Dionne would drop dead. Dad was the love of her life; Dad was the love of all of these women's lives. No one liked Dionne; they all wanted him. Stunned by the news of a baby brother or sister, Sam and I stood there. I didn't know what to say. For a moment I felt lost. I couldn't help but think this is it, we're going to be forgotten about. Dad pulled Dionne's face to kiss her. Dionne tried to pull away but soon gave in.

"Dad, can we go now?" I asked him. Dad ignored me and started the record again. He started singing really loud, it sounded like Jim Reeves.

"I've been accused, convicted and condemned, the trial is over and now I face the end," he continued to sing at the top of his voice. Dad swung Dionne around, holding her by the hand and began to dance with her. Dionne followed his lead. "Is this your way of telling me we're through, when all I'm guilty of is loving you," Dad sang out aloud to Jim Reeves this was one of Dad's favourite songs. Slowly, Sam and I drifted out of the room, unnoticed. That night I slept right through and Dad didn't come to see me. We had quite a few good nights' sleep. Dad wasn't coming home every night anymore and sometimes I would hear Dionne crying in her room. Dad would come and get washed, changed and kiss us all quickly before leaving again.

Chapter Six:
The Eviction

Age nine. "Well, if you weren't out all the bloody time, Joey, maybe we wouldn't have this problem!" Dionne yelled at Dad. The kitchen window was slightly open I could hear her voice from outside along with the sound of pots and plates banging.

"Oh, dear what's Joe done now?" said Neil. Neil is Dionne's brother – he came down most Saturdays to help Dionne out. He had an appearance like someone that was living in the sixties. Cropped, greasy-looking hair, like one of the guys out of the movie Grease. He has piercing blue eyes with dark brown hair. He would arrive at Dad's early, around 8 am every weekend. With a roll-up hanging from his lip, tight jeans and a biker jacket. Dionne was the only girl in her family, with six brothers.

"Well, you tell the fucking kids then," was the last thing I heard Dionne say before one of them slammed the kitchen door.

"Do you want a go of my bike?" Neil asked me. I looked behind me just to make sure it was me he was talking to. Neil's behaviour would change every now and again. Sometimes I felt as though he didn't like Sam or me. He would always make hurtful remarks about Mum.

"No thanks," I replied. Just then, Dad appeared at the front door.

"Hello fuck face," Dad said to Neil.

"Don't call me fuck face, you black enamel bastard," Neil snapped back. They both began to laugh. "What you done to my sister now?" he asked Dad whilst pulling a large bottle of Coca-Cola from his bag which he had strapped to the back of his bike. Neil loved Coke; he would drink bottles of it every day, along with at least one whole bag of sugar, which he would eat by the spoonful, and tins of Devon custard eaten from the tin.

"Ingrid, Samanta, come," Dad beckoned from inside.

What we done now? I thought to myself. Neil dropped his roll-up on the floor.

"We're coming, you black bastard," Neil shouted out. We followed Neil into the flat. Dad was sitting down in his usual armchair and wearing his blue silk robe, his face looked worried. Dionne sat on the sofa; her face was red, as though she had been crying. Dad stood up with his hands on his hips peering down at us sitting on the sofa. What had we done? Maybe we were playing with our dolls too much. Or maybe Mum's dead.

"Right, you lot, I'm gonna get straight to the point. We have to move out."

What? That's it? I thought, Sam looked as confused as I felt. Neil shook his head in disappointment. "How's this happened, Joey?" Neil asked him.

"Well, work has been really slow, so we couldn't keep up with the bills," Dad explained.

"What bloody rubbish, Joey, if you weren't out all the time and drinking away the money we wouldn't be in this mess. And we have another two mouths to feed, with one more on the way," Dionne snapped back. Neil went over and put his arm around Dionne trying to console her.

"Oh Dionne, be quiet, you told me to tell the kids so let me fucking do it then." Dionne got up and left the room.

"Where will we go, Dad?" Sam asked him.

"Look, we only have a week to get out. Don't worry, we won't be on the street. The housing will put us somewhere because we have you two and fuck face is pregnant," Dad explained. "It will probably be a hotel somewhere until they find us somewhere else." Sam and I smiled at each other.

"That sounds like fun. A hotel, wow," Sam responded.

Dionne didn't talk to Dad for the rest of the day. "Fuck this shit, I'm going out. I know where I'm not wanted," Dad said aloud.

"That's it, go on, disappear again like you always do," Dionne shouted back, banging things around in the kitchen.

"Right, Dionne, I'm off too, will you be okay?" Neil asked.

"Well, I'll have to be won't I? No one else gives a fucking shit," Dionne answered, finally smashing a few plates in the sink.

"Oh dear," Neil said faintly as he stepped out of the kitchen. Without saying goodbye to anyone, Neil slipped out behind Dad, slamming the door closed. There was an awkward vibe in the flat.

"You two may as well go sort through your stuff what you're keeping and what you don't want anymore," Dionne said eventually. We spent the rest of the day in our room. Every now and again, Dionne would come in to check we were doing what she asked. With clothes sprawled all around us, we manage to slip our Sindy dolls under the pile of clothes whenever Dionne came to the door.

"What if Mum comes to see us, Sam, and we're not here?" I asked her.

"I didn't think about that, Inx, she won't be able to find us. We could be going anywhere," Sam replied. Her eyes saddened.

"I bet Carl will like that, then we will be out of her life forever," I responded.

"Hmm maybe Mum won't be bothered at all, Inx, you know Mum cares about her boyfriend's more." It's true. I felt exactly the same as Sam. The reality of it was too much to think about so we put our dolls away and continued to pack.

Chapter Seven:
Central Park Hotel

Dad's Rover 3500 was packed to the brim with our bags; I could hardly see where we were going. "We're nearly there," Dionne told us. "And we get a cooked breakfast every morning, eggs, bacon, beans, and bread," Dionne continued.

"Wow, it must be really posh!" Sam responded. Dad laughed. As the car came to a halt, I noticed that the whole street was hotels. They looked very fancy.

"Look, Sam, it's gonna be so much fun living here," I told Sam whilst unloading the car.

"So what, who cares? Mum's not gonna find us here, is she?" Sam gave me a long stare. I felt sad for a moment, but I was so keen to get inside and see our rooms.

"Right you two, sit there while me and Dionne go check in and sort out any paperwork," Dad told us. The reception had large glass doors with brass edging and handles. The floor was shiny with a large marble counter. It was just as I expected. After the man at the desk checked us in, a second man came from behind and asked us to follow him to our rooms. We came out of reception back onto the pavement and went back into the building using a door right next to the reception. Sam and I looked at each other puzzled. The stairway was narrow with dark brown carpet. The stairs seemed endless. As we reached the second floor, a pungent smell like nothing I have ever smelt before hit me.

"Err, what's that? It smells like poo," I said aloud. Sammie laughed and Dad looked back at us, telling us to be quiet. A small Asian woman dressed in a sari appeared from a small kitchen with her baby clutched to her hip. The smell got more pungent. She was cooking with another two Asian women; she looked at us and smiled.

"Afternoon," Dad said as we passed her on the landing. She didn't reply, she just smiled.

"Next floor is yours," the hotel worker told us.

"Thank god," I said quietly, "my legs are killing me." There were lots of split landings and doors leading to other parts of the hotel.

"Inx, we are gonna have so much fun," Sam said.

"Here we are," the hotel man said, stopping outside room number 46. "The one opposite is also yours," he continued, pointing to the door with number 45 on it.

He unlocked the door and we walked in. It wasn't very big. There was a double bed, a sink and a large wardrobe. It wasn't what I expected at all. The walls were a mustard colour with green curtains with a few missing hoops, allowing the curtains to hang down in the middle. "Oh boy." Dad sighed disappointedly.

"Can we see our room now?" Sam asked. The man held out his hand with another set of keys.

"Shall I?" the man asked Dad's permission, still holding the keys out for Sam to take.

"Yeah, go on," Dad agreed. Sam snatched the keys and we ran to our room. We couldn't stop smiling. "It feels like our own flat, don't it, Inx," Sam said as she unlocked the door.

We were in; there were two single beds, a single wardrobe and a sink behind the door. "This is great, Inx," Sam said.

"This is my bed," I told her. I chose the one furthest from the door.

"Inx, we can lock our door when we go to bed." Sam looked relieved. Just as she said that Dad appeared at our door.

"And what would you want to do that for, Samanta?" Dad asked her with his arms folded, leaning up against the light switch.

"Um, um…I just meant it would be good to lock it in case a stranger came in, Dad," she stuttered.

"Well, I can tell you now this door isn't going to be locked and I can guarantee you there will be no strangers apart from me coming in here you understand?"

"Yes Dad," we both answered.

"Besides if there's a fire, how am I supposed to get you out," Dad continued as he left the room. Sam and I stared at each other for a moment in silence. After all the excitement of having cooked breakfast every day, and running up and down all the stairs, playing knock-down ginger on every resident, the days started to become long and boring. We still hadn't got a place in school. Dionne was getting, what she called, depressed. She was crying all the time and her belly got big really quick. Dad said she was really unhappy and couldn't take it anymore. He had arranged for us all to still be registered at the hotel but we would sleep and spend most of our time at Dionne's friend's house in Hackney. Just before we left to stay with Dionne's friend, Sam and I had got a place in school. Mine was called Gillespie in Finsbury Park and Sam's was a secondary school called Woodberry Down. I hated school. I wanted to be with Sam all the time. Dad would have to drop us to school on the nights we spent at Dionne's friend's house. On some occasions, Dad wouldn't take us back to Dionne. We would have to spend the night at the hotel with just him.

Most weekends were spent with Dionne and her friend Christine, I really liked Christine. She had long black hair and a pleasant face. Her flat was huge; it was on the ground floor of Nesbit House E5. Best of all, there was a massive swing park right outside. Dionne was very happy there; Christine spoiled her like she was her own child.

"Dad, are we going to Christine's today?" I asked him.

"Yes my angel, we're going to get Sam from school first," he answered, whilst peering back at me through his rear-view mirror. Once pulled up outside, Dad did not take his eyes off of the school gates. Not even for a second. He chewed on his spearmint gum, clearly in deep thought. "There she is, Ingrid," he told me, pointing over to the gates. Sam was walking with a couple of girls and a couple of boys. When she spotted us she smiled and waved. She said goodbye to her friends and came to the car.

"Hi Dad, hi Inx," Sam said, placing her bag down by her feet in the front of the car.

"Hm." Dad sighed arrogantly. "What, no kiss for your dad, fanny?" Dad said to Sam, holding a cold stare.

"Oh Dad, do I have to?" Sam felt embarrassed. I knew she did. Within a split second, Dad slapped Sam with the back of his hand at full force.

"Agh," Sam screamed out loud. I jumped my heart was racing.

"You fucking slag, how dare you fucking dismiss me. Who the fuck do you think you are?" Dad yelled, driving like a madman. Sam was crying uncontrollably and I cried silently. Dad looked back in the mirror at me. "What the fuck you crying for? Your sister's a dirty slag," he screamed.

"I knew she didn't do anything," I said to myself. At that moment, I hated Dad.

"Who were those boys? I bet you let them finger you, don't ya?" He continued. "You're not even thirteen yet and already you're behaving like your mother." Sam continued to cry. Sam glanced back at me; I could see in her eyes that she wanted me to help her. I couldn't do anything to make it better. Her lip was swollen and her gums were bleeding. "Ingrid, stop that crying you hear me. Right now." That was Dad's final word. Once we'd pulled up outside Christine's house, Dad jumped out and left us. He slammed the car door so hard I thought the glass was going to smash.

"You okay, Sam?" I asked her. *Thank God he's gone,* I thought.

"Yeah, I'm okay, Inx, are you?" she asked, concerned for me.

"Why did Dad have to do that, Sam?" I asked her. Sam climbed out of the car, still holding her mouth, and opened my door.

"Why does he ever do anything, Inx? It's what he does," she explained to me. "Now please stop crying, Inx, in case he hits you," she said. We took a slow walk into the flats. "I'm sick of this, Inx, we can't have any friends because he'll probably hit them," Sam told me, and she was right. When we reached the front door, we could hear Dad shouting and swearing. "I don't want to go in, Inx, he's gonna hit me again." Her eyes looked terrified. There was nothing I could say and nothing I could do. I knocked on the door hesitantly.

"Hi, Di," I said, gazing up at her. Sam said nothing. Dionne stood at the doorway looking disappointed. She obviously believed Dad's made-up story again. Dionne followed us to our bedroom door.

"Those who don't hear shall feel," she mumbled under her breath. "I don't understand how you would be kissing a boy outside school anyway Sam, you're only 12. It's disgusting," Dionne said before leaving the room. Sam slumped down on the bed and cried.

"I haven't got a boyfriend, and I never kissed anyone," Sam said out loud. To my horror the bedroom door flew open; Dad had heard Sam.

"Yeah, go on say it again, you lying cunt." Dad grabbed Sam by the hair, holding her up in one hand and slapping her with the other. I gasped for air. Dionne ran in and dragged me out by my arm.

"Ingrid!" Sam shouted. The door closed. Dionne forbade me to enter the bedroom; Sammie's pleas for help continued. Eventually, Dad emerged from the room with his belt draped over his shoulder. His face looked satisfied, the whites of his eyes were red.

"Ingrid, we've got visitors tonight," Dionne told me, trying to break the silence. All I could think about was Sam in the bedroom. There were no sounds from her anymore. I rested my head on my arm on the armchair and said nothing. "They're two sisters around yours and Sam's age, I think. Me and Dad are friends with their parents," Dionne continued. I raised my eyebrows to show I was listening when really, I wanted to ignore her completely but that would end up in me getting beaten. Christine entered the room with two cups of tea for her and Dionne. Dad was nowhere to be seen. It sounded like he was cleaning up in the bathroom. "Joey, they're going to be here in a minute. Can Sam come out now?" Dionne called out to Dad as he emerged from the bathroom. At the same time, she winked at me, as though she was doing me a favour.

"Yes Dionne," he replied, closing his bedroom door behind him.

"Does that mean I can go in now Di?" I asked her, sitting on the edge of my chair.

"Yeah go on, and tell her to make herself presentable," she replied. I opened the door slowly to find Sam asleep, curled up on her bed. Taking a closer look, I could just about make out Dad's handprint across her cheek and random red lines on her arms.

"Sam, Sammie, wake up," I said, nudging her gently. Sam began to stir.

"What, Inx?" she answered solemnly.

"We have got visitors coming in a minute, some girls. They're meant to be our age," I informed her. Sam sat up, her face showing the pain in her body.

"Agh," she said, as she pulled herself up against the headboard.

"Who are they, Inx?" she asked me.

"I don't know," I answered, trying my hardest not to stare too much at her face. "Dionne said you should get up and do your hair and stuff before they come."

"I don't want to see anyone, Inx, I'll just stay in here," she replied. Her response made me uneasy; this will just get her into more trouble. "Alright don't come out then, but at least do something, Sam, 'cos you'll just get into trouble again," I pleaded. Just moments later there was a knock at the door.

"I'll get it, Joey," Christine called out. Sam and I gazed at each other for a brief moment.

"Go see what they're like, Inx," Sam requested, tenderly brushing her hair.

"Hello, you sexy arrogant bastard," Dad said to the man standing at the door.

"Hello, you black enamel bastard," the man greeted back. They embraced each other with a hug.

"Come on into my humble abode," Dad stepped aside to allow them to enter.

"Joey, you know my wife, June," the man said. Dad leant over and kissed her on the cheek. "And this is my eldest daughter, Maggie." Dad was elated; I had seen this look many times.

"Hi Joey, I've heard lots about you." She smiled, then stepped aside.

"And this is Angie, she's my youngest daughter." Dad kissed her as well.

"And who's this handsome young man?" Dad asked, referring to an odd-looking boy.

"This is Terry, my one and only son," the man replied. Dad walked them through to the living room. I slipped away to go and tell Sam what they were like.

"Sam, there's loads of them, come see," I told her.

"Ingrid. Samanta. Come and meet our family," Dad called out. Sam couldn't help but laugh; she was quickly reminded of her busted lip.

"Ouch, what family? He chats so much rubbish," she said quietly. We both laughed.

"Dick, you know my other half, Dionne, already. And this is our good friend, Christine. Ahh, here they are. Everyone, these are my two beautiful daughters, Ingrid and Samantha." I felt like I was on show. "Ingrid, Samantha, this is Dick and his wife June." As he went down the line he continued, "then we have a beautiful princess Maggie, and another princess Angie, and finally this handsome prince Terry." Everyone laughed. Dick reminded me of a Smurf or a Gnome; he was a white short man with greasy grey hair, thick beard and dirty clothes. Dionne's efforts for that fresh-smelling home that she tried so hard to maintain had been diluted out by staleness. "Dick, follow me, captain. Let's get some drinks." Dick followed Dad into the kitchen. June was a small-framed woman with mousy brown cropped hair with slightly protruding teeth, she sat next to Dionne looking uneasy and a bit out of her depth. Maggie got up then walked over to Sam and me still standing by the living room door.

"Hiya, nice to meet you. I'm Maggie, which one's Sam and who's Ingrid?" she asked us.

"I'm Ingrid and this is Sam," I answered.

"Aw, what happened to your face, Sam?" she asked. There was an awkward pause.

"Oh, I had a fight at school," Sam replied.

"Aw you poor thing," she responded. Maggie was tall, slim, and blonde. She was pretty. She wore tight-fitting jeans, a black V-neck jumper and black leg warmers up to her thigh. "I'm 15, how old are you two?" she asked.

"I'm 12 and Ingrid's 9," Sam answered. Our conversation was interrupted by strange noises coming from Terry who was standing beside his mum who was sitting in the armchair. It was like a grunting, groaning sound like I had never heard before. Sam and I began to laugh.

"Shut up you two. Have some bloody manners," Dionne snapped.

"Don't worry about him, he's always like this when he meets new people, I think he's excited," Angie said, still sitting on the sofa. "Well, I'm Angie, I'm 13 soon to be 14." Maggie and Angie looked very similar, so similar that if they were the same height, I would have thought they were twins. She too had tight jeans on, thigh-length leg warmers and a black top. I had never seen a style like this before. Terry's sounds became more distracting.

"Is he okay, June?" Dionne asked concerned.

"Yeah he's fine, I'll just take him out for some space if that's okay, Di?" June answered. Terry was almost the same height as me with short shoulder-cut blonde hair and protruding teeth, as he walked past me, I noticed he had short ankle-length trousers with black shoes which looked like something we would see when going to the Jumble sale with Mum, the kind of shoes no one would buy. He had a weird look in his eyes. June held on to him and took him into the hallway. Dad returned from the kitchen with an armful of drinks while Dick carried the glasses.

"Christine, be a love and put some music on," Dad requested. Angie got up and followed Sam into our bedroom; I was fascinated by their confidence. "Oh, Dick how you been? You old son of a gun?" Dad asked with a wide grin on his face.

"Yeah Joey, I'm good thanks. You know what it's like, trying to get by," he replied, then taking a large swing of vodka.

"I know what you mean, mi old friend. God, I tell ya' these kids will be the death of me," Dad replied.

They raised their glasses to toast to friendship and knocked back their drinks. "Ah that's more like it, this will put chest on your hair," Dad said, they both laughed. Dad's jokes became tiresome but his friends loved it. "Here you are fanny," Dad said to Maggie, passing her over a glass of vodka and Coke. I suddenly felt uncomfortable but Maggie smiled. She had uneven teeth but that didn't matter. She was still very pretty.

"Mum, Mum!" a strange voice yelled from the hallway.

"Oh Terry, come on. Come into the living room you little fucker!" June shouted out. Maggie sat back in her seat and took a mouthful of drink flicking her hair back. Dad was staring at her. He had that familiar look in his eye again. Distracted by my thoughts of Sam, I got up and left the room. As I passed the living room, I could see Terry standing in the corner. *What was he doing?* I asked myself. He was rocking side to side; he had his hand in his mouth biting down on it.

"What you doing?" I asked, concerned. He began to make those loud groaning noises as I stepped closer. I could see his hand was bleeding. His cries got louder but no one seemed bothered.

"Fucking hell Terry, get your arse in err," Dick demanded. Terry looked as though he was scared to pass me so I stepped aside to let him pass. This was really strange, I needed to tell Sam what was going on. When I entered the room, Sam was sitting in the corner of her bed holding her pillow on her lap; Angie was sitting by her feet stroking her leg.

"Your sisters just told me what's happened, Ingrid. You know, about your Dad hitting her." I was horrified. Did my sister not learn? Dad would kill her if he knew that she'd told someone. "It's okay, Ingrid, I won't say anything. I give my word." Angie tried to reassure me. Sam looked relieved.

"Are you the same age as me, Angie?" I asked.

"Well, how old are you?" she asked.

"I'm nine," I replied sitting down on the cushions in the opposite corner of the room.

"Aw no honey I'm 13, I'll be 14 soon though," she answered. I thought she looked much older; she had tits. She was wearing makeup – blue eyeliner and blue mascara. Dad would never let us put makeup on. "Do you want to see something funny?" she asked, already standing up in front of us.

"Like what?" Sam curiously asked, while removing her pillow from her mouth. Angie began to roll down her leg warmers, revealing bare skin just above her knee. Sam started to laugh. What's so funny? I gave Sam a puzzled look.

"Well, we can't afford to buy new jeans, so what we do when they get too short is cut them down and put legwarmers on top. Then people think we're wearing full-length jeans," Angie explained. It was funny. I never would have guessed. She looked so nice, I wanted to be her; to have her long blonde hair, boobs and be allowed to wear makeup. With that thought, the door flew open. Sam jumped. She clearly thought it was Dad again. Terry stood there in the doorway.

"What you doing, Ange?" he asked her. His cheeks were red, he looked hot and bothered. That strange stale smell followed him into the room.

"Do you want to watch King Kong?" I asked him, but there was no response. He just stared at me, smiling.

"Yeah, go on, Ingrid, put it on. We can all watch it," Angie smiled. We turned the lights off so there was complete darkness. I was so happy; it was one of my favourite films. The black and white light from the TV was the only light in the room. I was completely comfortable with our new friends. Every now and again, Maggie would pop in to check up on us and with each visit, the smell of alcohol got more pungent. She would come in and sprawl herself across Sammie's bed, giggling.

The last few times I could hear Dad calling out for her. "Maggie, my sexy wife-to-be, where are ya?" The house felt unusually calm; Dad was extremely happy. I kept drifting in and out of sleep. I managed to catch a glimpse of King Kong getting shot down; I hated this part of the movie, but I still needed to see it. Terry was sprawled out across the floor, fast asleep with his jacket on top of him. Angie and Sammy were still talking.

"I bet you Ingrid's crying," I overheard Sam say to Angie.

"Shut up Sam," I snapped, wiping the tears from my cheeks. This was the first of many nights we got to spend together.

It was a cold, rainy Monday morning. I hated Mondays. I hated mornings. "Dad's got to leave early this morning you two, so you need to get washed and dressed quickly. You may even have time to eat breakfast," Dionne said, opening the curtains. Her stomach was massive; Dionne was due to have her baby any day now. Once on our way to school, I soon noticed Dad had changed from our usual route.

"Where are we going, Dad?" Sam asked him. Dad had a weird smile on his face.

"We're just gonna stop and collect a couple of friends, they wanted to see you two," Dad answered. The car pulled to a halt in Kingsmead Estate in Hackney. Dad beeped his horn a couple of times. The excitement was making me fidget; looking up at the flats, we waited patiently.

To our surprise coming out of the ground floor flat were Angie and Maggie walking towards us in their cut-down jeans, leg warmers and high-heeled shoes. "Samanta you can get in the back now," Dad told her. Sammie quickly climbed out of the car and joined me in the back. We shuffled over to make room for Angie. This was a complete surprise; we couldn't stop laughing.

"Hi Ingrid, hi Sam," Maggie greeted us with a warm smile.

"Hi," we replied.

"Ingrid and Samanta, I have one more surprise for you. You two won't be going to school today. There is something I want to do and so I thought it would be nice for you lot to get to know each other," Dad informed us. Whilst stroking Maggie's leg in the front.

"You alright, Jo?" Maggie asked Dad.

"I am now you're here." Dad laughed. Dad was in a great mood. I haven't seen him like this for the longest time. Just as the car began to pull away, Maggie waved goodbye to a man who was fixing a dirty, beat-up car parked outside their home.

"You remember my uncle, Jo?" Maggie said pointing at the greasy man with piercing eyes and greasy black hair. He resembled Catweasel from Worzel Gummidge.

"Yeah sure," Dad replied, winding down his window. "You alright, you sexy bastard?" Dad hollered out. The man stood there, not too amused, with his spanner in his hand.

Looking quite sheepish, he replied, "Yeah Jo, and you?"

"You know me, captain. Anyway, I'll catch up with you soon," and Dad pulled away. The man held a long stare as we drove past him. "You know what, Maggie. I know I've met him before but for the life of me, I can't remember his name. What was it again?" he asked her.

"It's Lesley, Jo! Lesley Bailey," (Lesley Bailey, convicted child killer and paedophile) she answered.

"Oh yeah that's it, I'll chat to him later if he's still around," Dad said as he drove us out of the estate.

The streets started to look familiar. Were we going to school and this was all a joke? Sam and I looked at each other confused. "So, where we going, Joey? Come on you can put us out of our misery now," Angie said.

"Is this it, Dad?" Sam asked as we pulled up outside our hotel.

"Ah what's this then, Joey?" Maggie asked with a cheeky grin on her face.

Dad kissed his teeth. "I told you, I wanted you lot to spend some quality time together." Sam looked at me, looking disappointed and concerned.

"Come on you two, this is fun! We get to spend the whole day together," Angie said while jumping out of the car. *Yeah, it will be fun*, I thought. Angie linked her arms into mine and Sam's as we walked alongside her, using our bodies to keep warm. Once inside Dad and Dionne's room, Angie asked us to show her our room.

"Not just yet, fanny," Dad told her whilst locking the bedroom door. Sam looked at me with that familiar look of dread. Maggie put her bag down on the back of the chair and hung her cardigan behind the door. Angie sat at the bottom of the bed while Sam and I took a seat on the two chairs in the corner. Sam looked over at me and shook her head from side to side, which spoke volumes. We're trapped, don't think of moving, just be still. Dad began removing his clothes layer by layer. Angie's face turned bright red whilst Maggie remained calm. This was like no other experience with Dad. My palms began to sweat. I just wanted to go to my room. If I were brave enough, I would have asked Sam to break me out of here. We both knew what was coming. Maggie laughed as Dad stepped out of his underpants. "Well, what you waiting for? Get undressed then," Dad ordered Angie and Maggie. "You two stay there and don't move, Daddy wants to show you something special," Dad said, unconvincingly. There was nowhere to go, Maggie and Angie were like our sisters by now. I didn't want to see them undress. Once they had removed their clothes, they lay waiting on the bed for Dad to join them. One by one Dad had what Dionne would call pudding – sex. Dad was in his element.

"Inx, do you think he's going to make us do that?" Sam whispered.

"I don't want him to, Sam," I whispered back. Before our eyes, Dad had done all of what we had seen in his X-rated videos. This became a regular occurrence; Dad would convince Dionne he was taking us to school but we would end up there. After a while, it wasn't so scary. One day we might watch, another day he would take either one of them into his room and we would sit in our room and laugh at the noises that echoed through the wall. Dad was happier with us and treated us nicer, as long as we never told Dionne.

Dionne had finally given birth to our baby sister. They named her Melissa. When Dionne brought her home, we couldn't contain our excitement, she was so small and cuddly. Although we never got to hold her much or even see her much. Dionne spent a lot of time in her room at Christine's. After a while, I would avoid asking Dionne if I could hold her because she would always say no. Dad said he had enough of it and that she puts her baby before him. He said that we made him feel special. He would tell everyone that he wasn't getting any 'Nookie' – that was what Dad called sex.

We got to spend more and more time with Angie and Maggie. It was like a second family. Today we were going to meet Angie and Maggie at their nan's house, which was in Kingsmead Estate but in a different block of flats. Everyone called her Nan. She was a large woman; sometimes she would wrestle herself out of her own chair. She had greasy, grey hair and would wear these brown bootie slippers with fur inside, and a brown floral dress. I wasn't sure what colour the flowers were as her dress was shiny and grimed in dirt. Underneath the dress, she would wear brown trousers. When we first got to know her, we wouldn't accept a drink because the cups were stained brown and greasy. Not even Mum was this bad at keeping things clean. Even walking into the kitchen was a challenge. We would have to hold on to the walls to avoid sliding over. The top of the cooker was so black from years and years of spilt food which never got cleaned up. We were there so often that it became normal. Nan was well known for her rock cakes; they were like heaven. Sam would have one or two but I would eat until I felt sick. They were made with so much sugar I was in sugar heaven. "Ingrid, Samanta, I'm leaving you two here with the nanny for a while. Make sure you behave," Dad called to us.

"Where you going, Dad?" I asked.

"Never you mind, I'm going to see a man about a dog," he replied. *What's that supposed to mean,* I thought. I was so confused. We had a great time; Nanny fell asleep in her chair, leaving us to watch loads of horror films. My favourite was Rabid and An American Werewolf in London. Around 2 am there was a knock at the door.

"It's for me," Maggie announced, running to the front door.

"Who do you think that would be?" Sam asked Angie.

"Oh, it's probably her boyfriend," she answered. I wasn't sure what to make of it. *Dad must be okay with it I guess, if he's coming here*, I thought. Maggie was now one of Dad's women that was how we saw her. Maggie returned hand in hand with her friend. He was slightly taller than Maggie and looked around her age with jet-black hair, dark brown eyes and olive skin.

"Hi everyone, I'm Jake," he said, smiling and giving us a swift wave.

"Inx, Dad will be back soon. I wonder what will happen when Dad gets back," Sam whispered. Angie's body language had changed; even she seemed as though she was flirting with Jake. "Come on, Inx. It's late, we need to go to bed now, Dad will be back soon," Sam suggested. Maggie took her seat on the sofa and Jake sat on the floor between her legs. I didn't want to go to bed; I wanted to watch the end of American Werewolf. Before I could answer I was distracted by the sound of footsteps coming from the landing. We all sat up and adjusted ourselves.

"What's wrong with you lot?" Jake asked, confused.

"It's our dads, they're back already," she answered. Maggie got up and went to open the door.

"Hello fuck face," Dad said, stepping into the flat.

"Hi Jo, hi Dad," Maggie said, walking briskly back to her place on the sofa. When Dad and Dick walked into the living room, the atmosphere changed. Sam and I both wanted to leave; I knew she did because she kept nudging me. That was my cue to get up and leave. Dad looked on in horror at Jake sitting in between Maggie's legs.

"Ah you're the famous Joey I've heard about," Jake stood up and reached out to shake Dad's hand. There was an awkward pause.

"All good I hope," Dad responded. There was a sigh of relief from everyone. I could feel Dad's eyes burning through me as he studied me up and down at what I had on. "Dick, go get some glasses, let's welcome this young man into the family," Dad added. Dick scurried out the door, leaving a trail of smoke from his roll-up behind.

"Oi Joey, what do you mean welcome him? It's not like we're getting married or anything," Maggie said, looking up at Dad and rubbing the back of Jake's neck.

"Nah seriously, Joey, it's nice to meet you at last. I have heard great things about you." Jake held on to Maggie's hand, still placed on his shoulder.

"It's nice to meet you too, although I haven't heard about you before from Maggie," Dad said. Dick returned with four glasses and a bottle of spirit. Poor Dick, he was like Dad's shadow. He actually thought he and Dad were like brothers, but I knew different. Dad just wanted Dick's daughters. Dad poured the drinks while Dick walked over to the old-fashioned Grammy in the corner and selected Tammy Wynette.

"I won't put it on too loud Jo 'cos Mum's sleeping," Dick said considerately.

"Ingrid, Samanta, it's time you get to bed now or is there something you're waiting up for?" Dad asked sarcastically. This comment confirmed Dad was not happy at all. If we didn't leave now, Dad would be accusing us of wanting to have sex with Jake. With that remark, we got up, said goodnight and went straight to bed. Sam and I had to sleep top and tail in the bottom bunk bed, Sam quietly laughed as our faces felt as though they were sticking to the pillowcases. The smell of mothballs and crisp clean sheets at Dionne's was deeply missed.

"Did you see Dad's face, Inx, when he saw Jake?" Sam whispered.

"Yeah. He was pretending to be happy. He'll probably beat him up later," I whispered back. We laughed quietly then turned over to sleep. "Night Sam," I said.

"Night Inx." And Sam was asleep. I was tossing and turning for ages. The laughter, music and loud conversation made it difficult to sleep.

"Stop, what you doing man?" An unfamiliar voice had woken me. In the darkness, it took a moment for my eyes to adjust to my surroundings.

"Be quiet." It was Dad's voice. Dad was standing beside our bed. I knew it was him because I could see his keys, which he had hooked on his trousers, shining from the light outside. There was movement above.

"Please stop," the strange male voice whispered again. I squeezed my eyes closed and moved back gently to the far side of the bed so as not to be heard or seen by Dad. I lifted my head slowly. I could just about make out that Sam was wide-awake, laying there, still. There was one more figure curled up on the floor. Eventually, I could see it was Angie, asleep on the floor. I knew it was her because of her large hooped earnings. Maggie was nowhere to be seen. My heart was beating loud and fast, I'm sure Dad's going to hear it. I couldn't crawl down to Sam because he'll hear me.

"Don't fucking move you hear me, you cunt," Dad whispered violently. He sounded like he was gritting his teeth. It was Jake, it had to be. His voice was muffled. I felt sad. I looked up again at Sam, she looked back at me placing her finger on her mouth and gesturing for me to be quiet. Eventually, Dad stepped back. I squeezed my eyes tightly and wished him away. When I opened them again he was gone. The bunk bed began to move vigorously, Jake jumped down from the top and in a hurry, he ran out of the room and out the flat, slamming the door behind him.

"Inx, did you see who that was?" Sam whispered.

"Yeah Sam, Dad must have done something to him," I whispered back.

"I can't believe Dad came to him. You know what he was doing don't you?" Sam continued. I knew what Dad had done. It all seemed like a dream.

"Yeah, Sam. He must have touched him," I guessed. There was movement outside of our room. It was Dad, I could hear his keys rattling. Dad had opened the front door. A cold breeze came gushing through, then he closed it. He must have been looking for Jake.

"Go sleep now, Inx, in case he comes back," Sam told me. Once again it took ages to go to sleep, but I made sure my eyes were tightly closed. After this night we never got to see Angie and Maggie much. Our relationship with them fizzled out over time. Dad said it was because Maggie was a slag and that he didn't want us around them, but Sam and I knew differently. Dad was just angry that he didn't get to have sex with Maggie's boyfriend.

Chapter Eight:
Brian House

Age ten. "Ingrid, Sammy," Dionne called from her bedroom. "Come quick, me and Dad have something to tell you." Dionne sounded excited. Dad and Dionne were still in bed, with Melissa in between them. Melissa's fat little legs were in the air while she was playing with her toes. Her fat belly hung over her nappy. I smiled at how cute her little body was.

"What is it, Dionne?" Sam asked curiously.

"We are moving," Dionne answered while waving a piece of paper around. I jumped on the bed to get a closer look at what Dionne was holding; I was so excited. "It's from the housing, they have offered us a three-bedroom ground-floor flat." Dionne sounded so happy and relieved.

"Yes," Sam said, taking a seat at the bottom of the bed. Dad was sitting up, still eating his fry up. Dionne made one religiously, every morning.

"So now you two can settle and start a new school," Dad said, placing his fork onto his plate. Once again, the thought of Mum's face was pictured in my mind. Somehow, I managed to block out any other thoughts by distracting myself by crawling over to Melissa and blowing bubbles on her chubby belly. Melissa laughed loudly, with dribble running from her mouth.

"Yes, no more having to go to the hotel," Sammie cheered. I immediately looked up at Dad. I knew there would be a reaction.

"It wasn't all that bad was it, Samanta," Dad said, sitting up and placing his plate on his side table. His face was fixed with no expression. I began to hum with no tune in mind, just a stupid hum. I often did this when I felt uncomfortable. Thankfully, Melissa started to cry. Probably because I stopped playing with her, she was bored. Sam got up and left the room. I knew this wasn't to be the end of this conversation. We pulled up outside our new home – number 3, Brian House, E3.

"That must be our one, Joey." Dionne pointed to the one that's boarded up. A ground floor flat, with a green metal style picket fence. "Come on Joey," Dionne continued, re-positioning Melissa on her hip.

"Calm down, Dionne, it isn't going anywhere," Dad responded calmly. There was a short white woman pacing up and down outside, with papers in her hand.

"Ah, you must be the Adams family." She chuckled.

"I was wondering who this beautiful, sophisticated woman was," Dad said walking towards her.

She laughed as though she enjoyed the compliment; women never minded anything that came from his mouth. "I'm Dionne, this is Ingrid and Sammie." Dionne held out her hand, still trying to keep a firm hold on Melissa.

"And who's this bundle of joy?" the woman asked, peering at Melissa over Dionne's shoulder.

"This is Melissa," Dionne answered.

"Just beautiful, don't you just love them at this age," she stated, reaching for the keys to our new front door. Once inside, Sam and I made a dash in search of our potential new room.

"Look Inx, this could be our one," Sam said excitedly.

"Will you two calm down I'll tell you which one will be yours," Dad said from the next room.

"The living room is a good size isn't it, Joey," Dionne mentioned to Dad.

"Do you like it, Dionne? Cause if you do let's just accept it now. Remember I have work later." Dad tried to hurry us along. Dad worked most evenings at the weekends as a nightclub bouncer. I hated Dad's job. I always thought he was going to be killed at work. He would tell us stories of the fights he had while working on the door. Sometimes he never came home at all. I didn't realise clubs were open all night.

It was recorded as the hottest summer in 1983, with temperatures reaching 32.8 C. We were in the middle of our school summer holiday. Our days were filled with water fights and playing games of canon with other kids from the estate. Sometimes Dad and Dionne would join in too. If we weren't playing on the estate, we would be spending all day at the Victoria Park lido. I had a good group of friends; only one of them was from my new primary school, her name was Tanya. I often got teased because the other kids said they couldn't understand why I had her as a friend; they would call her names and say she was

104

dirty. Well, she wasn't to me. Tanya was kind and loyal, she had a really good heart and I could tell her anything. Tanya's dad had left her mum when she was very young. She only had her mum and older brother. She looked up to my dad. Then there was Nicky and Pamela – two identical twins. The day we first met, Sam and I heard a woman with red hair screaming out their names outside our block of flats. I could hear them calling back from a distance. It was all so bizarre; screaming back to their mum, shouting to let her know they were near.

These two girls appeared from around the corner, both faces exactly the same. They noticed me and Sam sat outside our front door, playing with our dolls. One of them looked over and winked at us and their mum slapped them across the back of the head and continued to shout. We watched them walking off into the distance. The next day they came to our gate, again catching me and Sam playing outside with our dolls. I think Sam felt embarrassed because she hid her doll behind her back. "Do you two want to hang out?" one of the twins asked.

"Yes, if you want to," Sam answered. Without hesitation one of them unlocked the gate and walked over to us.

"I'm Pamela and this is Nicky," Pamela put out her arms for a hug from Sam. Placing my dolls carefully on the floor, I stood up.

"This is Ingrid, my little sister, and I'm Sam," Sam introduced us.

Dad appeared at the front door. "Hello." His frame took up the narrow space in the doorway.

"Dad, this is Nicky and Pamela," Sam introduced them to Dad. Suddenly there was a scuffle behind Dad; Melissa came crashing in her baby walker straight into Dad's ankles. The twins laughed heartily. From this day we became the best of friends, we were inseparable. Melissa was doted on by all of us; she was included in most of what we did. Dionne must have liked them because she never minded them spending so much time with Melissa. Melissa was getting fatter and fatter. She loved to eat iced buns. We used to call her 'tree trunk Lily' because her legs were so fat, she would get stuck when we tried to lift her out of the walker. It was a great summer.

"I don't want you two to go," I told Nicky as we headed back home after a long day of sunbathing and swimming at the lido.

"Well, we have had all day together, we will come over tomorrow," Pamela replied walking ahead, arm-in-arm with Sammie. Although the twins were the same age as me, Pamela seemed older. I guess that's why she was closest to

Sammie. "Unless," Pamela continued with a cheeky grin on her face. "Why don't we see if we could stay over?" Pamela naughtily suggested.

"Mum will not allow that, you know she won't, Pamela," Nicky told her.

"How will Mum know, Nicky? She works nights, we can pretend we're at Nanny's," Pamela answered.

"Great idea! Who's gonna ask Dionne?" Sam said. We all burst out laughing. "Nah I am not going to ask," Sam said, still laughing at the dreaded thought of asking Dionne.

"I'll ask, I'm not asking Dionne though. I'll ask Dad," I suggested, not expecting my offer to be met with such excitement.

"Yes, good idea," Sam agreed. I went in first to find Dad sitting alone, thankfully, in the front room, watching TV.

"Hello fanny," Dad said, acknowledging me briefly before getting back to his movie.

"Daaaadddd," I said. I would always drag out his name when I wanted something.

"Yes fanny, what do you want?" he asked, with a soft smile on his face. I could see he was in a pleasant mood.

"You know our friends Nic—"

Before I could finish, Dad interrupted, "Spit it out, Ingrid."

"Can they stay tonight, pllleeaasse?" I asked, stupidly.

"Is that it? Of course, they can." I didn't wait to hear anymore. I ran to the front door to tell the twins and Sam, who were waiting outside.

"Dad said yes," I shouted at them eagerly. Nicky and Pamela pushed passed me and ran to Dad.

"What's going on?" Dionne hollered from the kitchen.

The twins were jumping all over Dad. "Thanks, Joey," they said, almost in sync.

"Dad said the twins can stay tonight," Sammie informed Dionne. Dionne was holding Melissa on her hip with one hand and a supply of baby bottles in the other hand ready for the nights feeding.

"Oh I see, no one asks me anything, but then what do I matter," Dionne snapped. Sam pulled a mimicking face to Dionne's words behind her back.

"Oh Dionne it's only for tonight, anyway they don't have school tomorrow," Dad continued to explain his reasoning for not asking her opinion.

"Well so long as you lot keep the noise down. I'm putting Melissa to bed now." Dionne turned and walked away, slamming Melissa's bedroom door.

"Dionne, what did I say about slamming doors in my house?" Dad shouted aggressively. Dionne was silent; she didn't respond. "Right girls, can I get back to watching my film now?" Dad asked politely. "And make sure you all wash before going to bed," Dad continued as we left the living room.

"Yes Dad," Sam and I replied in sync. For a split-second Sam and I caught each other's eye, my thought as Dad requested, we washed before bed was, *surely not, Dad wouldn't do anything with our friends here.* I was sure Sam thought the same. Desperately trying to keep our voices low throughout the night so as not to ruin any future possibilities of the twins being able to stay over again.

"I wish we could be together all the time," Pamela announced in the middle of our talk about how much we loved Michael Jackson's Thriller video.

"Me too," Sam agreed.

"Your dad is so cool," Pamela said.

"Innit, Pamela, our mum just moans all the time," Nicky confessed.

"Well, sometimes things aren't always how they seem," Sam interrupted, looking uncomfortable as she spoke.

"Your mum does seem nice," I said, trying to distract them from Sam's statement about Dad. "She comes across a little scary at times," I continued, and we all laughed. Finally, after hours of talking, the twins fell asleep. I could hear Dad moving around outside. It sounded as though he was checking the front door was locked. I listened closely. Once I heard his bedroom door close, I knew it was safe to sleep.

"Right girls up you get," Dionne shook us awake. She threw open the curtains, the sun's bright rays had us hiding under our covers like vampires exposed to the sun.

"Why do we have to get up so early, Di?" I asked.

"You can't sleep all day. Isn't my fault you were up all night," Dionne snapped back. *How did she know?* I thought to myself. I poked Nicky from under the covers, trying to see if she had heard Dionne's comment. We giggled and crawled out from under our blanket. "I'm going to the market so I want you lot up and dressed," Dionne ordered, before leaving the room. One by one, we emerged from my room like zombies. I noticed Melissa strapped in her pram by the front door. Her chubby face was smiling underneath her huge pink dummy. Whenever I looked at her it gave me a warm fuzzy feeling in my belly. I walked over and kissed her cheek. In turn, the twins and Sam did the same, then Dionne appeared and left with her. We made our way to the living room and tuned into one of my favourite cartoons, Super Ted. We watched it on most Saturday mornings. It didn't seem long after Dionne had left that I was met with shock and horror. Dad's bedroom door flung open, his naked body walked slowly across the hall and into the bathroom opposite his bedroom door, it all happened so quickly. I prayed that Pamela and Nicky hadn't seen him.

"Oh," gasped one of the twins, they must have seen him.

"What the fuck," said Pamela, covering her mouth trying not to be heard swearing underneath her breath. "Wait, was that, Joey?" she asked. I wanted to die. I wanted to be invisible at that precise moment. Both twins burst out laughing.

. "I guess he couldn't hold it," Nicky said, trying to justify Dad's action.

"I'm so sorry," Sam said, apologising for Dad's nudity. At that moment the bathroom door opened. Dad stepped out, still naked, and casually stood in the living room doorway. He was so calm, as though nothing had happened. "What's wrong?" Dad asked, glancing his eyes across our faces while holding the door frame. I was screaming inside but I couldn't show it on my face as I knew I would get hit for disappointing him. "It's just a body, what's the big deal?" Dad questioned. He made no attempt to cover his willy; he just stood there holding onto the door frame. I looked to my left where the twins were sitting, their faces bright red. As my eyes met Nicky's she put her face in her hands, removing them every so often. There was a white hand impression for a second until the blood turned her cheeks back to red. Dad was talking away but my ears were deaf. I knew he was talking but I wasn't listening, Sam kept her head down the whole time. After what seemed like an eternity, Dad turned and walked away and then vanished into his room.

"It's okay, please don't be embarrassed," Pamela told us. How could we not? Sam cried silently. "Seriously, it's okay," Pamela continued, trying desperately to make us feel okay.

"I hate him," Sam whispered. I think it was at this moment the twins realised something was wrong and that there was a lot more to it. "If you both chose to not be our friends anymore, we will understand," Sam told the twins while wiping the tears from her eyes.

"Listen, we are sisters. We will not tell our mum, will we, Nicky?" Pamela indirectly ordered this secret be kept from their mum.

"No, we won't say anything. If we do, our mum will stop us from seeing you both," Nicky explained as she got off her seat. Placing herself at my feet, she looked up at me and reached out for a hug. We hugged for a brief second. I pulled away at the thought of Dad coming back out and catching me hugging or Sammie crying. That would anger him.

"I know, let's make it official and become blood sisters then no matter what happens no one can separate us," Pamela suggested.

"What are blood sisters?" I was confused.

"Come, we will show you," Nicky said. Sam and I got up to follow the twins into the kitchen. Nicky opened the cutlery drawer and took out Dionne's small knife that she would peel potatoes with. "Hold out your hand, P," Nicky told her sister. Pamela placed her hand in Nicky's, palm up. My mouth opened in horror as Nicky cut a three-inch opening into Pamela's palm. The blood slowly began to trickle out. "Now you, Sam," Nicky opened her hand, waiting for Sam to hold out her own. Sammie was fearless and without hesitation, she placed her hand in Nicky's. She sliced Sam's the same.

"Now give me your hand, Sam," Pamela said, placing her bleeding palm onto Sam's bleeding palm. I was so focused on what they were doing that I didn't notice Nicky take my hand and begin to slice. The pain was sharp but bearable. Nicky then sliced her own palm and placed it on mine for a moment. "Now we have to swap. Ingrid, you come to me," Pamela ordered. We swapped twins and did it again. There was no need for me and Sam to do it as we already shared the same blood. "There. Now we are sisters for life," Pamela concluded. I was so excited. This was like magic. Just like that were blood sisters; bonded for life. It was our secret.

Sunday morning, I was woken by the smell of Dionne cooking something and the sounds of Dad's music echoing through the door. Dad was singing a song by Ray Charles at the top of his voice. "I can't stop loving you, I've made up my mind to live in memories of a lonesome time. I can't stop wanting you, it's useless to say," Dad continued to sing. I soon noticed Sam was not in her bed. I got up quickly and put on my dressing gown to investigate. *What time was it?* I thought, heading to the kitchen. I could hear pots clanging. On my way, I noticed Dad stood in front of his record player wearing his leather slippers and Japanese-style black robe on top of his trousers. "Morning fanny," Dad said cheerfully, noticing me pass the door.

"Morning Dad," I smiled and he turned away. "Morning Di," I greeted Dionne.

"Morning Inx," Dionne replied, continuing to stir the brown stewed chicken in the Dutch pot.

"What time is it Di?" I asked, still wondering where Sam was.

"It's 10:30 am," Dionne answered.

"Oh," I was shocked.

"Yes, what time do you call this?" Dionne continued. Dionne did not seem angry or disappointed. The atmosphere was strange; Dad and Dionne seemed really mellow.

"Where's Sammie, Di?" I asked.

"I just sent her to Prestos to get me some bits for dinner," Dionne replied. It wasn't like Sam to go without asking me to go with her.

"So where's Melissa?" I distracted myself.

"She's having a nap," Dionne's face looked flustered from the steam coming from the pots.

"Aww, can I go see her?" I asked.

"No Inx, when she gets up you can have her. I need to get this food done and if she wakes now, I won't get anything done," Dionne responded.

"What's happening today, Di?" I asked before leaving the kitchen.

"Oh, your mum's coming over," Dionne told me like this was any normal day.

I paused by the kitchen door. "What? My mum?" I asked again, unsure.

"Yes," Dionne answered, now looking agitated.

"How comes? I don't get it," I continued to ask.

"I don't bloody know. Dad saw her somewhere and they seemed to have sorted things out, so she's coming with Carl." This was all so sudden. I hadn't seen Mum for so long; I wanted to see Mum but I didn't want to see Carl. *Why's he coming? And where's Sammie?* I thought, feeling frustrated. My blood sisters, Sam and I played Double Dutch skipping outside of the front garden, almost forgetting Mum was coming until she appeared from around the corner.

"Mum!" I yelled. Dropping my end of the rope, I ran to her. Carl wasn't far behind, carrying what looked like alcohol in plastic carrier bags. Mum looked well; she had coloured her hair a deep red. She wore a knee-length skirt and floral blouse with low kitten heels. Carl had a stupid grin on his face.

"Hello Ingrid, you alright?" he asked in his deep tone.

"Sam, Mum's here," I hollered, just in case she hadn't realised. "Hi Carl," I acknowledged him, reluctantly. Sam walked over slowly and hugged Mum coldly. "Mum this is our friends, Nicky and Pamela," I said. The twins politely walked over to shake Mum's hand. Carl didn't pay much attention; he made his way to the front door.

"How are you, Mum?" Sam asked as we walked with Mum to the front door.

"I'm okay. I've missed you two so much," Mum said, she sounded choked and her face was sad.

"We missed you too, Mum," I told her and squeezed her hand gently.

"We will talk later, Mum," Sam said as we stepped inside the front door behind her. We escorted Mum into the living room.

"Ah there's my Bernie the boat," Dad said, walking over to greet Mum. Dad leant forward and kissed Mum on the cheek. "I've missed you, my little Irish woman," Dad continued with a broad smile on his face. Dad gestured for Mum to sit. Mum looked slightly uneasy and unsure. "Dionne, bring these beautiful people some glasses," Dad called out to Dionne, who was still in the kitchen. Carl had already taken his seat in the armchair nearest to the living room door.

"There you go, Joey, we brought this for you. It isn't much," Carl held up the plastic bag for Dad to take.

"Ah, you're a gentleman and a scholar. You shouldn't have, Carl." Dad laughed heartily as he took out two bottles of Bell's whisky and placed them on the coffee table. Dionne eventually made an appearance.

"Hello Bernie," Dionne said to Mum, placing two extra glasses on the table.

"Hello Dionne," Mum replied. I felt as though I was waiting for them to fight. Once the initial meeting was over, I felt a lot more relaxed.

"Dionne, this handsome young man is Carl," Dad told Dionne. Everyone laughed; Dad's crazy remarks broke the ice.

"Come Inx, I think we can go now and play," Sam said. We turned and went back outside. As the evening came, more of Dad's friends turned up. The music got louder, Delroy, Tony and Fox all made an appearance, greeting us on the doorstep as they passed. Sam and I decided not to venture too far away. This way we can make sure everything stays calm in the flat. Every so often I would pop in to check on Mum. With each check-up, Mum got progressively more drunk.

"Ingy," Mum called out. Mum beckoned me over as I stood rooted to my spot; there were too many people in there. "Ingy, come to Mummy," Mum persisted.

"Ingrid, don't be so rude. Go see your mum," Dad shouted over the music.

"What is it, Mum?" I asked, looking down at her. She was slumped back in her seat, looking up at me.

"Come sit," Mum turned me by my hips to sit me on her lap. "I love my Ingy, isn't she beautiful? Look at them big brown eyes," she said, taking my hand and practically slobbering on it with wet kisses.

"Yes, she's a good girl," Carl said, looking at my dad and smiling. Sam looked back from the front door where she sat playing Jacks with the twins. Sam rolled her eyes to show she was sick of hearing how wonderful I am.

"Mum, can I go now?" I whispered to her.

"Yes love, I'm coming with you," Mum said, pushing me off her lap. Mum struggled to get up; taking her arm, I helped her get to her feet. Keeping a firm grip, I escorted Mum to the bathroom. I called quietly to Sam to come and help me. Too late. Mum was already trying to pull up her skirt before I had shut the door.

"Wait Mum," I told her, quickly locking the door behind me. Mum slumped herself on the toilet and began to cry. Thankfully, at that moment, there was a knock at the door.

"Inx, open it's me." Great, it was Sammie. I felt relieved as I let her in "Oh Mum, what is it?" Sam asked her.

"I don't know, Mum just started crying," I answered for Mum as she couldn't get her words out.

"Oh God, I love you two so much," Mum said, breaking down even more. The tears poured from her eyes and dribble fell from her lips. Her face was red and flustered and strands of hair sprawled across her face stuck to her cheeks.

"We love you too Mum," I replied. My heart hurt; I felt so sad.

"Why did you leave me?" Mum asked, now sobbing uncontrollably. "What?" Sam replied, looking very confused.

"What do you mean Mum? You let Carl get rid of us," Sam snapped, still trying to remain calm so as not to upset Mum anymore. With Sam's response, Mum cried even more. I unravelled some tissue to wipe Mum's face. I was suddenly aware we had probably been in here too long. I couldn't help but wonder if Dad thought we were talking about him. "You do realise, Mum, that Dad has custody of us now," Sam told Mum.

"Yes, but I always thought you would have come back to me," Mum responded, now trying to find her skirt, which had ridden up to her waist. Mum fiddled with her skirt, not seeing which way to pull it down from.

"Mum, stand up, then we can help you," we said after watching her struggle with it. Mum began to laugh and cry at the same time. What was happening? There was no point trying to talk to Mum when she was like this. I truly wished she didn't drink. She looked so helpless. Mum's heart was broken and we had been the ones to break it. As Mum stood to allow us to dress her, she said, "He's a wicked man ya know."

"Who is, Mum?" I asked, looking at Sam, so confused.

"Who, Dad?" Sam asked.

"No, not your dad. I love your dad and that bitch took him away. That fucking Dionne," Mum snapped. Suddenly she looked wide awake. Sam and I laughed at Mum's cheeky words towards Dionne.

"Mum shush. Dad will hear you," I asked her, so worried about what would happen if Dad was to hear her.

I didn't worry about Dionne hearing her as she was singing at the top of her voice, to the lyrics of Louisa Marks, "I know you're having an affair and I know who and I know where; It's that easy-going chick, just down there!"

"So, you said he's wicked, Mum, who?" Sam asked again.

"Carl," Mum answered, trying to find her way to the door. She looked angry.

"Wait Mum, you can't just say that and walk out. Why is he wicked?" Sam asked again, now looking fed up.

"He's evil Sammie. He's no better, he beats me too," Mum finally answered.

"I knew it. I bloody hate him. Fat pig, he makes me sick," Sam said, unlocking the door. I sat on the side of the bath feeling helpless.

"Sam please don't say anything," I pleaded.

"I'm gonna tell Dad though," Sam told me.

"Please don't, Sam. Carl might take it out on Mum," I begged. I wasn't sure if Sam heard what I had said, they'd already left the bathroom. The twins were still sitting where we had left them, playing a game of Jacks outside the front door.

"Is everything okay?" Pamela asked us.

"Yeah, I guess," I replied, shrugging my shoulders, not sure if it was alright. "My mum drinks a lot and gets really upset," I told her, unsure of what she will make of it all. Pamela didn't say anything. She squeezed her lips together and gave me a look of sympathy.

It wasn't long after Mum's confession in the toilet that Carl appeared at the door and said, "Sammie, we are going shortly. Your mum is tired, I've called a cab." Sam just gave him a blank stare – it was awkward. "Sammie, what's wrong?" he was pressing Sam for a reaction. I pleaded with her in my mind not to give in. "What is it Sammie, you can tell me," Carl persisted.

"Please don't pretend you care, Carl, because you don't," Sam said, continuing to stare at him. I was shocked that Sammie had said that to him.

"I do love your mum you know. You don't understand, she's a handful when she drinks," Carl explained. He was still trying to get Sammie on the side.

"Yeah, but who gives her the drink?" Sam asked.

"Okay, that's enough. It's been nice to meet you, Carl," Nicky said, standing up. Carl didn't like Sam's response. He turned and walked away.

"Bernie, come out. We need to walk out to Roman Road and wait for our cab," I heard him tell Mum from the hallway. One by one, Dad's friends began to leave. It was only after Mum left that I realised how tired I was. Finally, I could go to bed.

"Ingrid, Ingrid," I was woken by the sound of my name. No, it was Dad. No, no, no. I want to sleep. Without realising it, I said no aloud. Dad didn't like that. "What do you mean no? Don't you love me?" Dad whispered. It wasn't that I didn't love him, I just wanted it to stop.

"Of course, I love you, Dad, I'm tired," I said quietly. I could feel Dad's rough hands lifting up my nightdress. "No Dad, please," I asked, making sure to sound polite and not to offend him. I began to cry. My tears ran into my ears and drenched my hair and pillow. Somehow I managed to take my thoughts somewhere else. I lay there thinking about my friends, my school, my teachers, my mum and my baby sister. Every so often I was brought back to reality by the rough scrape of his afro rubbing roughly on my chin. It was like giving yourself carpet burn over and over in the same spot. "Dad you're hurting me," I said politely. Really, I wanted to scream at him 'I hate you please go away' but I couldn't. My fear kept me silent and I didn't want to hurt his feelings.

"Shut up Ingrid, do you want to disappoint me?" His breath was stale from cigarettes and alcohol. If I held my breath for long enough, I wouldn't have to be here for this whatever this was. His heavy body kept me breathless. My cries angered him. I knew this so I cried in silence; this was something I had mastered over time. I wondered if Sam was awake. I couldn't see her face, just her silhouette in the dark. I tried to think of someone, anyone, who could magic me away from here.

"Ouch Dad, that hurts. What are you doing?" I said. I was petrified, I clenched my fists. My whole body was tense, I tried desperately to wiggle up and away but it was useless. I tried to force my legs closed but it was pointless. I was exhausted. Dad held my head down with his head; how was he able to do this? I pictured Mum coming to rescue me but that was just another fantasy.

Finally, Dad's body relaxed. He sat up as though nothing had happened and said, "Don't you ever push me away again, do you hear me?" I couldn't see his face, just his large framed silhouette sitting at the side of my bed.

"Yes Dad," I replied. He was furious with me. His tone was threatening. I knew that he would probably not talk to me now for a few days. I had disappointed him and hurt him. He stood up and my eyes could just about make out in the dark him tying up his dressing gown.

"Now clean yourself up." And then he was gone. I lay there not knowing what to think. I felt paralysed and in pain; even my heart was in pain. I thought about waking Sam but decided against it, Dad might hear me. I felt empty. I had become nothing. Sort yourself out Inx, I told myself. You can't get Dad into trouble – just go to sleep. It felt like there were monsters all around me. I squeezed my eyes closed tight and did not open them again.

Chapter Nine:
Baby on the Doorstep

"Ingrid, wake up." I opened my eyes. It was Sammie, sitting up in her bed.

"Guess what, the house is empty, Dad and Dionne have gone out," she told me. I could not speak, I just cried into my pillow.

"What is it, Inx?" she asked, sounding really concerned.

I raised my head and said, "Nothing Sam." I did not want to cry. I don't even remember sleeping; I felt as though I'd been crying all night. Sam got up and sat on the edge of her bed.

"Did you hear Dad come in last night Sam?" I asked her.

"No, why? Did he? I was so tired Inx, I didn't hear a thing. I slept like a log," Sam said, looking slightly puzzled.

"It's okay, I just wondered if you had heard him or not," I explained. I couldn't and wouldn't say any more. I felt ashamed. Dad's secret was mine. Sam did not ask me anything, as she left the room to make some porridge. I got up once she had left and went to the bathroom, I pulled down my knickers to investigate the pains I still felt in my lily – that was our word for vagina. To my horror, there was bright red blood in my knickers. I began to cry again. I reached over and pulled the door open and shouted, "Sam! Sam!"

"What Inx?" Sam shouted back.

"Can you come please, I'm bleeding," I let go of the door handle and sat still on the toilet, waiting for Sammie.

"What do you mean you're bleeding, Inx, you're only ten," she stated.

"What should I do, Sam?" I asked her. I was trying to keep my lily covered by leaning slightly forward as I sat.

"I can't believe it, Inx. I didn't start my period until I was 13. Well, you will have to call Dionne, I think she's gone to Pat's house," Sam told me. As she walked away, I could hear her giggle. I didn't question Sam's diagnosis; I got up, after carefully rolling up some tissue and placing it in my knickers and headed for the house phone. Searching through the A–Z of Dionne's phone book, I came across Pat's phone number.

"Hello Pat, can I speak to Dionne please?" I asked.

"Of course, you can, who is this?" she asked. I had forgotten to say it was me calling.

"It's Ingrid, Pat," I answered.

"Ah, hello darling. Just one moment, I'll get her," Pat said as she placed the receiver down. I could hear her call out for Dionne.

"Hello, Ingrid."

"Hi Dionne," I answered.

"What's wrong, Inx?" she asked.

"Well," I said. I couldn't finish what I wanted to say.

"Come on Inx. I was just about to feed Melissa, what's wrong?"

"I've noticed I've been bleeding down there," I said. There were a few seconds of silence.

"Oh," Dionne said, and then a pause again. "Is that it, Inx? It must be your period," Dionne explained.

Before Dionne could say anymore, I interrupted, "Dionne, please can you not tell Daddy," I begged her.

"Why not, Inx? You're being silly," she told me. I could hear Dad in the background.

"What is it, Dionne?" he shouted.

"Dionne, please don't tell him," I continued to beg for her promise.

"Well, you're being silly Inx, why not?"

"Cos I'm embarrassed," I answered quickly. I was hopeful that Dionne would keep my promise; I was hoping Dionne would believe my reason for me not wanting Dad to know. It had dawned on me that the real reason was that if he knew I had a period, he would do what he does even more. I remembered when Sam started her period, she said that he told her she was a woman now. It happened to her more often after that. I didn't want to be a woman; I didn't want him to do it more. Dionne promised me that she wouldn't tell him.

"Ingrid, if you look in my bedside drawer you will see a packet of sanitary towels take one out, I will get you some more on my way home," Dionne instructed me.

"Why will I need more, Dionne? Isn't one enough?" I asked.

"No Inx, it will last at least five days. It might be a bit irregular at first but you will need more than one," Dionne told me before hanging up the phone. I'm gonna bleed for five days, *ew*, I thought on my way to Dionne's room.

The next day Dionne called me into her room. "Sit down, Inx," she instructed me. Dionne was changing Melissa's nappy so the room smelt foul. Dionne was trying hard to keep hold of both of Melissa's fat legs in one hand while wiping away the poo, which had gone up her back, with the other hand. Then came the freshness of Johnson's baby powder being sprinkled over her lily. "How you feeling, Inx?" Dionne asked. This was nice. It felt nice that Dionne hadn't forgotten what I told her; she wanted to know how I felt. Before I could answer she said, "Go you look over there in that plastic bag you will see the pack of pads I got you."

"Oh, thanks Di," I said appreciatively. I opened the bag and took out the packet of stay-free pads. I told Dionne that I felt okay, I did not tell Dionne that my lily hurt as she would already know this if this is what happens with periods. I also did not tell her that I had now stopped bleeding so I did not want to tell her she was wrong. Periods don't last for five days. As I left Dionne's room, Dad called to me from the living room. *Oh, what now?* I thought. I smiled as I walked towards him, pretending to be okay. Dad hadn't spoken to me all morning. He was still angry with me. "Yes Dad," I said while taking a seat in the armchair opposite him. I couldn't help but notice that Dad had a cartoon paused on the TV so he could speak to me.

"What did Dionne want?" he asked, adjusting his house robe. His legs were outstretched and crossed at his ankles; his face was serious. His eyes spoke volumes he was furious with me.

"Nothing, Dad, Dionne just gave me this," I answered. My eyes began to well up, I couldn't help it. My palms were sweating and my heart racing.

"What you crying for?" Dad asked, his tone was strange. He leant down and took off his slipper. He held it in his left hand and said, "Stop crying or I will give you something to cry for." He held the slipper tightly; his eyes were cold. I tried so hard to stop the tears from rolling down; I could feel my breaths starting to shorten. "Now, how comes you didn't want me to know you was bleeding?" he asked. I began to cry more. "Ingrid. Ingrid, I said stop it," Dad whispered firmly, glancing over at his bedroom door, checking Dionne was not there. "Look at me when I talk to you. I said stop it now," he insisted. "Do you hate me, Ingrid?" he asked. Why would he think this?

"No Dad," I answered. My thoughts went back to Dionne; she'd promised she wasn't going to tell him. I began to fiddle with the hem of my skirt and adjust my knee-length socks by pulling them up higher. I hated wearing skirts; I felt like Dad would look at me more. "What have I done so bad to you Ingrid that you would treat me like this?" he asked. I was so confused.

"I've stopped bleeding now, Dad," the words just fell out of my mouth. Why did I say that? Too late to take the words back now.

"Of course, you have," Dad replied. "Tell me, Ingrid, do you want me to go to jail?" he asked, his face saddened.

"Of course, I don't, Dad," I replied. I couldn't help but get distracted by the paused cartoon character on the TV screen. I wondered what he was watching.

"In future, you only talk to me. Do you understand?" Dad ordered.

"Yes Dad," I answered, focusing my attention back on him.

"Now go and wash your face." Dad pressed play on the VCR as I stood up, the cartoon character was sucking a fat lady's boobs. She looked like she had a crown on. I quickly looked away and left the room.

"Ingrid, Tanya's at the door for you," Dionne called for me. Dropping my dolls on the bed I rushed to the door.

"Ah, hi Tanya," I said; I was pleased to see her.

"You alright, Ingrid?" Tanya stood at the front door wearing navy blue jeans, a white t-shirt and white trainers. Her long hair was tied back loosely in a ponytail, her hand squeezed into the front pockets of her jeans. Many people said Tanya looked like a lesbian but not to me, Tanya was Tanya. She was one of my best friends.

"Come in then," I told her as I stepped back making space for her to step inside.

"Yeah, why not, if it's okay with Dionne?" she said as she walked into the flat.

Dionne came out of the kitchen looking disappointed to see Tanya standing in the hallway. "Hi Dionne," Tanya said politely. Dionne just grunted Tanya looked uncomfortable.

"Hello Tanya," Dad called out from his armchair in the living room.

"Hi Joey," Tanya greeted back. She gave him a friendly smile and made her way into the front room. Dad always made her feel welcome.

"Come here you beautiful young lady," Dad said, grabbing Tanya around the waist, picking her up and twirling her around.

Tanya's face turned bright red. I could tell she was slightly uncomfortable. Tanya always appreciated Dad's attention. Her mum was also an alcoholic and her brother used to beat her up, so any attention from Dad was welcomed. He made her feel beautiful and protected. Tanya took a seat in the armchair opposite Dad. "But wait, Tanya, you look like you're growing titties," Dad said, looking directly at Tanya's chest through her t-shirt.

"Oh, Joey." Tanya laughed uncomfortably.

"No, it's okay. You're growing into a fine young woman, isn't she Ingrid," Dad said, laughing. I felt awkward but Tanya didn't look upset, so it must be okay, I thought.

"Ingrid, come here please," Dionne summoned me from the kitchen. Baby Melissa was sitting in her highchair eating a dry Farley's Rusk biscuit. It was soggy, mashed into her fingers and smeared across her face. She also had bits dried into her eyebrows. "Come here a second," Dionne whispered. She quietly closed the miniature doors to the food serving hatch which led into the living room. "What is it Di?" I whispered back "What is she doing here, Ingrid?" Dionne asked. She looked disgusted, as though she had salt in her mouth.

"I don't know, Di, she just came to see me," I answered, feeling confused by the secrecy.

"Well, she ain't staying. I don't know why you hang about with her, anyway, she looks dirty."

"But she isn't, Di," I said in Tanya's defence. "She's really nice. I like being with Tanya," I continued.

"Where's the twins today anyway?" Dionne asked while picking the remnants of Melissa's broken biscuits off the floor.

"I'm not sure. They went away for a week I think," I answered, not sure why Dionne cared about the whereabouts of the twins.

"Well, she ain't staying so don't ask. I've got enough on my plate as it is," Dionne continued. She repositioned the small wooden stool in front of Melissa's highchair. The stool had red cherries printed onto white laminate, which Dionne proudly covered herself to keep up the red and white theme of the kitchen. Melissa started to get upset, kicking and wiggling in her seat. She wanted to get out. "Oh, wait a bloody minute Melissa," Dionne snapped. It wasn't like Dionne to be so short with Melissa.

"Should I take her for a walk in her buggy, Di?" Sam asked, walking in on our conversation. "I can walk her around the block a few times, she might fall asleep," Sam suggested.

"Yeah, go on then," Dionne said. Dionne struggled to lift Melissa out, her fat legs kept catching the tray of the highchair. With Melissa finally free, Dionne wiped her face and hands then handed her over to Sam.

"Dionne, get the phone please I'm talking to this beautiful young lady," Dad shouted out.

"Hello? Hello?" Dionne called out, then slammed the phone down aggressively.

"Dionne, who was it?" Dad asked.

"I don't fucking know, do I. They won't speak," Dionne shouted back.

"Tanya, you wanna come for a walk with Sammie? We're gonna walk Mim around the block," I asked Tanya, hoping she would say yes. I needed to get her out. With Melissa secured in her buggy, we left, closing the garden gate behind us. We could hear Dad and Dionne shouting at each other.

"I hope they ain't fighting 'cause I'm here, I can go home if it's a problem!" Tanya said, her face looking concerned.

"Trust me, it has nothing to do with you, Tanya. It's more like an issue with one of my Dad's girlfriends I bet," Sam stated, trying to put Tanya's mind to rest.

"Really, why?" I asked, trying to find out more.

"Because I answered it this morning, it was a woman. She wanted to talk to Dad. I asked her for her name but she wouldn't give it to me, anyway, Dionne took the phone and the woman put the phone down," Sam explained. Tanya looked at me with raised eyebrows but didn't say a word.

"Joey, can you get the door? My hands are full," I heard Dionne call out to Dad who was still sitting in the living room watching his animated cartoon featuring the midget king with a huge willy called King Dick.

"I'll get it, Di," Sam shouted out, leaving Tanya and me in the kitchen eating jam sandwiches. "Dad, Dad, come quick," Sam shouted out. I dropped my sandwich on the plate and rushed to see what was happening. Trying to see over Sam's shoulder was difficult, Dad and Dionne's frame took up most of the doorway. It was only when Dad stepped outside, I could see what looked like a baby wrapped in a blanket on the doorstep. Dionne shoved past me, rushing into her room and slamming the door shut behind her.

"What the rass," Dad said, looking at the baby intently, then scouring his surroundings to see who left the baby at the door. Dionne came back out of her room and picked up the baby. Tanya's face looked as confused as mine. Dionne took the baby inside while Dad went to search the estate. Dionne placed the baby safely on the sofa tucking a cushion in at her side so she couldn't roll off. Just then, Dad appeared, looking lost.

"What the fuck, Joey?" Dionne yelled at him.

"Ingrid and Samanta, do me a favour. See if you can see a woman on the estate with black hair walking around," Dad asked in a soft, exhausted tone.

"Come, Inx," Sam gestured for me to follow her.

"I'll wait here, Inx," Tanya said, sitting on the doorstep. Poor Tanya looked nervous. I was too curious to find out who left the baby than to sit and talk to Tanya. We searched the estate, not quite sure who we were looking for.

"Look Inx, over there." Sam didn't point in which direction I should look; she just signalled with her eyes.

"Where Sam?" I asked, getting frustrated.

"Not there, silly, up there!" Sam pointed behind me. As I looked back there was a woman with black hair on the balcony of one of the blocks of flats on our estate, she stepped back so as not to be seen but it was too late – we'd spotted her. "She must have been waiting, Inx, to see if Dad got the baby," Sam suggested. "Come let's go and tell Dad." Sam ran back ahead of me to tell Dad we had found the woman who dumped the baby. Before I had reached home Dad was already heading in my direction, still in his house robe and slippers.

"Go inside, Ingrid, watch the baby for me," he said as he passed me.

"Yes, Dad." The baby was still laying on the sofa, I wasn't sure where Dionne was. I had to see what the baby looked like; I walked over and began to unravel the blanket. "Aww, it's a girl Sam," Sam came to join me on the sofa. She was so pretty. She had dark brown hair, light brown skin and big dark brown eyes. Dionne appeared; her face was red she looked so sad. "Who is this baby, Di?" I asked.

"Ask your dad," she said sharply. The baby was a lot smaller than Melissa, her little face looked lost, as she gazed at the faces around her. Dad stormed in, snatched up the baby girl and walked out leaving the door open behind him.

"Come, Tanya, let's go look out the kitchen window," I said. Sam followed us to see if we could catch a glimpse of the woman with black hair.

"Oh, it's Miranda," Sam said, pushing me out of the way to get the best view out of the window.

"Who's Miranda, Sam?" I asked, trying to push back.

"Don't you remember her, Inx? She used to live at Mum's with us for a bit, Mum took her in. She was like 15 at the time, but Mum kicked her out because she thought Dad was sleeping with her," Sam explained.

"Nah not really," I told Sam.

"God, your dad is in shit if that's his baby," Tanya said looking extremely worried. "I think I should go," she added.

"No don't go," I pleaded. Miranda didn't look afraid as Dad handed her back the baby. She spotted us in the window then smiled and waved at us. After handing the baby over, Dad turned and walked away. We quickly ran to our room before Dad caught us spying. Just as we sat on our beds the door flew open, it was Dad.

"By the way, that was your sister," he informed us, then closed the door again.

"What the hell?" Tanya whispered. We giggled amongst ourselves and decided to stay there and play with our dolls. I expected to hear shouting but there was none. Just banging doors and clanging of pots and pans. Dad kept the volume of his movie on loud to drown out the bangs. "It's getting late, I'm gonna have to make my way home soon," Tanya said, looking at her watch. Just then the bedroom door opened, it was Dad again.

"Hey, girls what you all doing?" Dad asked. I quickly hid my Sindy dolls face. Dad didn't like the games we played with them. Once he watched us playing without us knowing and he confiscated them for days. "I just wanted to say if you want your friend to stay, Ingrid, it's fine with me," Dad said, stepping inside and smiling.

"Really, Dad?" I said, looking over at Tanya.

"Thanks, Joe, but I don't think I will be allowed to," Tanya said quietly.

"Well, the offer is there if you want, just thought I'd mention it and don't worry about face ache." He laughed as he left the room.

"Tanya, it will be great if you can stay, do you want to go and at least ask your mum?" I asked, hoping Tanya would agree.

"I'm really not sure, Inx. My mum's been in the right mood recently. Besides she doesn't know your dad or Dionne," she said.

"Well, why don't you go with her, Inx? It might be better that way. When you come back, we can keep playing Joey and Bernie," Sam suggested. Joey and Bernie was what we called our doll game; we always pretended they were Mum and Dad. Sam didn't usually pay much attention to Tanya so it was a nice gesture.

"Okay, I'm gonna see if my dad will let me come back with you to ask, yeah Tanya?" I was excited. Without hesitation, I went to ask Dad. "Daaaddd, we really want Tanya to stay. Could I go with her to ask her mum?" I hesitantly asked, trying not to disturb Dad's film.

"Why do you think her mum will say no?" he questioned.

"Well Tanya, thinks she will say no because she hasn't met you or Dionne before," I told him.

"Okay so I will come with you," Dad said, turning off the TV. This was great, Dad will get her to say yes. I was certain.

"Mum, it's me," Tanya shouted through the letterbox, after knocking three times with no response.

"Okay, okay. I'm coming," the voice said from the other side of the door. Dad stepped forward as the door opened slowly, the smell of alcohol breezed past in our direction. Tanya's mum looked as though she had been caught off guard; she wasn't much taller than Tanya. Wearing only a knee-length shirt dress with dark short cropped hair and heavy black eyeliner which had smudged around her eyes.

"Hi Mum, this is Joey. Ingrid's dad I was telling you about," Tanya moved aside so Dad could reach Tanya's mum, "Joey, this is my mum, Pauline."

"Well, hello," Dad said, reaching in to take Pauline's hand. Dad lifted her hand to his lips and kissed the back of it. "Tanya, you didn't tell me your mum was so beautiful." Pauline laughed.

"So, what is it you want, Tanya?" Pauline asked, looking uncomfortable.

"Well, I know Ingrid and Tanya are very close, so I came to show my face to let you see for yourself that your daughter is in safe hands. I said to the girls that such a beautiful sexy sophisticated woman such as yourself won't want to stop two kids from having a sleepover," Dad went on and on. It seemed to be working; the more he spoke the more she laughed.

"Oh, I'm not sure, I'm sure Dionne won't want another person in the house. I don't want Tanya in the way," she continued, looking at Tanya.

"Listen, Tanya is like family. Dionne is more than happy to have Tanya there," Dad concluded his case.

"Oh, okay then," Pauline surrendered. I ran into Tanya's bedroom to help her pack an overnight bag, leaving Dad and Pauline at the door.

"Night everyone," Dionne shouted from the hallway. Dad didn't respond; he kissed his teeth and turned his attention back to the TV. Sam looked over to me from the other end of the sofa. It was a silent conversation, whenever Dionne went to bed it was a race between us to see who would say is going to bed next. We couldn't be too eager as Dad would get angry. Neither of us wanted to be left up with him.

"Actually, I'm tired too," Sam said. My belly filled with dread; Sam got there before me. Then I realised Dad wouldn't touch me because Tanya is here. I smiled at Sam, as though to say, 'you haven't won, I will be okay'.

"Ah you see you're all leaving me," Dad said with a sad expression on his face. Sam got up and kissed Dad on the cheek.

"Night Dad, love you," she said, before leaving the room. I was so tired my eyes were burning, every so often I looked over at Tanya to check if she was still awake. Oh no, she'd fallen asleep.

"Hey fanny," Dad said, throwing a cushion across the room at Tanya's head.

Tanya jumped up. "I'm awake," she said.

Dad laughed. "Go to bed Tanya, you're shattered," Dad told her, without hesitation Tanya left the room. Now that leaves just me; I don't want to be here; I want to sleep. How can I tell him I want to sleep? He will be upset with me. I thought if I counted to fifty and then told him, it would be okay. 49–50. Nope, I still couldn't say it. I counted to fifty again. It didn't matter how many times I counted to fifty, it was never the right time. Dad undid his robe and began to stroke his willy. I wanted to cry. I wanted him to tell me I can go to bed too but he didn't. I stared at the TV, pretending not to see him. "Ingrid," he said.

"Yes, Dad?" I glanced at him for a split second then turned my attention back to the TV.

"Do you think Tanya is asleep yet?" I was puzzled by his question.

"Probably, Dad."

"Look at me when I talk to you," he said firmly, "I want you to go and take the covers off her."

"What Dad?" I questioned. What was going on?

"Ingrid, did you hear me? I said go and take the covers off Tanya." Dad's face was serious; his tone had changed, just like it does when he's gonna hit me.

"Okay Dad," I agreed. The walk to my room felt long. I opened the door quietly and stood by the light switch. I stared at Tanya, breathing heavily as she slept in the spare top bunk bed. I thought about what Dad would do to her if she woke up; what he would do to us. I couldn't do it. I could hear my heart pounding. I was scared to go back and tell him I couldn't do it. Then it dawned on me, I'll pretend I did it and say she woke up. Yes, that's what I'll do. I closed the door quietly and returned to Dad. "Dad she woke up." I felt as if he could see right through me – he knew I was lying. If Dad caught me in a lie he would beat me again with the buckle of his belt. Dad stared at me.

"She woke up did she?" he asked. Oh my god, he knew I was lying. My body tensed as I waited for the first blow. "Hm. She's nothing but a slag anyway," he said, kissing his teeth. "Oh just go to bed." Dad was furious. I felt discarded. I had disappointed him again. But at least I was able to sleep.

Chapter Ten:
Caught Smoking

Age 11. "Sam, can you pass me the milk please?" I asked her while pouring out enough porridge for the both of us. It was so early; normally we got to sleep in a bit later on a Sunday. We were woken by the sound of Dionne's Randy Crawford album playing, Dad was nowhere to be seen.

"Don't either of you ask me for anything today, you will have to fend for yourself. I'm done. I'm going on strike," Dionne told us, grabbing her cup of tea from the side and walking back to the living room.

"What's that all about?" Sam whispered to me.

"I don't know," I shrugged.

"I don't think Dad came home last night, Inx," Sam said quietly.

"Oh," I replied, not quite knowing what to make of it. Dad was often out until 7 am as the bars closed around this time so it was nothing new to me. Dionne stayed in the living room most of the day, singing her favourite tunes to Melissa. It was great for us; we got to play outside with no questions asked. There was no 'where you going?' or 'who you going with?' The twins had returned from their cousin's house, so we went to knock to see if they were allowed out.

"We will be down shortly. We have to clean our room first, so we will meet you at the camp," one of the twins said at the other end of the intercom.

"Okay we'll meet you there," Sam replied. We made our way through the estate to the block of flats where our camp was located on the roof. It was a small brick building with little electrical cupboards inside. It was our usual hang-out when we weren't allowed to go too far. It was near enough to our home where we could hear Dad or Dionne if they called us. We got bored really quickly with it just being us there, the excitement had gone. I began to feel deflated and fed up.

"I want to go, Sam, I don't think they're coming," I said eventually, hoping Sam would feel the same.

"Yeah, me too. Shall we go then?" Sam suggested. She was pacing around, kicking the dirt around on the floor with her shoe. I pulled myself up off the floor and dusted my bottom down. "Look what I found, Inx," Sam said, bending over and picking up a small white object.

"What is it?" I asked curiously. Sam opened her hand. It was an unused Benson & Hedges cigarette. "And what?" I questioned. Sam didn't answer, she just placed it in her pocket. "Why you keeping it, Sam?"

"Don't worry, come on let's go," she replied quickly.

I didn't question her, maybe she was gonna give it to Dad. I didn't really care. Just as we reached the green outside our flats, we spotted the twins. "Agh, I can't believe it, Inx. Now they come," Sam moaned. We laughed and walked towards them.

"We're so sorry we're late man, our mum had it in for us today," Nicky tried to explain. "We ain't even allowed to stay, we're on our way to the shop for her. Then we have to go straight back." Nicky's face looked disappointed.

"It's okay though we will try and come over tomorrow," Pamela interrupted. By this time, I just wanted to go home and watch the Wiz for the fiftieth time and eat porridge.

"Look what I've got," Sam revealed the cigarette from her pocket. The twins laughed naughtily.

"Haha, where did you get that Sam?" Pamela asked.

"I found it. Shall we light it?" Sam asked suggestively.

"Yeah, go on, I've got a lighter," Pamela told us. I began to feel slightly worried as we were directly opposite our front door.

"What if Dionne sees us, Sam?" I asked the concern was clear in my voice.

"We'll crouch down then, behind this bush. There's a bench there, so we can sit there?" Sam pointed out a wooden bench not far from where we stood. "Dionne won't care anyway, she's depressed I think," Sam said, giggling. I was convinced we would be okay. Sam handed the cigarette over to Pamela who reached out to take it. Placing it in her mouth, she lit the end. Pamela took a long pull on the cigarette – like an expert. Then she passed it over to Nicky who in turn did the same. This wasn't good; I knew it was coming around. Nicky handed it to Sammie. "No, give it to Ingrid first," Sam told her.

"I don't want any, Sam," I insisted back. "What about my asthma?" I reminded her.

"Oh, come on, it ain't like you haven't done it before, Inx. Remember at the adventure playground when we lived in hackney, and that boy passed us some of his? You smoked then," Sam argued.

"I was like six, Sam, and I didn't take it down like the twins just did." I knew I had a weak case.

"Oh, go on, Inx. We won't tell, will we Pamela?" Nicky begged, holding the cigarette.

"No way! Remember, we are blood sisters," Pamela concluded. I took the cigarette and took a pull on it, choking straight away. The twins and Sammie burst out laughing.

"Do it again, one more time. Like they done it, Inx," Sam instructed me. I took another deep breath with the cigarette in my mouth, choking again. My eyes were streaming.

"No more, that's it now. It's your turn now, Sam," I handed Sam the cigarette, but she threw it on the floor and stepped on it. "Why did you do that, Sam?" I snapped. I was so angry. The twins didn't say a word, they just looked on.

"Okay, we better go now before Mum comes looking for us," Pamela said. They kissed us both on the cheek and left.

"Hello? Hello?" Dionne shouted into the phone's receiver, then slammed it down. Sam and I looked at each other but we didn't say a word. I was still angry with her for not smoking.

"Inx, come here a second," Sam asked me to follow her to our room. "You know your grandad shirt. Would you mind if I wore it with your brooch?" Sam asked. I was furious. How could she ask me to use my stuff?

"No Sam, I don't want you to wear it. You have much nicer clothes than me, wear your own!" I answered, feeling proud of myself. It was probably the prettiest thing I had. Sam ignored me and walked over to my wardrobe. She opened the doors and began to rummage around, in search of the shirt.

"I got it," Sam said, holding it up in the air for me to see.

"No Sam, I said you can't wear it!" I tried to prize it out of her hands but she was stronger than me. I wasn't letting go.

"Inx, if you don't let me wear it, I'm gonna tell Dionne what you done," Sam raised her voice. Before I knew it, the bedroom door flew open.

"What did she do that you need to tell me, Sammy?" Dionne came bursting in. I immediately released my grip from my shirt. I looked Sam in the eye; I felt like someone had punched me in the belly. I prayed silently for Sam not to tell her. Dionne was persistent. "You better tell me, Sammie, I mean it," Dionne threatened. Sam looked worried. She put her head down and walked over to her bed. "Come on. Tell me or I'm gonna call Dad. I promise I won't say anything to him if you tell me," Dionne said. There was no way out, I knew it and so did Sam. I began to cry. "Don't cry, Inx, just tell me and I won't tell Dad," Dionne said one last time, this time with her hand on the door handle – one of us had to tell her. At least she won't tell Dad, I thought.

"Ingrid was smoking," Sammie mumbled under her breath, keeping her head down.

"What? I didn't hear you," Dionne said, stepping in closer to Sam so she could hear clearly what she was saying.

"I said, Ingrid, was smoking." Sammie quickly looked at me, then put her head down again.

"Right. You do realise I have to tell your dad, don't you?" Dionne said, rushing out of the room.

"No Dionne, please don't!" I screamed out. I was terrified.

"Ingrid, I'm so sorry, I didn't know she was there." Sam tried to apologise but it was too late. I was on my own. Dad was going to kill me. "She promised she wouldn't say anything, Inx, I believed her," Sam continued. It was hopeless. I threw myself on my bed and cried into my Dusty Bin Man pillow.

"Sammie, you better go to your party," Dionne reminded her. I didn't know anything about this party.

"You can wear my shirt if you want to," I said, sounding defeated. It felt like hours of torture waiting for Dad to come home, then there it was. I could hear Dad's voice coming closer to the front door; he was with someone, a man. I couldn't make out who the other person was. Dad opened the front door.

"Dionne," he shouted. "Where's my beautiful wife and where's my little princesses?" Dad was in a good mood and I'm going to ruin it. At this moment, I hated Dionne. Did she not know that he would kill me, I kept thinking. I grabbed my pillow and held it tight. There was silence outside; I couldn't hear Dad's voice. Dionne must have been telling him what I had done. God, what have I done? I was searching my mind to think of ways I could get out of dying, but there was no point; there was nowhere to go. "Tony, do not start without me. I need to go and sort my daughter out," Dad said loudly. It was Tony who Dad was with. He can't help me. My bedroom door opened slowly. I looked up to see

Dad standing there with his thick yellow leather 1970s-style belt draped around his neck, his hands placed on his hips, his stature looking bigger than ever. He was huge. My heart stopped; my hands tingled. There was no sound, just tears pouring down my face. "Ingrid, stand up," Dad ordered. I let go of Dusty and stood up, keeping my head down in case he struck my face. Dad walked over and stood in front of me. He was so close; my head almost touched his chest. He looked enormous. "Look at me," he ordered again. I couldn't; I kept my head down, my legs went weak. I couldn't stop crying. "I said look at me," he screamed so loud it hurt my ears. Slowly, I raised my head. I couldn't look him in the eye. I could only focus on his chin and mouth. With each word, I flinched. "So, you think you're a big woman, right?" I did not respond. I could not speak. "So, you want to smoke and be a whore like your sister?" he continued. The tears just kept pouring down. "Stop the fucking crying. Listen to me when I say this. You will never be anything. You are worthless. You'll end up being a slag like your sister, do you hear me?"

I responded, "Yes Dad." My heart was breaking. Why was he talking about Sammie like that? She wasn't a slag. I was so confused.

"You are disgusting, do you hear me? You have shamed and humiliated me," he continued. My breathing started to become more and more rapid. "Do you think an asthma attack will save you, Ingrid?"

"No Dad," I mumbled. With that response, Dad grabbed my wrist and was trying to raise my arm.

"Don't fucking fight me, Ingrid!" He screamed. I wasn't fighting. I would never; that would only anger him more. My legs gave way, I couldn't stand. Dad struggled as he put both my wrists together above my head and held them both in one hand. His grip was tight. Then pulling the belt from around his neck and struck me with the buckle. The pain was immense, I screamed out. "So, you want to smoke? You disgusting girl. And if you want to cry, I'll give you something to cry for." He screamed, over and over. With each word, he struck me across my back and legs. Finally, he let go of my wrists I fell to the floor. I struggled to breathe. All I was thinking was, *if he knew how much I loved him, maybe he would stop.* Dad continued to lash out with his belt, lashing me across my back with the buckle. I had stopped breathing for a moment. I am sure I no longer felt anything. "Now get the fuck up and come and say hello to Tony," Dad insisted, then left the room. I didn't want to go outside. I didn't want to see Dionne. I wanted Sammie. I knew it wasn't over. I could hear Dad cursing me to Tony, who just listened. As I left my room, Dionne glanced at me from the kitchen.

"That will teach you won't it?" She made it clear that I deserved it.

"Tony, look at her, can you believe my Ingrid would do this? She's turning into her mother." Tony put his head down, not saying a word. "Ingrid, you see these cigarettes...I want you to smoke them," Dad said, pointing to the box of twenty B&H on the coffee table. I looked at Dad, my eyes begging him to not make me do this. I couldn't refuse because he would hit me, and if I reached for them, he might hit me again. Tony got up and left the room. "I said pick up the fucking cigarettes and smoke them all. You're not going anywhere until you have done it," Dad ordered, kicking my foot as he spoke. Hesitantly, I picked up the box and took one out. My hands began to shake. I placed it to my mouth slowly and reached for the lighter on the table. My mind began to wander off for a moment. I lit the cigarette and blew it straight out. "Don't take me for a cunt, Ingrid, smoke the fucking thing!" Dad shouted. Tony returned to the living room and took his seat.

"Oh, Joey man!" but that was all he could say, as quickly as Tony entered the room he walked out again. No one could help me now. I took a second puff, inhaling it this time. Dad laughed hysterically as I choked. The cigarettes burned out fast in between me choking and crying and before I knew it I had smoked about half the pack.

"Now go to your room and don't come out!" Dad shouted. I was so sorry that I had disappointed him again. Maybe I really am nothing.

Dionne continued to get strange phone calls. Sometimes it seemed as though she was talking to someone and other times she just picked it up and slammed it down again. "Joey, I'm taking Ingrid to the hairdresser today so I'm leaving Melissa with you and Sammie for a bit," she told him. As far as I knew, Dionne was taking me to get my hair trimmed. She told me it was far too long and too much for her to manage. Sam said a trim was when they cut away a small amount just to even out your hair. Mum loved long hair. Even though mine was harder to manage than Sam's, Mum said our hair was her pride and joy. Dionne walked me to the black hairdressers at the top of Roman Road. "Go, sit Inx!" She pointed to the waiting area. She spoke to one of the ladies before coming to sit with me.

"Come, my dear, come sit in my chair," the lady said. I got up and took my seat as told, Dionne handed me some hair magazines. All the women in the spread were beautiful. The black ladies in them had long straight hair. There were a lot of adverts for hair relaxers; 'If you use this cream, your hair will be dead straight,' it said. My hair was long enough. *If only I could get Dionne to get me some of this cream,* I thought. Then she wouldn't get so angry when brushing it.

"Inx, I'm just gonna pop to the shop next door, you will be okay. I'll get you a chocolate," she said before leaving.

"You have lovely hair," the woman told me whilst combing through my mane of hair.

"Was that your mum?" she asked.

"No, she is my step mum," I answered politely, looking back down at the magazine. I could hear the scissors cutting away but I paid no attention. I had chocolate and a book with beautiful women in it. I looked up after some time had passed; my mouth dropped open. There was about two inches of hair left all over my head. I panicked and looked for Dionne in the mirror. "Di," I said.

Dionne looked back at me and smiled. "See how much better that is Ingrid. You will be able to manage it yourself now." She was so proud of herself. I hated it.

"But I look like a boy, Dionne."

She laughed back at me and said, "No you don't." I did look like a boy. The lady brushed the hair from my shoulders, and then picked up a mirror to show me the back. I couldn't bear it. I didn't want to see; there was nothing to see. I was worried that my friends would laugh at me in school. I cried all the way home. I was so angry with Dionne. Mum's going to kill Dionne when she sees this. Secretly, I prayed that she did. I never did get used to my new hairstyle.

Chapter Eleven:
Dad's Secret Exposed

"Hi Tanya," I said down the phone.

"Hi Inx," Tanya replied.

"What you up to today?" I asked her.

"Nothing really, I'm just home. My mum's away for the night at my nan's house," Tanya explained.

"Okay so do you want to come over for a bit?" I asked, hoping she would say yes.

"Yeah sure, should I come now or later?"

"You may as well come now if you can," I told her, that way we would get more time together.

Jim Reeves played through the house once again. I felt exhausted from constantly trying to predict what mood Dad was in; having to watch his body language, facial expressions and listen to the tones of his voice was all becoming too much. He was constantly on my mind. At least Tanya was coming today. I could hear Dad singing and laughing so that was a good sign. "Ingrid, Tanya's here," Sam called out to me. Taking a quick glance at the living room on my way to meet Tanya at the door, I noticed Dad had a room full of people. The air was thick with smoke.

"There's my little angel," Dad called as I passed through the hallway. "Oi, fanny don't be so rude. Come and say hello," Dad continued.

"I will, Dad, I'm just getting Tanya. She's at the door," I answered. I didn't want to go in there.

"Hi Tanya, come in." I greeted Tanya as she stepped inside.

"Hello Tanya," Dad called out to her. "This is my other daughter, referring to Tanya. isn't she beautiful?" Dad announced to his guests. His guests looked tired and washed out; the two ladies looked baffled, not knowing if Dad was joking or not. "Tanya, come and sit on my lap," Dad gestured to Tanya, tapping his lap and laughing.

"I'm alright Joey." Tanya laughed but I could tell she was uncomfortable.

"You see, Tony, no one loves me. It's okay though, I'll be dead and buried soon," Dad said, looking for sympathy.

"Aw, don't say that, Joey," one of the ladies said back, clearly falling for his attention-seeking ways. I couldn't help but notice her brittle, bleached blonde hair with black roots. Her skin was so pale, it was as though she was still wearing her tight party dress from the night before.

"Oh Joey, hurry up and die then," Dionne shouted out from the kitchen. Everyone roared out laughing. Dad's eyes were bloodshot red – it was clear that he had not slept.

Tanya discreetly poked me in the side. "Inx, shall we go and play now?"

"Inx, if you two want we can play Hopscotch when I've finished helping Dionne?" Sam suggested.

"Yeah, okay then," I answered Tanya smiled at Sam. Sammy never gave Tanya any of her time.

"We will be in the room, Sam, let us know when you're ready," I told her. For a split second, I was distracted by Sammie's long, flowing locks of hair. It reminded me of my hair that had been taken away. I was fed up with being teased in school and told how much I look like a boy.

"Ingrid, before you disappear can you tell Foxy I want him? He's in Melissa's room," Dad asked.

"Okay, Dad." Tanya followed me. I knocked the door twice before I got any response.

"Foxy? Foxy?" I called out.

"Come in," he answered. Foxy was standing at the end of the spare single bed in Melissa's room quickly doing up the button on his trousers.

"Dad said he wants you," I told him. I noticed Jackie in the bed our eyes made contact. She pulled the covers over her head and began to giggle. Foxy looked proud of his conquest; it was clear what had happened. Although, I was surprised Dad allowed Foxy to sleep with her. Dad had tried so many times to get Jackie into bed. I left the room quickly, closing the door so Tanya couldn't see.

"What is it, Inx?" Tanya asked.

"Don't ask," I answered dismissively, "come, let's go play." Dad's voice was getting louder and louder. I found it hard to focus on my game of dolls. I was waiting for the mood to change in the living room; like at any second Dad would erupt. His friends laughed as Dad recalled the story of him biting off someone's finger while out last night. Every so often one of them would fill in the gaps.

"Come Inx, let's go." Sam appeared from behind the bedroom door at last. Finally, I could relax and enjoy a game of Hopscotch. Melissa sat strapped in her pram, watching us play. She fell in and out of sleep, occasionally eating her custard cream biscuits.

"Sammie, Dad wants you," Dionne called from the front door, "and can you bring Melissa in now please." Sam had a look of dread on her face.

"What now?" Sam said, making her way inside with Melissa.

"You okay Inx?" Tanya asked if she knew me well enough to know that I was not okay.

"Not really," I replied. Suddenly I heard screams coming from inside the house and the sounds of glass breaking.

"You fucking slag!" It was Dad's voice. I ran as fast as I could, filled with dread about what I'm going to see. Sam was huddled up in the corner of the living room, her face tightly tucked into her chest with her arms covering her face; Dad was kicking her viciously. "You fucking slag, you want to fuck everyone!" he screamed. Every so often Sam would look up, her face covered with blood. I wanted that second to be frozen in time. I watched helplessly, searching with my eyes for someone to stop him.

I jumped up and down on the same spot as though I was jumping over hot coal, screaming, "Please stop! Dionne, stop him." Dionne just stared, unable to help, holding Melissa tightly in her arms. Melissa was screaming, burying her face into Dionne's chest. Occasionally, she looked around and flinched with each scream.

"Joey, come on man. You can't do this man." Thankfully Delroy intervened. Delroy was trying his hardest to pull Dad away from Sammie but Dad continued to lash out. Sammie looked up and, amongst the madness, I noticed a gap in Sam's teeth as she cried out, pleading for Dad to stop. It was clear that Dad had kicked it out of its place. My heart was being ripped apart. I desperately wanted to help but there was nothing I could do.

"Dionne, please make him stop," I begged. The room was dark and all I could see was Sam in the corner. Finally, Delroy managed to get Dad away from

Sammie. "Sammie come!" I shouted to her. Sam managed to peel herself off of the floor and followed me into the bathroom. Her face was swollen. Tanya unravelled some toilet tissue, wet it and handed it to Sammy, who was sitting on the side of the bath. She had stopped crying she had a vacant look in her eyes.

"You okay, Ingrid?" Sam asked me.

"Yes, Sam, are you?" I replied. My big sister was so hurt and there was nothing I could do. I cried silently, mainly out of anger and frustration. There was a knock at the bathroom door. "No, Sammy, don't open it," I whispered to Sam but she quickly reached over to unlock the door. Sam didn't seem to care; she looked as though she'd had enough.

"It's okay, Inx," she said bravely.

"Open, it's me, Delroy." I sighed with relief. Delroy was a tall, slim, dark-skinned man. Dad always suspected that he fancied Dionne, but then Dad accused everyone of everything. Delroy came in. "Sammy, let me see your face," he asked. He took the wet tissue and flushed it away. He soaked a clean flannel and dabbed Sam's face gently. The sight of Sam's face angered him. "What the fuck man, I don't business ya know. Joey can't be doing these fuckries with me," Delroy sounded choked.

"Delroy, I think my dad might hear you," I whispered.

"Sorry Ingrid, but right now I don't give a fuck. This is too much, he's gone too far." Delroy turned back to tend to Sam. Sam began to cry.

"He's angry because he found my diary. I had written in it that there was a boy I fancied, called Michael Reid. He's angry because he's jealous," Sam tried to explain. "I'm not even allowed out so where do I get time to sleep with all these people?" Sam continued to cry.

"But I don't understand. It's normal for a girl your age to have crushes." Delroy was trying to make sense of it all. I could hear some of Dad's friends leaving one by one. At last, I thought.

Realising there wasn't enough space for all of us inside the cramped bathroom, I left with Tanya. We took a seat in the hallway on the floor so as not to be too far away from Sammie. Dionne was sitting on the sofa next to Dad. He was still furious. "You see Ingrid, your sister is a dirty fucking whore." Dad wouldn't let it go.

"Okay Joey, leave it now," Dionne asked him politely. I knew Dad was jealous; he often accused me of seeing boys on the estate too.

"Ingrid, I'm gonna go now. I think it will be best," Tanya said. "I'll check on you tomorrow," she said discreetly, before slipping out so Dad didn't see her go. I quietly went to my room. I sat there silently, trying to listen to what Dad was saying in the next room. Suddenly there was a loud bang. I jumped off my bed and ran to the hallway; 'Please, God, don't let it be Sammie again,' I prayed. Delroy was shouting at Dad, he had cornered him in the living room. At last, someone was helping us.

"Joey, you touch your children?" Delroy shouted. I was so scared. What had Sammie told him? "No, I would never do such a thing," Dad shouted back in his defence. Delroy grabbed the end of the coffee table and threw it over, all the drinks and glasses smashed. Delroy was now out of control. Dionne and Tony stood in between them; Dionne pleaded for it all to stop. "Sammie, look what you've done," Dionne called out. Sam grabbed my hand tightly; she was as scared as I was. Dad managed to free himself from Delroy's isolation. He ran towards us. I thought he was going to hit one of us, but he pushed past us and ran out the front door, leaving it wide open. Dionne ran out after Dad. "I can't find him Delroy, you two may as well go. He probably won't be home tonight anyway," Dionne told Delroy and Tony when she came back. And then there was silence; everyone was gone.

"Do you think Dad will come back, Sam?" I sat swinging my legs at the edge of my bed.

"I don't know, Inx, but I do know if he does come back, he will probably kill me," Sam said, staring up at the ceiling. "He's back," Sam said, listening intently by the bedroom door. There was a strange sound of furniture moving around.

"No Joey," Dionne's voice shouted out to Dad in a panic. "Ingrid, Sammy, come and help me."

We jumped up and rushed to see what was happening. Dionne was struggling to pry the kitchen door open, it was locked tight. Dionne then ran around to the food serving hatch; she was pleading for Dad to come out. "Joey, please come out." She was crying. I went to see what was going on in the kitchen. I wondered why Dad had locked himself in there. As Dionne stepped aside, I could see Dad was on his knees with his head in the oven. He had barricaded himself in the kitchen.

"Daddy no!" Once Sam saw what he was doing, she started to beg him to come out. Dad was crying; the smell of gas was all around. I tried to climb through the hatch but I was too big. Dad's head was deep inside the oven.

When Dad heard our cries, he sat up, looked at us and said, "This is what you want, I know you don't love me. Let me just die in peace."

"Dad please don't! We do love you, I'm sorry," Sammy said in an attempt to stop Dad from killing himself. Dad crawled across the floor and opened the kitchen door. We ran in and cuddled him. Dad said that he had forgiven us both and that he loved us. We never spoke about it again. The only time anyone spoke about what Sam had told Delroy was when Dionne's mum called to speak to Sam. She told Sammie that she must have got it all wrong and that she should consider the possibility that maybe it was an accident; that maybe Dad's hand slipped one day when they were playing around. Sammie was devastated. She vowed to never tell anyone again because no one will believe her and that no one would ever be able to help. Dad was far too smart for us.

Chapter Twelve:
Nosebleed

"Ingrid, Sammie, Dallas is starting," Dionne called from the living room. "Oh, and grab your lasagnes on your way in. They're on the side," she told us. Wednesday evenings were always a night to look forward to. We would settle down to watch Dallas with a Findus lasagne, especially through the cold winter nights when we couldn't play out – it was something to look forward to. It was our little tradition. As per usual this winter, I was unwell. I had a runny nose and a feeling of hot and cold that lingered for what seemed like weeks. Even though I couldn't taste what I was eating I refused to waste my lasagne. With Dallas starting, I laid down in front of the TV; sprawled out across the floor, not far from Dad's feet.

"Ingrid, can you please stop sniffling," Dad asked, sounding irritated with me. "Go and get some tissue and blow the damn thing," he said. I was missing a crucial part of Dallas; Bobby Ewing was blackmailing Hicks into voting J.R. out of his position as Head of Ewing Oil so Bobby could take over. Dad's temper was running short. I'd had this cold for so long. I had gotten used to sniffling, even when I didn't need to; it had become a habit. Suddenly, I was stunned. Dad had hit me in the face with something; I wasn't sure what it was. I was taken by complete surprise. I covered my face immediately my nose was throbbing profusely. When I removed my hands there was a pool of bright red blood in the palm of my hands. It poured down into my mouth. The taste was salty and the texture thick and warm. My teeth began to hurt. I wondered what Dad had hit me with. "Jesus Ingrid, now you're bleeding," Dad shouted. "Go get some bloody tissue," he ordered.

"Oh, Ingrid, don't let it drop on the carpet," Dionne told me, "And keep your head back." I had done what Dionne had asked, but despite my efforts, my nose would not stop bleeding. Sam came to see if she could help.

"Dionne, it won't stop," Sam called out, sounding alarmed. I took a slow walk back to the living room to show Dad and Dionne that it really wasn't stopping.

Dionne got up and said, "Lay down on the floor, Inx, keep your head back as far as you can." I did as I was told and laid down on my back on the living room floor. Dad wasn't interested, he looked on in disgust.

I was interrupting his TV programme. Dionne tried to apply pressure to my nose whilst Sam went back and forth with ice and a clean damp flannel, but nothing worked, my face was tight with dried blood like I had a face mask on. I could feel the warm blood running through my hair. "Jesus, Dionne! Err, now it's going everywhere," Dad shouted, getting up from his seat. "Samanta, go get a large towel. I need to put it under her head," Dad told Sam. He took the flannel from Dionne and tried to make my nosebleed stop.

"Oh my God," Sam said, looking down at me. "Why won't it stop, Dad?" Sam asked. The fear on her face scared me even more. *Am I going to die?* I thought. I knew I was losing a lot of blood I began to cry.

"Fuck sake, Dionne, it really won't stop," Dad said, giving up.

"We're gonna have to call an ambulance, Joey," Dionne suggested. This really was it for me. An ambulance? I was so scared.

"Yes, I think you will have to," Dad agreed.

"What am I going to tell them, Joey?" Dionne asked.

"What do you mean? She had a nosebleed, it's simple," Dad answered. Sam continued to stare at me, in horror. I could hear Dionne talking to the ambulance man, telling them to come quickly.

"Ingrid, don't worry. They will be here soon," Sam said while pacing up and down. Dionne crouched down beside me.

"Ingrid, don't forget, you just say it was a nosebleed, no point saying what Dad has done. It was only a tap, you know your nose bleeds easily," Dionne said.

"Do you think they're near, Dionne?" Sammy asked.

"I don't bloody know, go outside and see if you can see them," Dionne ordered.

"Dionne, you ain't gonna believe this, I think Ingrid's nosebleed has stopped," Dad said, inspecting my nose closely. Dionne came over to take a look.

"Yes, Joey, I think you're right." Dionne looked relieved. "I better call them back and tell them not to come," she said, reaching for the phone.

"Oh Ingrid, you started to worry me," Dad said, looking relieved that I was going to be okay. "Ingrid, get up and go and wash your face," he added, getting back to his seat.

"And you're gonna have to wash your hair too, Ingrid," Dionne called out to me. "Sammie, you can come in now. Ingrid's okay," Dionne shouted to Sam, who was still outside looking for the ambulance. I just wanted to lay down and sleep. I couldn't be bothered to wash my hair but I knew I had to. Then there was all the combing after. The thought of it made me feel exhausted.

"Ingrid, come and sit here for a minute," Dad said softly as I walked through the hallway, still wearing the towel on my head. "You do realise, Ingrid, that I only did that to get you to stop sniffling. It's become a really bad habit, hasn't it?" he explained.

"Yes Dad," I replied. While Dad spoke, my attention was drawn to the advert on the TV. A lady called Esther Rantzen was talking about children who were being badly treated and said they should call Child Line. While Dad continued to speak, I reached for his pen and a small piece of paper from the coffee table, hoping that he wouldn't see. I was repeating the numbers in my head so I could memorise them.

"Oi fanny, what's the reason you're writing those numbers down?" Dad asked, kicking me at the same time.

"Nothing Dad," I replied quickly. How stupid of me.

"Is there a reason you need that number?" Dad continued to question me.

"No Dad," I answered, feeling worried that he was going to hit me again. Sam looked at me, surprised. She raised her eyebrows and then looked away.

"Get out, Ingrid, I don't want to look at you," he added finally. I felt like a fool. I got up and went to my room, realising I'd had a very lucky escape. What was I thinking anyway? What would I tell them? No one will believe me anyway.

As time went on, Sam and I never discussed anything that Dad did to us. My school friends still thought Dad was amazing, his friends thought he was amazing; there was no one who would listen to us. Dionne told us that we would be moving in the near future. She was pregnant again and our new baby brother or sister was due any day. Dad explained that our rooms had black mould in them, which was bad for my asthma, so the housing made us a priority to get a new home. We got to spend more time with our friends as we knew there was a chance, we may not get to see them again when we move. Tanya was allowed to stay over one last time before we had to move from Brian House. That night, we were all woken by the sound of the front door slamming at around 3 am. We all got up to see what had happened. Tanya had vanished in the night. Dad didn't seem too concerned and neither did Dionne, neither thought it strange that an 11-year-old girl ran out at 3 am. I was so upset because I knew Dad had done something to her. I desperately wanted to go and see if she was okay or even if she had got home okay, but Dionne said she was just being silly and probably wanted to be with her mum.

Chapter Thirteen:
Sam Ripped Away

Aldgate East E1

Age 12. Our baby brother was born, and we were finally in our new home. Sam and I shared the biggest room on the top floor of our four-bedroom townhouse. We had both settled into our new school, Mulberry high school for girls. I loved being in the same school as Sam. She was so popular, I put it down to her beauty. This made it easier for me to settle in and make new friends. "Dionne, is that Ingrid and Samanta who's just come in?" I heard Dad shout.

"Yes Dad, it's us," I answered before Dionne had the chance to.

Dad kissed his teeth. "You two come here."

"For God's sake, what now?" Sam mumbled under her breath. Hanging our school coats on the rail, we made our way upstairs. Dad was sitting in the living room, still wearing his house robe, watching one of his porno films.

"What time do you call this?" Dad asked, his face serious. I could tell he had been working himself up.

"Dad, we finished school at 3:25 pm but then I had to sit a 15-minute detention, so I asked Ingrid to wait for me so we could come home together. I just thought it would be safer," Sam answered.

"It's fucking 4:20 pm. You mean to tell me it takes you this long to get back?" he continued, not listening to Sam's explanation. The sounds of the moans and groans on the TV were distracting.

"Yes, Dad it did," Sam answered. I knew there was no point; Dad's mind was made up.

"You fucking slags. I bet you were both talking to boys!" Dad shouted. I put my head down, I couldn't look at him. To look him in the eyes while he spoke was a challenge that no one wanted. With my head lowered I noticed Dad was naked under his robe. "Oh, get out you two, you had best make sure you come straight home from school next time or you will have me to deal with." Without hesitation, we left the room.

"I bloody hate him, man, he's so nasty what's he watching those films for?" I said to Sam, feeling safe inside the four walls of our bedroom. "I know, Inx. I hate those films, they make me sick," Sam agreed.

I couldn't wait to get back downstairs to see Melissa and Jace. They were so cute. Only a year apart, they looked like twins. It was clear to us that Melissa was Dionne's favourite. Poor Jace was always in trouble, sometimes for things he never did. I always felt that Melissa was more protected by Dionne but that was okay. I knew Dionne would never allow Dad to hit her so I didn't have to worry too much. It was different for Jace. Either way, the older they got, the more I was on edge, needing to know where they were at all times. I knew that the older they got the more they would be on Dad's radar. The fact I felt Melissa was the favourite never made me love her any less; in the same way I knew that Sam loved me regardless of the fact I knew our mum loved me more. "Ingrid, Sammie, your dinner is ready," Dionne called from the kitchen. Taking my plate off the side, I couldn't help but notice that Dad had curried pork chops with rice while we had sausages and mash. Dionne always made Dad separate dinners. I always wanted what he had but I was always thankful that I had a meal, unlike with Mum. I felt relieved it was a Friday; Dad would soon be heading out for his security work at Maxim's Night Club in Hackney. This meant he probably wouldn't be home until Sunday or Monday, so we had a weekend of peace to look forward to.

"Inx, I spoke to Mum today," Sam announced out of the blue.

"When did you speak to her?" I said as we finished our dinner. I felt suspicious that something was going on behind my back.

"She called while you were in the toilet. She didn't talk for long, she ran out of money in the phone box, but she did say she will call you tomorrow," Sam explained. "I wish I could go live with her, Inx, she said she has a new place now in Brixton," Sam continued once we were safely in our room, out of earshot from Dionne.

"Oh, so she has left the Refuge then?" I asked curiously.

"Yes Inx, although I think she's back with Carl," Sam said. Her face saddened.

"What? You would want to live with Mum and Carl, Sammie?" I was confused by the logic of her working out that she would be better off there, with them both drunk every day and Carl beating Mum to within an inch of her life.

"Yes Inx, I would be able to protect Mum. Anything has to be better than living here," Sam said. I understood what she meant but I knew Dad would never let either of us go. Even if he did, I couldn't go. Who would watch over Melissa and Jace? "Oh well, maybe one day, Inx. Night," Sam said as she got into bed.

"Night Sammie." I lay there for a while, thinking about what Sam had said. I loved my mum so much. I knew we had hurt her by leaving but I wasn't sure where we would be better off.

"Ingrid, wake up. Dad wants you," a voice whispered, waking me up. It was Dionne. I could vaguely see her in the dark room, which was only slightly lit by the streetlamp outside. Nudging Sam, Dionne whispered, "Sammie get up, Dad wants you both."

"Oh Dionne, I don't want to go downstairs. It sounds like Dad's got loads of people there," I complained. I sat up, dreading having to see Dad. He sounded loud and angry. "Just listen to what he's got to say and don't answer back. He's come home with a whole load of bloody riff-raff," Dionne advised us before leaving the room.

"I'm scared, Sam," I confessed.

"Me too, Inx. Come on, before he gets angrier." Sam took my hand and led me downstairs. The living room was filled with smoke the air smelt stale. There were a lot of unfamiliar faces; ladies with their heels kicked off, with blackened soles of their feet. Men were listening to Dad talk as though he was a God. The setting was all so familiar, even if their face weren't. Dad spotted us standing in the doorway.

"Oi fanny, come here," Dad called to us. He was kneeling down by his record player with his glass of whisky in his hand, his cigarette burning away while it rested in his ashtray nearby.

"Aww, you have beautiful daughters, Joey," one of the ladies said, trying to be heard over the loud music. We stepped inside for the whole room to see like we were on show.

"Yes, they are beautiful, but they lie to me," Dad complained. I asked myself what he was talking about, trying not to let my thoughts show on my face. "Don't you, fanny? You both think I'm stupid," he asked us.

"No Dad," we replied in unison. I knew this wasn't going to end well. I glanced at Dionne, silently asking for help. I knew there was no point, we were on our own. Dad's friends looked on in disappointment. I, as always, began to cry. Dad filled me with terror. All the while I'm scolding myself, *Ingrid don't cry. Stop it. You will anger him even more.* My thoughts never worked.

"Fanny, stop it. I said stop it. You want something to cry for?" he threatened. I couldn't speak; I wished I could just stop it. "Ingrid, come here," Dad ordered, slowly undoing his belt. My legs were frozen; I couldn't walk. "Ingrid, I said come here. Don't make me come get you," Dad said again, his tone was calm but threatening. Sam stepped forward. "I didn't call you, did I? I called her," Dad asked, aiming his words at me. "Don't worry, Sammie, it's your turn next," he said, now clutching his belt tightly. I wasn't sure what was worse, knowing it was coming or the actual beatings. Dad stood up; his frame towered over me. Every time he spoke my body flinched. He looked down at me, screaming in my face, his nose touching mine. I could feel his breath and specs of saliva hit my face. Dad grabbed my arm so fast. Within a split second, he had both of my wrists, again in one hand. His grip was so tight, there was no point fighting. With every lashing from his thick leather belt, he shouted, "You will never be anything, Ingrid. You are disgusting, like your mum. And, like Sammie, you have become a whore." Then, the strangest thing happened. I realised that I didn't feel the beatings anymore but still I screamed out; as if I was trying to convince him that it hurt, in the hope, it would make him stop at some point. I was aware of all his friends and Dionne watching. No one seemed to care. This was so normal. Maybe I was really bad, maybe I will be nothing. After years of being told I am nothing, I realised that maybe Dad was right. Dad was pumped up. Throwing me aside, he grabbed Sammy. He was unable now to hold Sammie in one hand because she was much bigger than me. Instead, he lashed out at her with his belt. She tried to cover her face but every so often his belt caught her. I stood there helpless. I was more upset by watching him hit my sister than I was for myself.

"Joey, you're gonna wake the kids," Dionne interrupted. I was completely bemused by Dionne's comment. Dad must have listened to her because he stopped. *Yes, we mustn't wake Melissa and Jace,* I thought. Sam got to her feet I could see her hands shaking. I just wanted to hold her. I knew Dad didn't believe all the things he was saying to us. I realised by now that Dad actually enjoyed beating us but I also knew that he loved us. Didn't he? Dad turned and faced his friends like he was up for an award. He stood tall, full of confidence.

"Now, Ingrid. I want you to show these lovely people how you can dance," Dad blurted out. I looked at him in disbelief. Why would he ask me to do such a thing? Did I hear him right? His friends perked up and started to take money out of their pockets. Sam didn't speak. I could hear the strangest noise come from her – like a deep gasp. It sounded like it had come from her gut. I wanted to vanish. I wanted to die right there at that very moment. "Sammie can't dance as well as Ingrid," Dad told his new friends. There it was again, playing us off on each other. I wished I could speak, but I couldn't. I knew I couldn't. My mind was focused on the pain I started to feel on my body from Dad's belt. I was confused that I'd only just started to feel it.

"Dad, can I go to sleep?" The words just fell out of my mouth.

"Ingrid, I said dance," Dad persisted. He was not going to let me leave until I had done it. Leaning over, Dad put on his chosen record, Barrington Levy, Here I come. He turned the volume up as loud as he could.

"For fuck sake, Joey, you're gonna wake the babies," Dionne shouted over the noise. She got up and left the room slamming, the door behind her. Everyone was waiting for me to do something. I hated feeling like I was on show. His friends began to place money on the coffee table. I didn't even know what dance to do.

"Ingrid, I mean it. Do it!" Dad's face had that look again. I began to dance. I didn't know what I was doing; I just knew I had to do something. They all laughed and cheered. Some of the women stood up and started to dance with me. Finally, it was over. "Aw, come give your dad a big hug." Dad was proud of me. He held out his arms and then hugged me tightly. "And you fanny, come here," Dad said to Sam. "You do realise that the only reason I hit you is because I love you," Dad said, kissing us both on our foreheads. After he released us, we stood there for a moment waiting to be dismissed. "Oi fuck face, pour me two shots of whisky," Dad ordered from one of the men. He looked up at Dad, confused.

"You want two, Joey?" he asked. What was this guy even doing here? He looked like a schoolteacher. He definitely wasn't like the people Dad would hang around with. He was a white hippy-looking man. "Sure, Joey," he replied immediately, jumping to attention to do Dad's order. He handed them over to Dad, who then handed the glasses to me and Sam. We looked at each other, not sure if Dad was testing us or not. It wasn't the first time Dad had given us alcohol, but it was the first time he did it with other people here.

"Go on, take it. It will put chest on your hair," Dad said, laughing at his own stupid joke. His friends laughed along with him. Taking the glasses, Sam and I drank it quickly. I could feel burning in my throat and chest as the whisky made its way down to my stomach. At last, we can go to bed. As tired as I was, it took ages to try and sleep. Mummy was on my mind; the sunrise was shining through the window and Dad's music was still echoing through the walls.

"Ingrid, please come and help me in the kitchen or you can take Melissa for a walk around the block. And ask Sam too, if she can push Jace in the buggy. Just so I can get stuff done," Dionne asked politely. Dionne seemed stressed and exhausted maybe even more so because she was pregnant again. Dad had not been home all night he returned this morning around 10 am. I could hear him singing from my bedroom window. He often did this when he was 'in the doghouse', as Dad would put it. He'd returned with a whole bunch of new friends and one of his best friends called Stratton. He was a black man, of average height and quite skinny. His hair was an untidy, unkempt afro. Me and Sam called him Dad's little helper; whenever Dad said jump, he would ask how high. Although we knew he was harmless. Along with his friends, Dad told us that Mum and Carl would also be coming to spend the day. This became a regular occurrence over the years – a day spent doing nothing, just drinking. Mum would still sit there crying while she fantasized over Dad and blamed Dionne for taking him away from her. Carl knew he was living in my dad's shadow, yet he still wanted to be around him. It made no sense to me.

"I can't wait to see Mum, can you, Sam?" I asked her. I was trying to keep a hold of Melissa's hand when all she wanted was to run free like a big girl.

"Actually, Inx, I'm not looking forward to it as much as you. She's only gonna get drunk, it's not as if she really comes to see us, is it?" Sam replied. Thinking about what Sammie said, I knew she was right. We never had any quality time with Mum, it was always about Dad. "What I do know, Inx, is that we need to keep out of the way. You know Dad likes to show off when his friends are there," Sam suggested. As we completed our last lap with Mim and Jace, Mum was standing at the front door.

"Hi Mum," I called out.

Mum waved. "Hello my Ingy," she said, smiling. Mum looked nice, her hair was long and thick with loose curls.

"Hello Carl," I said reluctantly. Carl's presence was just about bearable these days I knew he was no good for Mum. I knew that no matter how much I told her that, it made no difference. She complained about him when she was drunk but when she was sober, she would beg us to forget what she had told us and ask us to be polite to him.

"Hi Mum," Sam said, kissing Mum on the cheek. Sam glanced at Carl quickly and then looked away. "Hi Carl," Sam said, as reluctantly as I did.

"Hello Sammie," Carl responded.

"Mum, before we go in, could you try not to get drunk too quickly? Like, there's no hurry. Maybe hold off on the drink for a couple of hours," Sam asked Mum. I knew this was a big ask; I was surprised Sam asked such a thing. I knew Mum wouldn't listen.

"Oh Sammie, don't start," Mum moaned.

"Don't worry, Sammie, I'll keep an eye on your mum," Carl said as if he was doing us a favour. Carl desperately wanted us to like him. We both knew that I didn't mind him. I just didn't want him to hit my mum. Once inside, Carl passed Dionne a few carrier bags full of snacks that he had bought from the shop. He made sure he kept a hold of the bag with bottles of whisky in it. The music was extremely loud. Every so often I noticed Dionne feeling irritated when one of the strays that Dad had come home with would come downstairs to use the toilet.

"Dionne, is it okay if we take Melissa and Jace to our room?" Sam asked.

"Yeah sure, keep them up there for a bit," Dionne answered.

As the evening went on Dad got louder. Occasionally we would hear Carl tell Mum to stop crying. I wanted to go and see Mum but I knew that Dad would capture me. "Ingrid, be quiet for a second," Sam told me as she jumped up and ran to the bedroom door, listening intently to what was being said downstairs. I sat Jace on the floor next to Melissa and went to join Sam at the top of the stairs.

"What is it, Sam?" I whispered.

"Shh. Just listen," Sam whispered back.

"Dionne, you're a fucker you know, you ruined my life," Mum shouted at Dionne. "Ya think ya good," Mum said again, her Irish accent thick and clear. I could hear Mum still crying. There was no response from Dionne; I think Dionne was used to it. All the years that Mum's known her, she always attacked Dionne when she had a drink. At least we had reached a point where they were no longer smashing each other's heads on the corners of furniture.

"I'm listening, Inx, cos some of the women are bad talking Mum," Sam said, sounding very concerned and protective. Of course, the women sympathised with Dionne; they didn't know that Dionne used to be our babysitter when she was about thirteen years old. Then Mum found out Dad was sleeping with her. The ironic thing was that the same women who were sympathising with Dionne were probably sleeping with Dad too. We were used to women pretending to love us or to like Dionne just so they could get to Dad. There was a car horn beeping constantly at the front of the house which drowned out the voices from downstairs. We both ran to the bedroom window to check it out. It was Eileen and Tina. I tried to get a better look to see if Lorrinda was there but she wasn't. We had not seen Lorrinda for a long time. "Oh no," Sammy said, laughing.

"What you laughing at, Sam?" I asked her.

"Well, this will be interesting, all of them together," Sam said, still laughing. "Come. Let's go and see Eileen," Sam suggested. We picked up Jace and Melissa and made our way downstairs.

Eileen had already reached the living room before we got there. "What the fuck is all this?" Eileen shouted. Eileen never cared about what came out of her mouth or who she offended, she had no filter.

"Oh look everyone, it's my second wife," Dad announced to the room. The strange ladies started to look uncomfortable by Eileen's presence.

"Hello Bernie," Eileen said to Mum with a genuinely warm smile.

"Aw, hello Eileen," Mum peered over her glasses. Surprisingly she was pleased to see Eileen. Then Mum began to cry again.

"Oi, I hope you're looking after her, Carl," Eileen said to him, poking him on his knee.

"What? Of course, I am," Carl replied, with a stupid grin on his face. Eileen dismissed him, turning her back, not allowing him to finish what he was saying. Eileen knew he was full of crap, she often told us so. With Eileen there, we felt safe to enter the room.

"Oh, my Ingy," Mum called out. It was too late she had spotted me.

"Yes, Mum?" I felt embarrassed. Why couldn't Mum be like Dionne or Eileen? I could feel the other women judging her. I went and took a seat beside her.

"Oi fanny, what do I owe the pleasure of your company?" Dad asked Eileen while slapping her on the bottom.

"Oh, piss off Joey, who's all the riff-raff anyway?" Eileen replied. The unknown guests did not look up. They continued to talk amongst themselves as if they couldn't hear Eileen talking about them. Only Eileen could be so rude and get away with it. She had her fair share of drama with Dad after he was imprisoned for throwing her out of her flat window. "I don't know how you put up with it, Di," Eileen commented.

"Oh, you know what he's like. He doesn't ask me anything. I'm just the servant," Dionne replied sarcastically.

"Eileen, you didn't tell me you brought Tina with you." Dad's face lit up when he noticed Tina standing in the doorway. "Come here princess, come give me a hug," Dad attempted to persuade Tina to go over to him.

"No, you're okay, Joe. I'll stay here if that's okay," Tina replied. She looked uncomfortable.

"You see what I mean? No one loves me, I'm just a black enamel bastard. Well, I'll be dead soon," Dad said. No one in the family entertained Dad's words anymore. His new friends tried to reassure him that this was not the case and that surely, we must all love him. What did they know? We were just sick of hearing it.

"You gonna get me a drink or what?" Eileen asked, taking a seat on Dad's lap.

"Dionne, go and get two glasses please." Dionne tutted and left to get the extra glasses. Mum kept pulling my face and slobbering on my cheek.

"I love you, my big brown eyes." Mum sounded like a broken record. "Where's my cheeky Sammie?" Mum asked. She tried her hardest to focus but she was far too drunk.

"She's there, Mum," I pointed over to Sam. Mum laughed once she realised Sam was sitting opposite her the whole time.

"So, Tina, where have you been all my life, my sexy sophisticated young lady? Isn't she beautiful?" Dad continued asking his friends what they thought of her.

"I'm gonna go downstairs, Joe, and make a coffee," Tina said politely. I knew she wasn't coming back to the living room. She had been trying to find a way to excuse herself the entire time she was there.

"Inx, you wanna come back upstairs and finish our game?" Sam asked me discreetly, so as not to be heard. I just nodded.

"Oh, Dad you made me jump," I said once I realised Dad was standing at our bedroom door. I did not see or hear him come up, he just appeared.

"Hello, my angels," Dad said, stumbling across the room and knocking over the Monopoly pieces we had left on the board. He slumped himself down on my bed, banging his head on the wall in the process.

"Oh Dad, be careful," I said.

"Why? It's not like you two love me," he answered. "But it doesn't matter because I love you. I always have and always will," Dad continued, now adjusting his seating position so he was on the edge of the bed. "Ingrid, has Sammie told you that she doesn't love me?" he added. Here we go.

"No Dad, why would you say that?" I asked, purely because I had to. I didn't really care.

"Because Sammie won't let me have full sex with her," he answered. I was shocked by Dad's bold words. He had never really spoken like that before. Sammie looked horrified, her cheeks went red. "Isn't it, fanny? You must be saving yourself for someone else," Dad continued, poking Sam in the head hard.

"Ouch Dad," Sam said, putting her head down.

"Do you think anyone in here will ever believe either of you if you told them what I do to you?" Dad's words were spiteful and chilling. I couldn't believe what I was hearing. "You see, the fact that you're not my biological child, Samanta, means that when I do decide to sleep with you, in the eyes of the law it doesn't mean anything. It will not matter because you are not my flesh and blood." Dad's gaze was cold, Sam put her head down. I knew she was hurt; Dad was being ruthless. "Ingrid, have you had your period?" Dad asked.

"No Dad," I replied, keeping my head down, careful not to make eye contact.

"You see, Ingrid, I asked Samanta if she would let me put a Tampax in her but she said no. Do you know how much that hurt me?" Dad asked, holding his chest as though he was in physical pain. I didn't dare say a word. *When was this?* I thought. Sam began to cry. There was no sound, just tears rolling down her face. "So, Ingrid, when it's your turn you have to let me know. It will mean you are a woman." Dad's words terrified me. I was scared in a way I've never felt before. Without warning, Dad grabbed Sam by the throat. His quick movement startled Melissa she began to cry still keeping her dummy in her mouth. He looked back at the door, making sure no one was there to see him. "I don't want you, Sammie. I don't want you here anymore." Dad looked vicious; he had a look in his eyes that I wasn't familiar with. Looking deep into her eyes he continued to squeeze.

I cried out, "No Dad, please, you're hurting her." Every part of me hated him. I wanted to help Sam so badly but I couldn't. As Dad squeezed, more tears rolled down her face.

"I want you out, Sammie," Dad said, releasing her.

"Where is she gonna go, Dad?" I asked. I was worried; I had a vision of Sam, 15 years old, sleeping on the streets.

"Your mum is probably home now. Carl took her ages ago. Go and live with her," Dad said coldly. It was as though he had no emotions; he felt nothing. Dad walked out, leaving us both crying and so afraid. Sam and I cuddled for ages, neither wanting to let go. Melissa looked on curiously her cheeks still wet from her tears. I had never felt a pain like it. There was a knock at the bedroom door. It was Dionne.

"Hey, what's happening? Dad is in the right mood, what happened?" she asked, looking puzzled.

"Dad has told Sammie to leave, Di, please don't let him send her away," I was choked, I could hardly speak.

"Oh," Dionne responded, clearly not knowing what she should say or do. "Well, what's brought this on?" Dionne continued her questioning.

"I don't know Dionne, I give up," Sam answered while grabbing her clothes and stuffing them into plastic bags. I was devastated. I needed my sister. The thought of her leaving left me breathless. I cried so much; I couldn't cry anymore. Dionne left the room without saying a word holding Melissa in her arms.

"Please don't go, Sam," I begged her.

"I have to, Inx, he will probably end up raping me or you one day." Sam's words sent chills down my spine. "I just wish you could come with me, Inx." She began to sob. "Ingrid, promise me you will be careful now that I'm not here. He will probably come to you more often." Her words terrified me, thinking about what she was saying had me screaming inside. It was like an out-of-body experience. I knew what she was saying was true. I didn't want him to come near me, ever. Even if I could go, I wouldn't have because of Jace and Melissa. I was trapped, there was no escape for me. "Ingrid, will you walk with me to the bus stop?" Sam asked kindly. Within this brief moment, my sister, who has looked after me for almost 13 years, was ripped away from me. She wasn't just my sister, she was also my mum. Taking a slow walk down the stairs, we saw Dad sitting in his armchair. He sat without a care in the world; he didn't say goodbye. And never broke his gaze from the TV. The walk to the bus stop was long and painful. I couldn't believe this was happening. As Sam's bus approached, we hugged each other one last time. I wanted to fall to my knees and just scream for someone to help us right now. Anyone. That would never happen; it was clear Dad would never be stopped. Sam let go and stepped on the bus. My body let out a cry like no other. Suddenly, Sammie was gone, her face looking back at me from the rear bus window suddenly disappeared.

Sammie would call me when she could, often telling me that I need to tell someone before it's too late. My nights were filled with fear and horror. There was no horror film I was scared of more than him. I was always on edge, always listening to the front door so I knew when he was home. Dreading hearing his footsteps as he climbed the stairs, quietly closing the door after making his way to my room, then creeping back down and slamming the front door as if he had just come home.

Chapter Fourteen:
Self Sabotage

1986 Age 13. Sammy was right. As the months went by, Dad did come to me more often. I was no longer able to sleep without some kind of aid. I would sneak Dad's beers out of the fridge, which tasted disgusting, just so my mind would switch off. I never slept peacefully again. The arrival of my new baby brother Andrew meant Dad got more resentful of Dionne's time being occupied by my younger siblings.

I started to self-harm, using Dad's razor to cut my arm. Not in slices so it would be obvious; I would just hold the corner of the blade to my skin and press down hard until it punctured me. I would wait until I felt something, anything. I was like a robot. For a while I managed to persuade Dionne to let me have Melissa in my room; it was the only way I knew he couldn't get to her. I knew it angered him that Melissa was so protected by Dionne. It meant he never got an opportunity to get to her. He would take his frustrations out on Dionne in other ways; giving her the silent treatment for days for no reason at all or staying out for nights on end. He would tell me that Melissa was spoilt and that since she came along Dionne neglected him. That was why I was there, to serve his purpose. I no longer felt loved. I knew I was an object. I always felt dirty; even after I bathed I could still feel him on my skin. I began to bathe in Dettol. This is one habit I have never been able to break, even to this day. Every day felt hopeless without Sam. I didn't want to live. I felt conflicted because at times I wanted to die but I knew I had to live, for Melissa and Jace. I resented them for it in my own way only because I couldn't leave. But I needed to know they were okay. Dad always reminded me that I would never amount to anything and I believed him. The only thing I knew for certain was that I would be a good Mum. I fantasised about having six children and all of them would feel loved and feel safe. I started to bunk off school. I would sit on the stairs in a block of flats in Watney Market and drink alcohol I'd taken from Dad's stash. I even managed to persuade a few of my friends at times to come with me, they never understood why I was such a troubled soul. I hated lying to them. By keeping his secret, I felt alone.

There was no one to talk to, no one I trusted. I felt let down. I even started resenting Sammie for leaving me even though she had no choice but to go. My friends would ask why I had bruises on my body, which were impossible to hide during P.E. and Dance lessons. I would make up stupid excuses like I fell downstairs or off my bike or roller skates. The list was endless. They called me clumsy. I did manage to make sure that none of them ever came to sleep over. I would watch children innocently climbing and jumping on their dad's and wonder if their dads touched them too. Dad terrified everyone; Dionne included. He may not have beaten her like he did my mum and Eileen but he had other ways of keeping her under his control. She knew not to step out of line she knew what he was capable of. "Ingrid, it's Daddy," his familiar voice woke me again. *How did I not hear him come in?* I thought. I must have drunk too much of Dad's beer! Dad climbed on top of me, kissing my face roughly. I could see his face clearly as the streetlight outside my window shone through. He no longer looked like Dad – his face seemed to morph into something I couldn't explain.

"Dad please don't," I asked him. I had given up; I just didn't care about my safety anymore.

"Ingrid shut up," Dad whispered in my ear.

"No Dad, I want you to stop," I told him again. Dad froze for a moment and stared at me. I could not see the whites of his eyes; they were all black, like the eyes of the devil.

"Ingrid, don't push me away." Dad's tone was threatening. I began to wiggle as much as I could, making it difficult for Dad to pin me down. I started to cry, pushing Dad away. He felt like a wall I just couldn't budge. He was furious.

"I said no Dad, stop!" I shouted. I no longer cared if Dionne heard, or anyone else. He placed his hand over my mouth, covering part of my nose. He pressed down so hard that the inside of my lip was cut from my teeth and I could taste blood. I began to panic; feeling suffocated.

"Ingrid, I said stop fighting or I will kill you right now," Dad whispered in my ear. There was no doubt that Dad would have followed through with his threat. I don't know what was worse, gasping for air or him on top of me. I surrendered. I tilted my head back, gazing at the dark sky and the lights from the streetlamps and drifted off to my happy place. I was an expert at doing that by now. It was like an outer-body journey. I was soon brought back to reality by Dad's body going limp. The weight pressing on me made it even harder to breathe. As Dad got up, I rolled over and started crying silently. "If you ever fucking do that to me again, Ingrid, I will strip you and tie you up outside," Dad said. It wasn't the first time he said he would do this. I did not get back to sleep. I stared into the dark, blank space around me for hours.

Before I knew it, Dionne called me to get ready for school. I was exhausted. I poured half a bottle of Dettol into my bath that morning. I stood there gazing at my body in the mirror hating everything about me; my thighs, arms and wrists were bruised. I looked at Dad's razor and thought of cutting my wrists. I don't know what stopped me at that moment. I couldn't eat and I barely spoke to Dionne who was sitting in the kitchen bottle-feeding baby Andrew. I kissed Jace and Melissa goodbye and left.

"Ingrid, what's happened? You look rough today," my friend Abbey told me as I walked into class. I took my seat without saying a word.

"Ingrid, are you okay?" Mrs Burton also noticed. I shrugged my shoulders and sat down. Mrs Burton began calling the register with every name she called out she would glance over at me. "Ingrid, can you stay behind after registration please?" she asked. Now everyone was looking at me. I just nodded.

"Ingrid, what's happened? Is it your mum? Sammie?" Abbey kept prodding away, wanting to know more. I put my head on my desk in front of me, hiding my head in my arms and cried.

"Right Abbey, can you take Ingrid outside, please? I will join you in a moment," Mrs Burton said. Abbey cleared space for me to sit on the bench outside our classroom by throwing bags and coats to the floor.

"Ingrid, sit here. Please tell me what's wrong," she said.

"My dad hurts me," was all I could say. I couldn't stop crying. I felt a surge of release and fear. Mrs Burton came out to join us, taking a seat next to me.

"Right Ingrid, can you tell me what's going on?" she asked. I couldn't speak.

"Miss, Ingrid said that her dad hurts her," Abbey spoke for me. I was pleased as I couldn't get the words out. Mrs Burton's face dropped.

"Right, Abbey, can you please take Ingrid down to Mrs Rowbottom's office? I will meet you there, I'm going to get Mr Wilson to cover my lesson," she said, taking my hand. She squeezed gently. "Ingrid, it will be okay. Go with Abbey, I will be with you as quick as I can." This was it; there was no backing out now.

The walk to Mrs Rowbottom's office was daunting. I never liked her; she was so strict; I don't think she liked me either. I noticed Abbey's eyes were filled with tears. "It's okay, Inx, I'll stay with you," she reassured me. *Mrs Rowbottom is probably gonna tell me I'm lying,* I thought. She was like the ice queen disguised as the deputy head. Once inside the office, Abbey was made to wait outside. When I told Mrs Rowbottom what was happening her reaction shocked me; her eyes filled up straight away.

"Oh my God, Ingrid, I'm so sorry." It was the first real emotion I had ever seen from her. Mrs Burton came to join us.

"I'm so sorry, Ingrid, this is so unprofessional of me I know but I'm just stunned," Mrs Burton tried to explain why she was crying. Before I knew it the police were called. I wasn't prepared for this. I started to worry. If Dad found out I was talking to the police, he would beat me. It all seemed like it wasn't really happening.

"Ingrid, these two policewomen need you to tell them all of what you have told us," Mrs Rowbottom said. The hours seemed to pass by. I missed my break and lunch. Abbey and three of my other friends held a piece of paper to the glass of Mrs Rowbottom's door for me to see. Written on it was "We love you, Ingrid". It was so nice it was exactly what I needed right now. I went over and over the things that Dad had put me and Sam through. There was so much going on, I just wanted to go home.

"Ingrid, we have a social worker coming to see you. Her name is Kim, she's lovely. She will be here any minute," one of the policewomen said. "Ingrid, you have given us a brief statement, but at some point, we will need a more in-depth one," the policewoman continued. *I don't know how she was going to get another statement from me with Dad around,* I thought. I didn't want to speak anymore, both Mrs Rowbottom and Mrs Burton were still with me in the office well after 5 pm. The office door opened and in walked a little lady with short, spiky hair, wearing dramatic eye makeup and bright red lipstick. She was dressed all in black.

"Hello Ingrid, I'm Kim from social services," she introduced herself, reaching out and shaking my hand.

"Sorry but my dad is gonna worry as to where I am," I announced. It was all I could think about. They all looked at each other strangely.

"Ingrid, that doesn't really matter right now. A few officers will be going to see him to explain what's happening but right now we need to sort out getting you to a place of safety," Kim said, taking out a notepad and pen.

"No, you don't understand, I need to go home," I said again. Why weren't they listening? I began to cry; I was sick of crying. My eyes were swollen and my cheeks sore and I kept wiping the tears away.

"Ingrid, because you have disclosed such serious allegations, we cannot let you go home. We need to investigate this further," one of the policewomen explained. She crouched down beside me. "So, we are going to work together, Ingrid, with social services to sort this out. For now, we need to get you somewhere tonight," she continued. I was devastated.

"Wait? Why do I have to go? Why isn't my dad made to go?" I asked. I was getting irritated. "Hang on, what about Jace and Melissa? They're still there, how can he stay around them?" I asked again. No one was listening to what I was trying to say.

"Ingrid, if we think your brother and sister are in danger we will remove them too," Kim explained.

"But that will make things worse! It makes no sense for them to leave Dionne. It's my dad you need to take, not me!" Now I was crying out of anger and frustration. The two officers and the social worker left the office to talk. A short while later, they came back.

"Right Ingrid, we are going to be taking you now to a place not too far from here. When we get there, Ingrid, you will need to be examined by a doctor; that is standard procedure. And then we can take that final statement," Kim told me while picking up my coat and school bag. Mrs Burton stepped forward and hugged me tightly. I could see she was trying not to cry after hugging me. Mrs Rowbottom hugged me too, the tears rolled down her face.

"I'm so-so sorry, Ingrid, I feel like I should have known something was wrong," she said. I didn't know what to say. I suddenly felt like everyone was overreacting. I just wanted someone to make Dad stop. My friends had all gone home by the time we left the office. The school grounds were empty and silent like a ghost town.

I sat in the back of the unmarked police car with Kim. I didn't know what to say so I just stared out the window. What will Melissa think because I'm not home? She will be so upset. And poor Jace. These thoughts were rushing through my head. I was in so much pain, I felt like it was all out of control. Then Dad crossed my mind. "So did you say you are sending police officers to my house?" I asked.

"Yes Ingrid, so you don't need to worry. He will know that you are safe and that you won't be returning," the policewoman in the passenger seat told me. "Does that worry you, Ingrid?" she asked, looking back at me.

"Yes, because he's going to go mad, he will be so angry," I answered. My palms started to sweat.

"Is he a dangerous man, Ingrid?" she asked.

"Yes, you don't understand! He will find me. And if you go there you have to have plenty of policemen because he's huge," I tried to warn them. They gave each other a strange look that I couldn't quite work out. We had not been driving for long when the car stopped.

"Right Ingrid, we are here," Kim said, undoing my seat belt.

"It's a hospital," I said, confused.

"Yes Ingrid, it's Mile End hospital, remember I told you we need to do an examination. Well, there is a doctor here who is expecting us, they're all very friendly." She tried to reassure me but it didn't work. All I could think of was home. Once inside, we were asked to take a seat in another room just off the children's ward. The two policewomen sat in front of me and Kim sat beside me. A tall white man entered the room everyone stood to greet him; I remained seated. Not sure why, I just felt awkward.

"Hello Ingrid, I'm Dr Davies. How are you?" he asked while reaching out to shake my hand.

"I'm okay," I answered, "I just want my brother and sister," I told him, then breaking down into floods of tears.

"I can understand that, Ingrid. Hopefully, you will see them soon, but for now, Ingrid, I need to do an examination. Is that, okay?" he asked.

"Okay," I replied. I was asked to sit on a bed hidden behind a curtain in the corner of the room we were all sitting in.

"Right, Ingrid, I will be right here. These two lovely officers will be with you to hold your hand. Then we can get on with our report, is that okay?" Kim asked.

"Yes okay," I agreed. I climbed up onto the bed.

"Sorry, Ingrid. I should have explained in a bit more detail," Mr Davis said, walking back to me after washing his hands. "I need you to get fully undressed and put on this gown. Then if you can just lay down for me, please," he explained while placing a hospital robe at the end of the bed. "Ingrid, I need to look at all the injuries you have on your body and any that may be internal," the doctor continued.

"What do you mean internal?" I asked as I started to feel uncomfortable.

"I need to look internally to examine your hymen to see if it's still intact," the doctor concluded.

"What's that?" I asked, looking at the policewoman behind him. She looked away.

"Okay Ingrid, because you have told these police officers that your father would force himself onto you, I have to check if he penetrated you so we can log it as evidence. There is a small piece of skin which, if he did, would no longer be intact. This is what I need to look for." I felt ashamed, as though I had done something wrong. One of the officers stepped forward and held my hand. I felt stupid. I didn't want to get undressed. I was so annoyed at myself, thinking I should have never opened my mouth.

"Ingrid, we do need this report, so we know how to move forward," she said while stroking the back of my hand. They continued to talk amongst themselves as I got undressed. I lay on the bed with my hands covering my face; I didn't want them to see me.

"Ingrid, can you place your legs onto these stirrups please?" the doctor told me, tapping my arm to get me to uncover my eyes so I could see where he was pointing to. The examination began. Keeping my eyes covered, I wandered off to my happy place. I didn't understand what they were all talking about. His nurse assistant made notes while he spoke. "Okay Ingrid, it's over now. You can get dressed." The doctor removed his gloves and then went to wash his hands in the nearby sink. "Ingrid, you will be pleased to know that your hymen is still intact," he concluded.

"So can I go home now?" I asked, feeling hopeful.

"Unfortunately, Ingrid, there are other injuries that we need to address. They need treating, so we would like to keep you here just for a few days until you are well enough to go home," he explained.

"What injuries?" I asked without giving him a chance to explain. I cried. The reality of what was happening, the reality of what I had done, hit me. I noticed through the window that it was now dark outside. I pictured Melissa asking where I was and Dad being held in prison, just like he said would happen if I told. I felt so bad. The nurses were told to watch me constantly. The main door to my ward was locked a code was needed to get in and out. There was a little white girl in the bed opposite me; she was so cute. She made me laugh because she kept waving at me. She was tiny, with long blonde hair and large blue eyes. "How old are you?" I asked her.

"I'm five," she answered. She hopped off her bed, walked over and stood by my bedside and just stared at me. It made me laugh even more.

"Are you unwell?" I asked her, trying to find something to talk about.

"No, my daddy hurt me so I have to stay here," she told me. I was surprised; she looked so normal. *Who would want to hurt her?* I thought.

"Come on, Sarah," the nurse said, walking into my cubicle and escorting Sarah back to her bed. The nurse helped her back into bed. Sarah looked over at me and waved again. "Are you okay, Ingrid?" the nurse asked, walking back towards me.

"Not really, I just want to go home. My sister will be so upset," I answered. A small tear rolled down my face. "And how can anyone hurt that little girl?" I asked now crying out aloud.

"How can anyone hurt any child, Ingrid? As far as I know, you were around the same age when your dad hurt you," the nurse replied. Her words were true but I didn't want to think about it. I just wanted to go home. "Ingrid, please try to sleep. You must be exhausted. If you need me, I will be at the nurse's station. I just have some medications to give out then I'll be back there." I couldn't sleep. I watched her walk away to her medication trolley. My head was pounding my eyes sore and puffy, the ward was silent and dark with only a few lamps to light the ward. There was another nurse who had arrived not too long ago. She had taken over the night shift.

"Can I call my mum please?" I asked the night nurse, hoping she wouldn't question me.

"Of course, you can, do you know the phone number?" she asked, picking up the phone and bringing it over.

"Yes," I replied, looking around me to make sure the head nurse didn't see me standing there. The night nurse pressed a button and then handed me the phone.

"I've already pressed the outgoing code so just dial the number you want," she told me. She turned away to continue with her paperwork. It wasn't Mum I wanted to call it was Dad. I had to. I felt so bad and riddled with guilt.

"Hello, Dad it's Ingrid," I said.

"Ingrid, is that you?" he replied.

"Yes, Dad." My heart was racing.

"Ingrid, how can you do this to me? Do you know what you have done? I've had the police here, Melissa is crying, wondering where her sister is," he said quickly.

"But Dad," I tried to explain, but I didn't get a word in.

"Ingrid, I don't know why you would make up such a thing," he interrupted; Dad was crying. It sounded like he had dropped the receiver.

"Dad, Dad I'm sorry. I just." Before I could say any more there was someone else on the line.

"Hello, hello Ingrid," the voice called out.

"Yes?" I answered unsure who I was talking to.

"Ingrid, it's Eileen," the voice said. For a split second, I felt relieved; she would understand, I thought. "Ingrid, what have you fucking done?" she screamed at me. I was stunned, she had never spoken to me like that before. "Ingrid, you have to tell them you made it up. I can't believe you have done this." I dropped the phone on the floor. I cried out so loud, the night nurse came running over. She sat next to me on the floor. Taking the receiver, she ended the call.

"This is why we have to watch you, Ingrid. No good will come from you contacting your mum right now," she said.

"It wasn't my mum. It was my other step mum. I wanted to speak to my dad," I told her. She took my hand and looked into my eyes.

"Ingrid, what did you expect him to say? This is typical, I see it all the time. Your dad will not admit to what he has done. It will just upset you more," she spoke softly to me. I was listening but it made no difference. I felt dreadful.

"But I wanted to speak to my sister too." I tried to make her understand.

"I can understand that, Ingrid, but right now you need to focus on yourself," she said. I could tell she didn't know what to say. I wished I didn't tell anyone. I've ruined everything; my whole family hates me and I will never see them again. This was the reality of telling the truth.

"I'm never gonna see my sister and baby brothers again?" I sobbed.

"It's a shock, Ingrid, I think you are very brave to speak up about what's happened to you, but you must not contact your dad again. He will hurt you with his words and make you feel worse. Please can you promise me you won't do it again?" she asked. I gave her my word then returned to my bed. Each night I was there, I cried a little less than the night before. No one knew for sure how long I had to remain at the hospital. After about six days my injuries started to heal. My physical pain was nothing compared to what I felt inside. After seven or eight days there was still no word as to how long I had to stay, and no contact from my family. Thankfully, I had Sarah. I would read to her and brush her hair. She said she was waiting for a new family to come and get her. I didn't want a new family; I just wanted Sammie, Melissa, Jace, Andrew, Lorrinda, Val and my Mum. In a strange way, I even wanted Dad. All I could do was hope that one day they would forgive me.

My Diary

2006 Age 33. "Hello, can I speak to Miss I.R. Dujon, please?" A softly spoken voice asked.

"Speaking," I replied, wondering who it was at the other end of the phone.

"Ah, hello Ingrid, my name is Margaret Bishop, calling from Tower Hamlets Social Services." The stranger sighed with relief. I listened patiently. "We spoke a few months ago. I must apologise to you, Ingrid, for not contacting you sooner, but we have been so busy," she explained.

"That's fine," I politely interrupted. "I had been meaning to call you. I thought it had been too long since we last spoke," I continued.

"Now Ingrid, can you speak?" she asked. Her tone was soft, with a hint of concern that she wasn't intruding.

"Go ahead," I requested.

"Now Ingrid, I have copied your files and I'm just in the process of reading them," she explained. "I have to ask you, are your parents still alive? And are you in contact with your siblings?" she asked routinely.

"Um yeah, well my mum has since passed, but my dad is still alive," I answered, feeling slightly uneasy. I always did when asked about my mum. It was a very sensitive subject for me. "Yes, I am in contact with all my siblings," I continued.

"Right, well the reason I have to ask, Ingrid, is because I will not be able to leave certain information in the file due to data protection, however regarding your mother, it will be fine as she is deceased." I wasn't paying much attention after I heard that. All I wanted to know was that vital answer is in my file as to, *why I had paid for what I feel was a sentence, a life sentence for the abuse that my dad inflicted on me, my friends and family?* My thoughts were interrupted by the sound of her voice. "Now all I can say, Ingrid, is that I will be calling you back again. Hopefully within the next week, and then we can make arrangements for you to come down and read your case files. Then perhaps discuss where you would like to take it from there."

"Okay," I responded. Eager to get off the phone, not sure of how I was feeling.

25th September 2006

I received a letter from Margaret Bishop telling me to contact her, as my files were ready to view. I called her that day and made arrangements for Wednesday 4th October at 10 am.

4th October 2006

That day had finally arrived. As I walked into number 62 Roman Road, the most pleasant-looking lady greeted me. She was just as I expected, warm and embracing. "Hello Ingrid, finally I get to meet you after all this time." I smiled; I felt anxious but I also felt safe. I knew I had nothing to worry about. She led me through the building into the little office in the Archive Department. "Take a seat, Ingrid," she told me.

"Thank you," I replied. She pulled out a chair for me from behind the desk and suggested I would feel much more comfortable sitting there.

"Can I get you anything? Tea, coffee, a cold drink?" she asked. My attention was drawn to the folders with my name on it. Five folders lay on the desk labelled:

Ingrid Adams D.O.B 22.05.73

File redacted by Margaret Bishop.

That was it, my life in those folders. "Oh my god," I said, "Are those all mine?" I started biting my bottom lip.

"Yes, Ingrid they are all yours, are you okay?" she sounded concerned.

"Yes, I'm fine. It's just that I've waited so long," I replied. "I'll have a coffee please if that's okay?" replying to her previous question. She picked up the folders and placed them in front of me.

"Now Ingrid, I'm going to get your coffee, you can start taking a look at these. When you open your files you will read from the back to the front," she explained. "If it's okay with you, Ingrid, I will sit with you and I will carry on with some work that I need to do. I will be quiet but at least I am here if you need me, is that okay?" I smiled, I wouldn't have asked her to stay but seeing as she mentioned it, that was fine. I had so many questions. Margaret left the room to get my coffee. As I opened the first file from the back, there was a brown A4 size envelope. Curiously, I picked it up, eager to see what was inside. It was my baptism certificate, which I had never seen before. I gasped; I never expected something like this to be in my file. There were two birth certificates and a letter from my secondary school telling me to collect my G.C.S.E results.

I couldn't believe it. The thing that stood out most were three pieces of paper that I had drawn on, in 1986, in the presence of my child psychologist. Names of all the people in my family were circled in different colours; each colour symbolises who I like a lot and who I hate, those who were alright and those I found stressful. I was speechless; I was so amazed. The people I hated most were my stepmother Dionne and Dad's ex-partner Eileen. This surprised me but I knew immediately why I would have said that. They were the two I thought would have stuck by me but they didn't.

There were many emotional moments as I read through my files; I am so glad that Margaret helped me through it. The missing part of my life was down on paper in black and white. It saddened me to see how I started off as everyone described; a mature, pleasant, quiet, well-mannered girl who was a joy to be around. Then slowly, I read myself deteriorate. It seemed to me the more I felt I wasn't being heard, the more I started to rebel. I started to mix with the wrong crowd. Absconded every chance I got. I wasn't an angel anymore. I searched frantically for the answer I needed so badly; why wasn't anything done for what my dad had done to me? Maybe that's why I have felt so worthless all my life. I wasn't that important back then that my abuser walked free and lived the life he wanted. It's only now, at 33, I am trying to live the life I have always wanted. I'm not perfect but I'm a good Mum, I would die for my children. There were lots of tears, anger and guilt that came from reading my files. In no way do I regret it. I needed to do this for me. There was no police investigation, which broke my heart. It turned out that my social worker had decided for me; that it would be too distressing for me if the police were involved and if charges were brought against my dad. My decision did not count. I had spent many years trying to get some kind of justice for what happened to my sisters, my friends and me, but there was none. Margaret comforted me and explained that now I have read my files I need to put them away somewhere; 'bury it', so to speak. I agreed with what she said but I have always been a fighter.

167

It's not my files that made me want to fight one more fight but to see if I am worthy of justice. It's amazing how much you learn to block painful stuff out in order to live and protect yourself from the things that distress you and cause your heart to ache. As I wrote about intimate details in this story, memories came flooding back. Not forgotten memories, just details that I had to shut away in order to exist. My father isn't just an abuser, he is a monster. For the first time, I was able to appreciate myself and commend myself for turning out the way I am. God's plan for me was not to let me slip into the net of no hope.

I have five beautiful children who I adore and they adore me. I have been able to hold down a relationship and build family values and morals.

So, I am thankful.

My Final Attempt for Justice

12th October 2006

Following the advice, I received from a telephone call with Margaret Bishop yesterday. I called an officer who deals with child abuse cases that are more than ten years old. "Hello Ingrid," he said. He was already aware of my situation as he had spoken to Margaret yesterday, who had given him a brief rundown of what had happened to me.

"Hi, Paul. I don't really know where to start," I explained.

"Well, let me start first, Ingrid, I'll tell you what I do and you can tell me if I can help you," he explained.

Relieved, I said, "Okay then," and just listened.

"Now Ingrid, I deal with child abuse cases that are more than ten years old where the victim would have been under the age of 18 years old and been abused by a family member or by a legal guardian, does that describe you?" he asked.

"Yes, it does," I replied. I didn't realise there were officers who deal solely with this sort of thing. I explained to him that I have tried many times to prosecute my dad and that nothing had ever come of it. I also told Paul that I contacted my social worker, Siobhan Pearce; I asked her why nothing was ever done as it still affected me. Siobhan's response was, "I'm surprised, Ingrid, that you still go on about it even now." I was shocked at the time but maybe I was just harping on about it. I asked her to meet me, not only to discuss my dad but I wanted to tell her about me now and show off my children. I wanted to thank her for all she had done for me. She took my address and telephone number. Siobhan arranged that we would meet the following week. She never did make that call. I arranged to meet Paul the following Thursday with Margaret Bishop. This was my first step. The first of thousands yet to come. Paul had asked me to write down the names of people who I knew at that time, twenty years ago. Out of a list of around twenty or more people, there were at least fourteen children on this list that my father had abused. This included friends and family.

19th October 2006

11 am at Bow Road Police Station, Margaret Bishop was waiting on the steps for me. A lady officer came out to meet us. She explained that Paul was not able to be there to speak with me as he was called away urgently. Her name was DC Debbie Walters. She was plain-clothed and softly spoken. She took us through to a quiet room. "Hello Ingrid, I'm Debbie." She shook my hand firmly. Margaret was not able to come in at this point as Debbie needed to speak to me first. Margaret did not mind at all, she sat in the waiting room and occupied my youngest child, as she too was not allowed in at this point. "Ingrid, can you explain to me exactly what allegations you are reporting?" she asked, picking up her pen and notepad. I felt slightly uncomfortable.

I swallowed and took a deep breath. "Sexual Abuse, which happened over twenty years ago, I was around six years old as far as I can remember."

"I do have to ask you, Ingrid, who was it who allegedly abused you?" DC Walters asked.

"My dad," I replied.

Debbie didn't look up at this point; she kept her pen on the paper, then asked, "Can you tell me, Ingrid, in brief detail, what it was that he did to you? If we decide to investigate this, Ingrid, you will be asked at a later date to give a full detailed statement of what took place, do you understand that, Ingrid?"

"Yes, that's fine," I replied. It came as no surprise to me; I had done this a few times before.

I explained to Debbie that I had reported it before and that nothing was ever done, and how it had always bothered me, which was why I got my files in the first place. And since reading my file I had felt an intense need to try again and get justice; some kind of closure. I gave her my list and explained who everyone was and which ones I had witnessed being abused. I had to tell her, in brief, the dates and places that my abuse had taken place and give some description of what took place. This made me very upset. Maybe I underestimated how I would feel and part of those feelings was severe embarrassment. Debbie was very sympathetic and calming. Knowing Margaret was waiting for me outside was also very reassuring.

For the first time, I had real support. My meeting with Debbie was my second big step. Our talk lasted around an hour and she said that she would get back to me by mid-next week to let me know if they will be doing a full investigation.

Even if they decide not to prosecute at least I have tried. At least I was able to decide and no one else.

Disheartened

31st October 2006

9:30 am. "Hello, can I speak to I.R. Dujon please?"

"Speaking," I replied. Immediately I knew who it was.

"Hello Ingrid, it's Debbie Walters from child protection," she introduced herself.

"Hi Debbie, how are you?" I asked her. Placing my cereal bowl down, I sat upright, waiting to hear what she had to say.

"Right Ingrid, I have gone through your files, and there doesn't seem to be a police report. However, Ingrid, on the system it is showing that there was an investigation, are you aware of that?" I sat forward on the edge of my seat, wondering what on earth she was talking about. Before I could answer, she then said, "Your father had also been arrested and interviewed." I couldn't believe it. My heart sank to the floor.

"No, I didn't know there was an investigation and if there was, how come no one that I had mentioned that I witnessed my dad abusing was interviewed?" I snapped. I felt very defensive and in a way I guess I clammed up.

Debbie remained calm, she explained to me that she wanted to investigate my case, but she was having difficulty obtaining police reports from twenty years ago. All I could think was, *what was the point? He will get away with it again.* "Ingrid, please don't lose hope. I am trying my hardest. Be patient, I have to see what I can dig up." As she spoke my thoughts drifted off. It was too late; I already felt let down. How could you be unsure if he had been arrested and unsure if he had been interviewed? Even worse than this, Debbie told me that if this was the case and he was interviewed and released without further charge she would be unable to arrest him again to question him. I couldn't believe what I was hearing. Are you telling me that if I murdered someone, and you had no proof at the time that it was me, then ten years later you had new witnesses come forward showing

172

you that there is a high possibility it was me, that the police would not be able to arrest and interview me again? Of course, they would. What bloody rubbish.

I do understand that at the time it was my word against his, but now there are others who had chosen to come forward. I strongly believe that if a full investigation had been done the victims who were afraid to speak would have. They would have felt safe in the presence of the police. A thousand thoughts went through my mind. I was furious. What on earth did he and his wife tell them that was so convincing? Did they just ask him if he abused me, he said no, and that's that? I wanted to confront him but that would just make me feel worse. To see his smug face, knowing there is nothing I could do would be a detrimental blow to my state of mind. I have to stay focussed and hope for the best.

Debbie asked me to give her a few weeks to try to get hold of this so-called interview; it really felt as though there was some kind of conspiracy. Someone somewhere had not done his or her job properly.

8th November 2006

"Hello, is that Ingrid?" a female voice asked at the other end of the phone.

"Yes, this is Ingrid," I replied.

"Hi Ingrid, it's Debbie Walters here." I smiled. Then I realised this call had come much sooner than I expected.

"Oh, hello Debbie, didn't expect to hear from you so soon," I continued.

"I'll speak quickly, Ingrid, as I can hear you have children around you."

"Yes, I'm at the kid's school," I told her. I signalled to my son to be quiet so I could hear all of what she had to say.

"Now you know I was having problems getting certain papers regarding the arrest of your dad, and the interview," she continued. I was desperately hoping she was going to say she had found them. "Well that still hasn't changed I'm afraid, but as it still stands, Ingrid, he was arrested and was interviewed."

I had to interrupt, "So what now then?" I snapped.

"Well, the only thing I can do, Ingrid, is to send all the information off to the CPS and see if they will allow for a second investigation." There I was, standing in the middle of my kid's school in complete shock. How can the system be so unfair? I felt as though I had gone back 20 years. There is no protection for our children. Just because it's my word against his doesn't mean it's not worth the fight. I know I'm not lying and so do all of my friends and most of my relatives, who he abused too. But for some reason, there is this wall of silence.

I got in my car and just cried; I thought there is no way the CPS is going to allow another investigation. As the evening went on, I was once again withdrawn. I sat in my room like a schoolgirl in trouble. For tonight, I know I can't function. I love my sister Sam, but deep-down today's events have made me resentful. Why won't she speak up? Why would anybody let someone get away with doing so wrong? I loved my dad unconditionally, but he hurt me in a way I will never forget. I wish I didn't have this fighting drive in me but I do. Why can't I just let things lay? Like everyone else, just sweep it under the carpet. I hate my step mum for protecting him all this time. I was a child; I know I was not her child, but a child who was innocent. Why didn't she protect me? There is nothing in my life that I have ever started and finished, even this book I don't know if I will ever finish it. As days go on, I don't know if I will ever get it all out of my system. I know where my story began; I don't know where it will end.

13th February 2007

I had a voicemail. "Hello, this is a message for Ingrid, it's DC Debbie Walters here. I was hoping you would call me back ASAP. It's regarding the allegations you have made towards your father, I have been contacted by CPS who have made a decision. I need you to call me by the end of today because I will be away for a month from 5 pm this evening. Thank you." I sat there for a moment; my thoughts were all over the place. I had to hear the message again. My heart was pounding. This is it, the final word.

"Hi, can I speak to Debbie Walters please?" I said shakily.

"Speaking," the voice replied. I took a deep breath.

"Hi Debbie, it's Ingrid." I felt anxious. I picked up a pen and started doodling on a piece of paper.

"Ah Ingrid, I was hoping you would call me. I'm away as of this evening and really wanted to speak to you." I couldn't help but interrupt.

"I'm really excited, Debbie, I don't know how I feel."

"Well, I wouldn't get my hopes up, Ingrid, it's not good, I'm afraid," she said, sounding solemn. I sat back in my seat feeling flustered.

"Go on," I snapped.

"The CPS has looked at your files and decided that they will not allow us to investigate again," she explained. Again, I felt as though I had been stabbed in the heart. I've never had a voice; what is it going to take? I couldn't see any evidence of an investigation in my files.

"But," I interrupted, "I don't understand."

"If you just let me, explain, Ingrid. It shows on the system that there was an investigation and that he was arrested, as I explained before. So, therefore, we can't do it again unless someone else comes forward. That would then make it a new enquiry," Debbie explained. I felt sick to the stomach. I just wanted to get off the phone. "I am away as of tomorrow so I want to give you the name of another officer you can call here if you need to speak to someone or have any questions." I said goodbye and hung up the phone. I sat there for a while in silence, shaking my head with disbelief. This was it I have hit a dead end. I didn't get as far as the bedroom door before I broke down crying. I knew there was no full investigation; none of the victims had been spoken to. Nothing had been done.

The days that followed, I did what I do best and just dismissed it from my head. As if none of this ever happened. I'm back to reality; get the boys to football and the girls to ballet. Wash, cook and clean.

27th Feb 2007

I'd left home, as usual, to take my eldest son to football training, when it all came to a head once again. "Are you okay, Mum?" my son asked. I was driving and knew where I was going, but my mind was elsewhere. A thousand thoughts were rushing through my mind. *Why won't these thoughts leave me alone?* I wondered.

"I'm fine, son," I replied, continuing to stare out the window. Once he left the car I sat there in silence in the middle of the car park, watching the kids happily walking by. I can't explain what happened, but I just sat there for the whole hour sobbing uncontrollably. I still didn't have the answers that I wanted. When was this going to end for me? I spent the rest of the evening in my room; my poor babies were wondering what's wrong with their mum. I just wanted to shut myself away. In my heart I know I'm right when I say the police investigation was not completed and that was what hurt the most. Now I have to accept that there is nothing else I can do. The nightmares persist. Sometimes they appear during the day. Nightmares.

I'm standing in a shop, looking at some bags with my sister and our friend. For some reason, I left my youngest outside in her buggy. I didn't want to disturb her while she was asleep. Chatting away, I glance outside to check that she was okay.

Then an overwhelming feeling of fear takes a hold. "Come on let's go, I don't feel right," I told the girls. Just as I'm about to step out the shop door, I notice a small Chinese man heading in the direction of my baby. I start to run; I can sense he means harm. He picks up the buggy with my baby in it and tries desperately to shove it into his car. I grab hold of him punching his arms to let go. I get her free!

I'm in a room with a good friend of mine. A tall white man who's quite feminine takes me on a tour around his home. I praise him for the beautiful decorating he has done. As we step into the lounge, I notice the cutest little boy crawling around. I wasn't aware that he had a child. The room begins to darken. From the streetlight outside, I can see my friend's silhouette standing by the window. "What's going on?" I ask him. I get no reply. I'm distracted by the sound of scurrying coming from the floor. The little boy was being sick on the floor. I rushed over to help him. The boy held me tight. As I looked up at my friend, I felt a sense of fear. Something told me to walk to the door. Pulling at the handle, I realise it's locked. I turn and notice my friend wearing my dad's house robe, but his face was the same. Holding the child tightly, I tried to scream. There was no sound. As he steps towards me, it dawns on me this is not his child, but somebody else's. He was not my friend, he was my dad, who wanted to hurt me.

The nightmares were back in full force.

7th March 2007

Today I had a meeting with my eldest sister Sam. We'd had a confrontation last week. After 20 years, I finally told her that I was angry with her for not supporting me back then. It didn't go down too well. Anyway, I had asked her to meet me at my sister, Melissa's house so we could talk. That too was a disaster. She made me feel as though I was mad, she was analysing me, dissecting me bit by bit. Sam could not understand why I wanted to do this. She said that she has forgiven Dad. That she was over what he had done and that she wanted no part in this.

I have to respect what she wants, but it hurts so much. I know that if she was as troubled by what he did, I would have helped her get the closure she needed. And once again, she was turning her back on me. I sat and thought long and hard about everyone and everything. I have fought enough and don't see why I should fight my own sister – who thinks I'm mad. I wrote her a note telling her that I was going to take time out and that she would not hear from me for a few months. I needed time to heal. Then I wrote to Dionne, my step mum, asking her to please put my mind to rest and answer my questions. Did she turn a blind eye because we were not her children? And did she ever want to come and look for me when they took me away? Even to ask me why I said what I did? Does she truly believe that it is all lies, or can she see that he is capable of doing these things? I ended the letter by saying that I know she will not contact me and that I wish her all the best for the rest of her life.

8th March 2007

I was driving home from an appointment with my dentist when I received a call from Tina. Tina is the aunt to my sister Lorrinda. "Hello Ingrid, it's Tina," she said.

"Hi Tina, how are you?" I asked.

"I just thought I should let you know that I am at the police station. I am going to make my statement against Joey." I couldn't believe what I was hearing, trying my hardest to concentrate on my driving.

"Really?" I asked as though I didn't believe her.

"Yes, I will call you back after and let you know what they say," she said, then hung up the phone. I had to pull over; I sat there for a moment and cried. Is this for real? After 20 years, finally, someone is going to do something. I was in shock. Once I reached home, I sat patiently waiting for her to call me back. The strange thing is that I know she was a victim of my dad, but there was not much more I knew about her. We saw each other on and off over the years and that was it.

Around 4 pm, Tina called me back. "Hi Ingrid, I've just left. The officer I spoke to was very nice. I explained the best I could as to what he had done to me. I also told her that I had heard that you had tried before to prosecute your dad and that nothing was ever done, so I gave her your phone number for them to contact you if needed." As Tina spoke, I was still speechless. She continued, "The policewoman explained that my allegation will be handed over to child protection and they will contact me." Tina sounded calm and strong. As far as I know, Tina had been in psychotherapy for nearly all her life. She was just as dysfunctional and troubled as I was. "I told the policewoman that I am under no illusions that he will go to prison, Ingrid, but if it means he can't do this to anyone again then that's good enough for me," Tina explained. She felt the same as I did. That was exactly it; he must be stopped.

9th March 2007

The house phone rang, displaying 'withheld number'. "Hello," I said.

"Hi Ingrid, it's Dionne," the voice said. I sat down. She had called back. "How could you think I would not contact you, Ingrid? I love you," Dionne said. She started to cry.

"I'm glad that you did call, Dionne," I replied. It meant so much.

"I did try to see you when they took you but your social worker wouldn't let me. She said that because I wasn't your real mum there was nothing I could do," she explained, still crying. I felt sorry for her.

"Do you believe that he had done it, Di?" I asked.

"Yes. Well, and no," she replied.

"You mean you do believe it, Di, you just don't want to accept it," I told her. My heart was pounding.

"It's hard for me, Ingrid, you see so much of it in the papers you just don't think it will happen at home," she told me.

"I think you need counselling, Di, you have never accepted anything," I told her. Now I began to cry. "You see, Di, he will never know the impact of what he has done. I look at my daughter and think how on earth would someone want to touch her. It's beyond me." Dionne began to cry more and said that she wanted to die. She said that she has had enough and wants to take an overdose; she said she had been thinking about it for weeks. I couldn't imagine what that man had put her through. She can't separate what is normal and what is wrong. It's so sad. Dionne told me that she will come to see me on Monday, then we'll talk some more.

The Universe Works in Mysterious Ways

21st May 2007

I haven't been able to write what has been happening for at least two months. A lot has happened, which, emotionally, has been a major setback for me. Tomorrow is my 34th birthday. Of which I will be spending a few hours with D.C Tony Weed, at Stoke Newington Police Station, giving video evidence. I feel really anxious about what might happen. In a strange way, I also feel quite calm. I'm just going to backtrack a few months to fill in the missing weeks.

22nd March 2007

I received a call from Tina, telling me that she received a call from Child Protection, asking her to come to Stoke Newington Police Station to give more information regarding her allegation. Tina made the arrangement to meet DC Tony Weed on the Tuesday after next.

3rd April 2007

Tina went to Stoke Newington Police Station, to meet D.C Tony Weed. Her sister Eileen went with her for emotional support. Eileen is Lorrinda's mother. As far as I know, all went well. Tina later told me that Eileen also made an allegation against my dad.

23rd April 2007

It was evening. I was relaxing, watching TV, while the kids ran around doing what they do best – screaming the house down – when I received a call from my brother Val. Immediately I could hear he had been drinking. It was hard to hear him clearly over the noise the kids were making so I left the living room and went to my bedroom for some privacy. Val sounded sad and upset. He told me how he hates himself for drinking and being the way that he is.

I tried to comfort him and told him that he should not be too hard on himself and that in no way was his drinking his fault. I explained to him that any child who is brought up feeling so unloved and beaten for nothing would most definitely find comfort in something else. Most commonly they find something that is self-destructing to them – drinking, drugs, or even self-harm like I did. For a moment, I thought I was getting through to him when suddenly he started screaming and wailing. The hairs on my arms stood up, I knew something was seriously wrong. "Val, what's wrong?" I asked him.

He continued to cry. It was difficult but I heard him say, "Yeah, but it wasn't just Mum who hurt me, it was Joey too." It sounded as though he had dropped the receiver because his cries sounded distant. My heart began to pound; I sat on my bed calling for him.

"Val, what are you saying?" I asked him. Don't know why I asked him because I knew what he was going to say. I guess I needed confirmation.

Val eventually spoke, "Joey abused me too, Inx," he said, sobbing. My heart felt like it had been ripped out by a wrench. Although Val is now 40yrs old, to me, he is my teenage brother.

My mind was swimming with questions that I needed to ask him but I didn't want to frighten him away. "Val, I need to ask you this, you don't have to talk about it if you don't want to, but when you say he abused you did he go all the way?" I asked him. It's mad, I sounded just like everyone else. Abuse is abuse I should know that. So why did I ask him that.

Val began to cry uncontrollably, I was scared. "He raped me, Inx, when I was eight years old. It really hurt, Inx. I wanted him to stop but he wouldn't." Just when I thought it couldn't get any worse, it did. I had visions of my little boy, who was around the same age, going through that and having no one to turn to. My head exploded; I couldn't take anymore. Inside I was screaming but, on the outside, I had to hold it down, for the sake of my brother's sanity. I could never explain the pain I felt in my heart at that moment. I tried to calm Val and tell him that everything happens for a reason, and if just the release alone from this dark secret that he has carried with him is finally out, then maybe he can move on. After speaking to Val. I was literally bouncing off the walls; I couldn't cope. One thought played over and over in my head; I'm going to kill him. I couldn't bear this pain. I thought I knew in some mad way what my dad was about, but even I had underestimated him. I drank and cried myself to sleep.

The day after Val's confession, I tried my hardest to carry on around the house as I would normally; wash, cook, clean. It didn't matter, visions of my brother at eight years old being raped was too much for my heart. For the first time in my life, I can say I truly snapped. I kissed my baby's goodbye, with only one thing on my mind. To get to my dad and confront him. Then murder him. I had no fear for my safety. I just didn't care anymore; I felt numb. I felt as though my body was not my own; I couldn't control anything. Only God knows how I didn't crash my car on the motorway. I was screaming and shaking, holding tightly onto the steering wheel. I was wailing like a mad woman. Never before had I felt like this. My experience did not come close to what my brother had gone through. If only I could take that pain from my brother. I was helpless. I received a call from my younger sister Melissa on my journey. I told her what had happened, not thinking anyone would feel the way I do. To my surprise, Melissa started crying. I couldn't believe it, someone else felt like me. I kept asking her, "Am I going mad, Mim?"

"No Ingrid, come to me first, and we will go together," she told me. Poor Melissa had a fight on her hands trying to keep me from going to my dad's and doing what I would later regret. It was a long and emotionally draining night. The next day, I thanked Melissa for stopping me from going. I still wished Joey was dead but I was glad I hadn't ended my life by ending his. Again, thank you, Melissa.

Since that day, my dad's wife Dionne had walked out on him; Dionne at this point does not know what is going on. She knows nothing of this investigation. She left him for her own reasons. She'd finally had enough. It's funny because I thought she was the weakest of them all but has proven to be the strongest. There is no way on earth any of my dad's women would leave him. He left them. Dionne is happy, safe and truly content now.

Video Evidence

22nd May 2007

I woke up this morning feeling like I had been hit with a sledgehammer. I had been up most of the night thinking about my visit to the police station to give my video evidence. It was a weird feeling; even though I have spoken about my abuse many times, it didn't change how I felt. My heart was pounding, and my palms were sweaty. I had to keep a handkerchief in my hand to absorb the sweat. Today is also my 34th birthday. I'm going out with my family for dinner to celebrate tonight. If I could get out of it, I would. I know I'm going to break down at some point and even thinking about going out tonight was far too draining. I kissed my kid's goodbye; inside I wished someone could come with me. I'd convinced everyone that I would be fine, when inside I was petrified.

As I parked my car outside Stoke Newington police station, I noticed Eileen crossing the road. *She must have just finished giving her evidence*, I thought. I watched her for a moment; I wanted to see if she had been crying. I was trying to read her body language. I thought that this would help me prepare for what I had to do. Eileen noticed me sitting in the car. She smiled and walked over to me. I stepped out of the car and she threw her arms around me. A cuddle was what I really needed. I asked her how it went and she assured me that it was fine. I knew that D.C Weed was a nice guy and was easy to talk to. Eileen wished me luck. She said she would wait for me if I needed her support but I told her I would be fine. Tony Weed came out to meet me. I followed him through to a small room.

There was a female officer sitting in another small room, which led onto my room. I noticed that she was sitting at a desk with TV monitors. I took a seat, anxiously wiping my palms. There were no social workers with me this time. I was on my own. "Hello Ingrid, how have you been?" Tony asked me.

"Fine thanks," I replied, with a smile on my face. Why did I do that? I don't want to smile; it's a nervous smile I know but why can't I just keep a straight face? That's what I really want to do. I began to fidget and pull at my hanky.

"Would you like a drink?" he asked me.

"No thanks I'm fine." I just wanted this over with.

The female officer came into the room. "Hello Ingrid, I'm WPC Clarkson. I have been looking forward to meeting you," she said, taking a seat on a small sofa opposite me. I smiled and continued to pull the edges on the hanky.

"Now Ingrid, I have to put you out of your misery," Tony said, crossing his arms. "You don't have to give a statement." I couldn't believe what I was hearing. I just looked up at him. "After talking with my colleagues, we have decided that your original statement should be enough evidence."

"Wow," was all I could say. I sighed with relief. "Do you have my statement here now?" I asked him once I'd gotten over the shock.

"Yes, would you like to read it?" Tony replied. I was so pleased that I didn't have to go through it again. I reached over and took my statement from his hand. I was amazed at the amount of detail I had given so long ago. I began to cry, as the tears rolled down, I kept thinking stop it, stop it. I didn't want to cry, I wanted to be strong. I looked over at them and stupidly laughed, I didn't know if I wanted to laugh or cry.

"I swore to myself that I wasn't going to cry today," I told them, wiping my nose and eyes.

"It's okay to cry, Ingrid," the policewoman interrupted. "You are feeling overwhelmed," she continued with a sad look on her face. "You aren't the only one who has reacted like this. I have seen many victims behave like this."

I fought hard to hold back the tears. "Tina was quite emotional too," Tony told me. "You have all done extremely well. Eileen was amazing, she gave us so much information that she probably thought was irrelevant, but is actually really helpful," he continued.

"What happens now?" I asked.

"Well as I told you before, Ingrid, it will be some time before we can physically go and arrest him, as you know I have moved to another section, but I have requested that I be allowed to stay on this case until it is over. So, I can't promise you a time that this will be dealt with because new cases will be dealt with as priority over historical ones," he explained. That was fine with me; the fact was that something was being done.

It's October now and nothing has happened yet. Since May I have been up and down, still fighting with myself. Still not liking myself and still struggling with not wanting to let my kids out of my sight, but my biggest issue is within me. How I feel about me, Ingrid, a 34-year-old woman, still trying to survive. I haven't seen or heard from my brother Val. Dionne is still separated from my dad; she has filed for a divorce now and I am in regular contact with her. In fact, it has brought us much closer. Tony will drop me a text message every now and again, just to let me know he hasn't forgotten about us. I have not written in my journal for a very long time; it has been almost a whole year since I have put pen to paper. I guess I lost my heart and motivation. I stopped believing that writing will make me feel any better.

January 2008

I received a call today from D.C Weed. I could tell by his tone of voice that it wasn't good news. "Ingrid, I'm here with the lawyers going through your case. It's not good, Ingrid. It still stands that we cannot prosecute your dad for what he did to you," he told me.

"Why?" I asked him.

"Well because your dad had been questioned already, Ingrid, my hands are tied. The law will not allow me to re-arrest him without new evidence," he explained. There was a moment of silence. "Are you okay, Ingrid?" he asked me. I didn't know how I felt; I just stood there staring into space.

"Yes, I'm fine, to be honest, Tony, I'm not surprised, I don't suppose it matters too much really, at least he will be charged with something," I replied. I genuinely meant that something was better than nothing. Tony sounded more upset than me, poor guy. He has tried endlessly to help me. I probably sounded cold for a while; I guess deep down I didn't expect any justice for myself or anyone else.

"I'm so sorry, Ingrid, truly I am," he continued.

"It's okay, Tony, honestly. All I can do is be there for Lorrinda and Tina now." And I had to be. I sat there for a moment, still wondering how I felt. Suddenly, I felt a bit lost. Poor Lorrinda and Tina. They are going to have to go through this alone. I felt as though I had abandoned them. My eyes began to well up, why I don't know. I held back my tears for the first time. That's it, I'm fed up of crying. I can't do this anymore. This was the moment of realisation for me.

11th April 2008

3:55 pm just getting ready to leave work when my mobile rang. D.C Tony Weed was flashing on my mobile screen. *Why would he be calling me?* I wondered. "Hello Tony," I said.

"Hello Ingrid, how are you?" he asked.

"Fine thanks," I replied hesitantly.

"Are you sitting down, Ingrid?" he asked me. I sat back in my seat and glanced across my desk at my colleague sitting opposite.

"I am now, why?" I asked back.

"Ingrid, I have great news for you, the CPS have decided to investigate and charge your dad with what he did to you," Tony said excitedly. This was an almighty blow, a good one of course.

"What? Why? How come?" I asked him. Tony began to explain that he had made a closing statement to the CPS telling them that he felt that I had been badly treated by the police and the state. Based on that, they made a decision. To be honest, he did explain more but I couldn't hear him. I sat forward in my seat, keeping my head down. I broke down into tears but at the same time a burst of laughter came out, I was in complete shock.

"Ingrid, Ingrid, are you okay?" Tony shouted down the phone. I looked up to see my colleague looking at me, concerned. I didn't care. This was it.

"Yes Tony, I'm fine thank you. Thank you, Tony, so much," I kept saying, over and over again.

"Now, everything is in place, all we need to do is to arrest him. You will be the first to know when we have got him," he told me. I was still speechless. I hung up the phone; my colleague just looked at me. I felt stupid because I was crying uncontrollably. Once I had calmed down, I explained as much as I could to my colleague, who is also a family member. It wasn't until my drive home from the office that I even realised how important to me this was. Over and over in my head, I thought, *I don't have to feel worthless anymore, I really do mean something.*

Out loud I said, "Thank you, God, I know you love me." I felt as though a massive weight had been lifted off my shoulders.

Sunday, 13th April 2008

Two days after my good news. I'm sitting here in my room, listening to my kids running and playing around the house. No one will ever know how I feel – how I really feel. Deep down in my soul, I feel a positive change; a change in me. I guess in a way I was slightly empowered, slightly more important than yesterday. Maybe this is God's way, maybe it was meant to be like this. Maybe if he had been arrested all those years ago, I would have got no justice. I don't know. I am ready; I know this is just the start; the start of a long fight. I feel as though I have been training for 20 years and now the fight is here. So yes, I am ready. Ready for all he is going to throw at me.

Sunday, 29th June 2008

Age 35. I wrote Dionne a letter today. It probably wasn't the best way to tell her how I felt but I couldn't face her. I couldn't face her tears and I didn't want to feel her pain or hear her excuses. Over the past few months, I have spent more time with Dionne. Since money was tight for her, she asked me to get rid of my ironing lady and give the job to her, so she could earn more money. I did not have a problem with this. At the start, it didn't feel very comfortable – having my step mum work for me. Dionne seemed to enjoy what she was doing though and it was nice having her around. It has been at least 21 years since I have spent this much time with her, on a one-to-one basis. After a month or so I started to feel emotionally drained and stressed out. I couldn't put my finger on it straight away. It's not that she did anything, it was more what she would say.

While Dionne would be ironing, she would talk of my dad as though nothing has happened. This, of course, would make me feel uneasy. As time went by Dionne would tell me of her concern for him, her pity for him. Knowing what she knows now, Dionne made her choice without realising it. She swore on her life that she knew nothing of the abuse he did to us when we were growing up. What she didn't know then, she sure knows now, and still it is not enough for her to cut all ties with him. This didn't surprise me really, because I was used to my own mum putting her men before us.

I realised I had to make a choice. You see, Dionne did not show much emotion; she cried when she had to and talked the talk, but her actions told me a different story. I knew I had to let her go out of my life if I wanted to move on. My letter did not go down very well. I don't think she will ever realise this was one of the hardest decisions I have ever had to make. I feel as though I am grieving; I miss her and I am angry with her, but more than this I feel relieved. I don't have to convince myself that she loves me. I believe she truly cares but it's not love. Sometimes I wish I could just put everything behind me like Sam has – but I can't.

To my family, you would think I have committed a worse sin than my dad. I have since lost my brothers and sisters. They think I am sick because I told Dionne what I thought. Maybe I should have kept my mouth shut and let it eat away at me. I am realising that I am starting to go down that road of depression, and I don't know if I can bring myself out of it. I just feel so hurt and let down by everyone. My family is so dysfunctional, and so far gone that no one seems to see what's right from wrong. I know I have to keep going. My brother Mitchel asked me, "How would I feel if Dionne was to kill herself?" because of what I said to her. He wasn't even around when I was growing up; he knows nothing of what went on. Every waking day of my life, my dad crosses my mind. Would it be best for all of them if I wasn't around? Maybe it would. It wouldn't be best for my kids, so stuff them. My kids come first. I believe in karma and I believe in being born again. If I'm to be reborn again, I have to make sure I don't go through this in my next life. I have tried all these years to protect my brothers and sisters, for them to turn around and tell me I'm sick. That's a knife in my heart. As much as it hurts, I would do it all over again, because I love them. Maybe one day they will realise that.

Monday, 7th July 2008

I received a phone call today from Sam. She asked if I was okay. I told her I was fine; I had no choice but to lie. I was far from fine. I made sure I came across to her as though I was really happy.

I had to do this because any doubt or sadness would have let her think that I regretted cutting Dionne out of my life. Sam told me that she had called Dionne and Melissa the day before to see if they were alright. I didn't mind, as my problem with Dionne is not hers. She asked me if I have thought of Dionne's feelings, and that she feels I have condemned her for something that happened all those years ago. As she spoke, I felt pain in my heart. I wanted to scream out loud and tell her I have always put everyone's feelings first – what about me? Not one person has asked me how I feel. I just listened and said nothing. It's not because I couldn't; I'm just sick of talking. I'm not being heard. The only person who could possibly hurt me now is Sam; I love her so much. I just wish she wouldn't demand I feel like her.

I told Sam that I have no regrets whatsoever and that I'm not condemning Dionne, this is just the best thing for me. For the first time, I am doing what is good for me. Sam told me that I was not a person who can forgive. She said she had to forgive Dad a long time ago for her to move on. In a calm voice, I replied by telling her that she had just hit the nail on the head so to speak. That was exactly what I was doing; ending my relationship with Dionne means I can move on. I do forgive her but that doesn't mean that I have to be around her. I can forgive from afar. I could tell Sam was having none of it. The fact that she even thought I was an unforgiving person hurt like hell. What I really am is a woman, not a child, who won't be bullied into changing my mind – not anymore. If I live to regret my decision, then so be it. Sam expressed her concern about how she will feel on the day of her daughter's christening, and that she was not comfortable with what I have done. She was worried about having me and Dionne both there. I am not a malicious or spiteful person; it's her baby's day. I would never cause a problem or be rude to Dionne. I most certainly won't speak to her. I don't know what she wanted me to say. I can't change what has happened. When I made my choice, I never had Sam in mind. If this makes me selfish, then that's okay. Once again, I couldn't believe my ears. None of this is about me; it's all about her and everyone else.

Tuesday, 8th July 2008

I've been feeling even worse today; I feel completely on my own. I'm scared as hell. Even though I have my sister Lorrinda by my side, I still feel alone. I'm sick of depressing everyone. So now I keep things to myself. I feel as though my head is going to explode. Am I wrong for what I'm doing? I am literally asking God every moment of the day for strength. Why am I being made to feel like this? I have been pulling my hair out, literally, over the past few days. I can fight my dad; I just don't know if I can fight my family. I made an appointment with my doctor and told him how I feel. I told him I did not want antidepressants, I wanted counselling. I have taken medication before. They did work but I want a clear head. I will not drug myself for those who don't give a damn about me. He was very understanding. Hopefully, I will hear from a counsellor in the next few weeks.

Tuesday, 6th August 2008

I received a text message from D.C Tony Weed this afternoon. The text read, "Just want to let you know. Plan to arrest next week. We'll get a better idea within the next few days, so fingers crossed." At first, I laughed, then my heart began to race, I got butterflies in my stomach. I felt strange. The first person to call me was Lorrinda. She was laughing excitedly. Was this really going to happen, after all this time? I'll just have to have faith and wait to see. It's mad; I thought that if ever this day came, I would have all the support of my family. Apart from Lorrinda and close friends, I had no one. No one else in the family wanted to support me. I shouldn't be too surprised. There was no one to help me all those years ago, why should I expect any different now? I realise it's time for me to grow up. It's no one person's fault that it's like this; it's what you get when you have such a dysfunctional family like mine. I look to no one for help now; I will do the hard work alone. I'm not referring to my dad, I mean the hard work of healing me. These people have taken up a lot of my thoughts and a lot of my energy, they will not take up anymore.

Self Help

Wednesday, 7th August 2008

It's 6 am. I have been tossing and turning all night. I have a banging headache; my eyes feel strained and my head feels tense. Finally, I surrender and leave my bed. I grab the nearest piece of paper and a pen and begin to write my thoughts. It's almost as though it was this night that I realise the changes this whole situation has brought out of me.

I have been reading quite a lot; mainly books on therapy for adults who were sexually abused as children. One book, which really hit home for me, is a book called Rescuing the Inner Child by Penny Parks. It took two days for me to read this book; I could not put it down. I found almost all of the answers I have been waiting for, like *who am I? Why do I feel like this? Why did my dad do this? Why do I carry guilt?* It was truly enlightening. I have been made to feel bad for feeling the way I do about my step mum, by those who don't understand me. I have questioned my decision to not want to see her anymore. Penny Parks talks a lot about abused adults and their inner child. I could not understand it at first, so I read it over and over again. A child does not understand the logic, only emotions. It is the adult in me who understands that my past was not normal or right. As a child, I could not express or show my emotions. I had to switch it off when I wanted to scream out not to be touched. I could not refuse when I was younger, there would be consequences. So, a child who is being abused pushes those emotions deep down inside, even the emotions of anger towards those adults who should have protected her.

When that same child grows up, sometimes they keep their emotions buried, which causes a lot of pain and damage without realising it. They begin to self-sabotage through drug abuse, crime or even prostitution. You see these are all ways of hurting yourself. My way of dealing with my pain was self-harm and self-sabotaging. It wasn't until I decided to get help, did all these things about me come to light. Reliving the past brought back the feelings of abandonment, resentment, pain, and new memories of the past.

My inner child was surfacing and I didn't even realise it. My whole world, my every thought and every feeling, were being consumed by him, my abuser. *Am I going mad? Am I losing myself?* I repeatedly asked myself these questions over the next few weeks.

I tried one exercise that I thought might help. You write two letters to yourself. The first letter is from the adult version of the victim. The adult allows the image of herself as a child to become clear as possible. She begins the letter by giving love, information and support, saying all the things the child wanted and needed to hear so much all those years ago. Mine went like this:

Dear Ingrid,

I know you are sad and feeling a tremendous amount of pain and confusion. I know you feel abandoned and let down. Ingrid, I want you to know that whenever you need me, I will be there for you. When your dad calls you in a tone that you are familiar with, and you know you are going to be beaten for being bad, I want you to come to me. I will sit with you and hold you. When your dad tells you, you must touch him and he must touch you, I want you to know I will be there to tell him NO. When your dad threatens you and says you must show him how much you love him by making you do things that make you scared. I will tell you that this is not real love. Real love is what I have for you, Ingrid. I will protect you and make sure he never hurts you again. You do not need to feel abandoned by your family, because I am here for you, with you always. Your dad was wrong to hurt you the way he has. He betrayed you. You are in no way to blame for what he has done; he is the adult; he knows fully what he has done.

Then a second letter, once contact has been made and the child feels reassured. Here it is time to ask your inner child her feelings. And in turn, your inner child will respond.

Dear Ingrid,

I know this must be very hard for you; I would like you to try and write down some of the things that your dad has done to you and how he made you feel. It will be very hard and painful but I want you to know I will be there for you all the way. He can't hurt you now. Do you remember the first time he touched you? When he called you into the bedroom along with your other two sisters, and he made you do things that you didn't want to? The things that scared and confused you. Your dad was wrong for doing this. You were seven years old. He took advantage of you. You were powerless; he took your father-daughter relationship and made it sexual. He then told you it was your secret. It wasn't your secret; it was his secret. His dirty secret that made you feel bad. Well, you are not bad, Ingrid, do not blame yourself. I will help you. I will help you not fear him. He is rubbish.

Child's Response

Hello Ingrid,

I was about six when my dad first touched me. Once Dionne left to go shopping; I was home playing with my two sisters. Dad called us into the bedroom. He told me off because I slept with my knickers on. I felt very dirty. My sisters laughed at me until Dad told them off because they had theirs on as well. Dad told us all we were nasty and we should get undressed. I felt really exposed and scared. I didn't want to do it but Dad made that face, the face that tells me he's angry. I was scared. I wanted to cry but I think if I did he would've hit me. He made me put my face on his willy; he was laughing and making noises. I just wanted it to stop. My little sister sat on the bed looking at me. I wished I could disappear. I loved my dad lots but I didn't want to do this. Not long after, some white stuff came out of his willy, he pulled my head down onto it. I wanted to be sick. I didn't like the smell or the taste. I began to heave. Dad just laughed, he told me that he loved me and that I was his special girl. I wanted to be his special girl. I just wanted him to stop. I never felt comfortable again with him.

Whenever he took me into a room or I was left in a room with him, I was scared. Inside I wanted to scream, but I never did. I didn't want to disappoint him, I wanted him to carry on loving me. I didn't want him to beat me with the belt and tell everyone I was a bad girl when I wasn't. When he told me to stop crying, I would stop immediately or he would take his belt off. I hated when my dad would pick me up by my neck, he would pick me up with his two hands around my neck, lift me off the floor then let go. Dropping me on my back for no reason.

Adult's Response

Dear Ingrid,

Thank you so much, Ingrid, for telling me. You will always be a special girl to me because I really do love you. I will never hurt you. You were right to be scared when he did those evil things to you, he was a scary man. You did what he wanted you to do, Ingrid, because you had to. It's called survival. And you trusted him. If you can't trust your own dad, you can't trust anyone. Well not anymore, Ingrid, you can trust me. You don't need to count on others to help you or shield you. You don't have to hold back the tears; if you want to cry it's okay. You are human, you have feelings. One day you will stop crying. I will cry for you. So, you can rest peacefully without fear that he is coming to use you again. He is a disgusting man who shouldn't be a father. He did all he could to keep your silence. Well, you don't have to be silent anymore. On the outside, he looks clean but, on the inside, he is vile, like an infection; his body is rotten to the bone. You have every right to be angry that your parents failed you. No one has even asked how the abuse has left you feeling. When you get older you will see that touching is okay, so long as you love the person who is touching you. You don't need to feel dirty or guilty, it is natural. You will not be trapped or scared, you have the right to say no. No one can make you do what you don't want to do. You cry all you want to, Ingrid. You are not weak, you are brave.

This is just the start of the letters that I will write to my inner child. I will not believe I have nothing to feel guilty for by writing one letter. It will take many, I'm sure, before I truly believe this. This for me was a great way to comfort myself. Once you get started it really does feel great. It's almost like going back in time to cuddle myself. To see and hear my pain. I always wished as a little girl I would not cry but now I realise, no wonder I cry, for God's sake I couldn't say how I felt because I would get hit. Even my sister, Sam, I know my crying aggravates her; still does to this day. Well, I don't care. I've had it with trying to be who others think I should be, this is who I am.

16th August 2008

I am able to put words to feelings that I haven't used or thought of for years. Fretful – I am feeling very fretful right now, extremely on edge and afraid. I have spent the whole night awake, tossing and turning. I wanted to cry with exhaustion but couldn't, my scalp feels tight and my eyes are burning. For a short moment, I must have drifted off when I heard a noise. I jumped, grabbing my pillow tightly. I was up and down the stairs; checking the children, checking the windows and doors. For the first time in over 20 years, I was weak and afraid of his presence. I lay in my bed afraid of the dark, trying to make sense of the shapes in my room. *Was that him? Is that his silhouette outside my door?* There is a small green light outside my door which is the light from my house alarm. I figured that if it went black and then green again that would mean he had walked past. Bloody hell, am I going mad? Maybe I have gone too far. I can't handle this anymore. Maybe someone in my family has told him what is going on. That's why he wants to get me, before they get him. I can't take feeling vulnerable like this. Maybe I was anxious because of the endless waiting for the police to arrest him. I'm not sure. I need to speak to my doctor because this is seriously affecting my health.

1st September 2008

Holiday in Florida. It's 8:15 pm and I'm in our villa in Florida, just about to make my way down to the water park with the kids. When I receive a missed call from Lorrinda. My heart is pounding. I texted her back and asked her to call me. "He's in custody," she said as soon as she answered. I sat down; I felt confused. I couldn't say how I felt.

"When? What happened? Oh my god I can't believe it," were all the words I could find.

5th September 2009

Age 36. I can't believe it's now been a whole year since I have written in this journal. It will be three days from now that my dad will have another birthday. And three days from now that I first started to write. I feel a bit disappointed because it's taken me so long. In all honesty, I'm actually pissed off with myself. The 8th of September will always be a day for me to remember Dad's birthday and the day I began to write. I have had to block all of this out as it was making me feel ill; I needed time to heal again. Now my trial is about to start, it's creeping back. I haven't told anyone but it's all I've been thinking about. I've got about ten weeks until it starts. I'm scared; scared of what all this might do to me. But still, I have to continue.

11th Nov 2009 will be the start of our trial; everyone is going through the motions. I have a thousand questions; *will I be too upset to get out what I want to say? Will he admit to it?* Will he fight us all the way and use his intellect to crush us? I don't know what I'm talking about right now, my feelings are all over the place. If anything, I need to do this for my kids. Like I have said before, we as people can't help but to judge each other on what we look like from the outside. I believe that this past year I have challenged myself to the max.

Can you believe that I actually got a job with weight watchers? This was a massive achievement for me. There were many times through my training that I wanted to give up, just run away. I knew I wanted to do it but something kept banging away at me telling me I will never be able to but I did. Even though just before each meeting, I would pull out a thousand hairs from my head telling myself I wasn't good enough. They will see right through me; I really am scared and insecure. I was to lead at least thirty women and men four times a week to a massive achievement of their dream of losing weight. All I can say is that if they could see through me, they would be shocked to see how afraid I was of them. I don't think they were afraid of me, but felt they had to answer to me when they had a bad week. I connected with them emotionally. I wanted to help them pinpoint what made them 'comfort eat' to begin with. Everyone, different colours and sizes but beautiful to me. The number of times I had been told off by the caretakers for running my meetings over time. I just couldn't treat them like cattle; it's not always about the sales. I miss them all. I have since left weight watchers. My time was cut short due to a back injury. My manager Michelle told me one thing before I left and that was, "Ingrid, don't be sad or feel low, just remember as one door closes another will open." I hope so. Not sure what will be in store for me yet, I'll just have to wait and see.

Thanks, Michelle xx

The Court Viewing

5th November 2009

As Lorrinda and I drove through the gates of the Snaresbrook Crown Court, I felt overwhelmed and intimidated by the size of the building. I glanced over at Lorrinda, *poor little thing*, I thought. Nervously, I began to laugh. "Oh my God, men in wigs," Lorrinda shouted shuffling around in her seat. I couldn't help but laugh. My stomach began to churn; I felt sick and wanted to go to the toilet.

"How do you feel, Lori?" I asked her.

She just gazed out the window, replying, "Bloody sick." I bit my lip and sighed. I think we both felt off key today. Along with this, Lorrinda was adjusting to her antidepressants, and I was adjusting to my higher dose of 40 mg of fluoxetine. Reality had kicked in; there was no going back. All these months, I've been emotionless due to my medication but not today. I desperately needed the toilet and my palms were sweaty. Looking over at Lorrinda, I could see she was bewildered. She climbed out of the car, I felt concerned for her. After all, she will always be my baby sister. Then it dawned on me that I had experience of talking about my feelings and my past. She had some, but not much and this was far from easy for me or anyone else in this situation. We strolled towards the court in silence; we were met by court security waiting to search us. Lorrinda has a habit of mumbling under her breath when she's nervous. I couldn't understand a word she was saying. Once inside we didn't know where to go or what to do.

"Lorrinda, I need to find a toilet," I told her again.

"Don't leave me, come let's look on the board," she suggested.

"Are you serious?" I asked her. I wanted to stay but my body had to do something else. "I can't Lori, I need to go now," I told her. When I returned from the toilet, I found Lorrinda sitting down in the waiting area, fiddling with her phone. "You, okay?" I asked her, feeling really relieved.

"Yeah, a woman called Hailey will be meeting us, she's Tony's colleague."
I sat down beside her. I couldn't help but wonder who was here for what, what
had all these people done? Maybe they hadn't done anything, maybe they were
here for the same reason as us.

Lorrinda got impatient and went to the information desk. Just as she returned,
a lady called Hailey came to collect us. She seemed very pleasant. We followed
her through the corridors of the court. I'm sure she could tell how nervous we
were. The tour didn't take very long, 30 minutes maybe. Once inside the court,
we were shown where the jury will sit, the judge, the barristers and the public,
but most importantly where Dad will sit and then us. Dad will be behind glass.
Hailey explained to us that there will be screens up when we enter the court and
that everyone but the judge and jury will remain in the court until we are seated.
Hailey was very attentive and caring. I took my seat in the witness chair and took
a deep breath, in a way I tried to savour every moment. For me, this was the most
important thing in my life. I tried to visualise everything. Hailey reassured us
that Dad would not be able to see us at all. There was clearly a lot of support,
this was it, our one and only chance to be heard by those who mattered, I couldn't
afford to get a nervous block. *I can do this,* I said to myself. Lorrinda then took
her place. I know she was overwhelmed; I just wish I could hold her hand when
it's her turn to give evidence.

The Countdown

Maybe I should choose my words carefully, but a countdown is how it feels. Just eight days until it all starts. I wonder what he is thinking. Is he going through what we are going through? I'll never know. Today is a good day. I'm feeling focused; tomorrow may be a different story. Either way I think I'm prepared. After 23 years, how can I not be?

The Trial

The trial was postponed, new date, 16th Nov 2009.

Monday, 16th November 2009

This is it. I had a good night's sleep, all thanks to fluoxetine. The kids were all sorted and my youngest was at breakfast club at 8:15 am. I'm feeling a bit worried about the fact that I feel so numb. I'm not expecting to be called today as Tony did say that it's a lot of legal stuff on the first day, so I expect to go up tomorrow. Around 12:30, Tony came to see us in the witness room with our lawyer – a really nice woman called Gillian – to give us the rundown on what's happening. "Ingrid, we expect to get your evidence by 2 pm," the lawyer told me. Suddenly, I felt overwhelmed. My palms started sweating and my hands began to shake. Inside I was screaming, *I can't do this*. I was nowhere near prepared. I had been to the toilet three times; on the last time, I thought I was going to collapse. My legs just gave way from underneath me as I went to sit on the toilet. I kept going over and over in my head what had happened, my mind felt confused, what if I end up speechless? As the day grew to a close it became apparent to me that I was not going to be called. It was around 3:30 pm that they told me that I would be the first one up tomorrow.

I've just had my dinner and given my children a big hug and kisses, and I am reminded of the reasons why I am doing this. It's not just for me, but for my kids too.

Tuesday, 17th Nov 2009

I got up at 6 am. I'd had a restless night and kept going over and over in my head about what's going to happen today. After a shower, I started to feel even more confused and decided not to take my antidepressants. I need to be completely in touch with what I am feeling I need a clear head. At 9:20 am I arrived at court, where I was met by Lorrinda, Tina and my best friend Kathy. My palms were sweating gallons. Strangely, my heart wasn't racing.

I think that was down to my medication still being in my system. I couldn't help but keep visiting the toilet; I had gone at least four times. At midday, I was called by the voluntary witness staff, "I.R. Dujon." I took a deep breath and sighed. This was it, everyone stood up and we hugged each other. Kathy walked with me down the large corridors. I felt as though I was walking into a death chamber. If I felt like this, I wonder what he was feeling. Maybe nothing. When we reached the doors of courtroom 9, I began to feel nervous but the need to fight was stronger.

Kathy was shown to her seat before me. I waited patiently, looking through the big glass doors, wondering where he was. Rubbing my palms frantically with my tissue, Joy, who was my assigned volunteer, walked ahead of me and showed me where to sit. I glanced around the courtroom before taking my seat in the witness box. This was truly it. No way out now. I swivelled around on my seat like a kid in her classroom chair. Directly behind me was Kathy. She smiled an encouraging smile at me. I could see nothing to my right, as this was where the screens were placed so I couldn't see my dad. To my left were the judge and his clerks, all quite intimidating. And of course, in front were 12 seats for 12 jurors. In front of them was my barrister, and of course his barrister. Doors opened and everyone stood up. I didn't know what to do so I remained seated – not the right move, I know that now. In walked the judge, Judge Lamb. As he walked towards his seat, he gave me a very subtle friendly smile. This was very comforting. He took his seat and then everyone followed. Strangely, Judge Lamb glances at me again. "Are you okay?" he asked me.

"Yes," I replied unsure of his reason for the question. With that response he stood up and walked towards me.

"Please stand, I would like to sit in your seat to make sure everything is in order," he said. I stood immediately; everyone in the court looked surprised. Judge Lamb sat down in my seat and checked the screen was in the right position. "All is in order," he said as he stood and walked back to his chair. "Bring the defendant in," he ordered someone at the back of the court. It was time for Dad to join us. My legs began to shake uncontrollably; my palms and armpits began to sweat.

Once Judge Lamb ordered the defendant in, he then requested the jury to enter. Still swivelling on my seat and obsessively rolling then folding my tissue, the jury entered and took their seats. The court clerk stood in front of me and asked me what holy book I want to swear on. I replied, "The Holy Bible."

"Please hold it up in your right hand and repeat after me," he told me.

I took the bible in my right hand and repeated after him, "I do solemnly swear to tell the whole truth and nothing but the truth so help me God." And then handed it back to him.

"Please sit, Ingrid," he told me, then walked back to his chair. Keeping my eyes firmly fixed on Gillian (My Barrister) I took a deep breath. Gillian was brilliant. She took me through my story slowly and patiently. Her calm manner drew out things that were stored in my mind, that even I didn't know were there. Every so often I would glance over at the jury. There were too many faces for me to focus on so I kept my gaze fixed on Gillian. I told the court that my father had a scar on his penis that ran from top to bottom; I couldn't believe I remembered it. He would tell us to kiss his scar and think of it as a snake. He told us that his first wife had cut his penis because she found out that he was cheating. He always told us that this was the reason why he would never go out with another black woman. There were a lot of tears but this didn't matter to me, this was the last time I would have to tell my story.

The court was then adjourned for lunch at around 1 pm. I was taken to a different room to make sure I would not discuss the case with anyone else. Eating was the last thing on my mind. At exactly 2 pm, I was taken back to court. When Judge Lamb entered, he asked me if I had eaten. I replied, "No." To which he just smiled. The second half of my evidence lasted about half an hour.

"Make sure she eats," Judge Lamb told Kathy as I got up from my seat. I was to be cross-examined tomorrow by Dad's barrister.

Once again, I could not sleep. I kept going over and over everything in my head – was I ready for my dad's defence? I know I'm going to have a fight on my hands. One thing with Dad, he has the gift of the gab.

Wednesday, 18th Nov 2009

Today started off great; I woke up feeling positive. I felt I was ready to fight. I reached the court around 9:30 am and Tony came to see me in the witness room. He had a massive smile on his face. "Ingrid, you aren't going to believe what I found in your care files," he challenged me. Tony rooted through his bag and pulled out a document. "Do you recognise this, Ingrid?" he asked me, handing me this mystery A4 document.

"No," I replied, reading it quickly. As I read, my mouth dropped open. I couldn't believe it. It was a sworn affidavit that I had made to my social worker back in 1986; it was almost a word for word account of the abuse that I had gone through.

"Do you give me your permission, Ingrid, to submit this document to the court?" Tony asked me. We never discussed what was in it; he just wanted to know if I gave my permission.

I said, "Of course, if you think it will help, that's fine." I was more taken aback by the amount of description I had given my social worker. I wondered again, *how could I have said all of this and they still did nothing?*

Tony went into court around 11:30 am and said he would return shortly to collect me when the court is ready. Tony didn't return until 2:30 pm. Tony returned with Gill, our barrister. She told him to wait outside whilst she had a word with us. Something was wrong, we all knew it. Gillian sat facing us, her face looked sad; her efforts to try to disguise it weren't working. Gillian went on to tell us that because Tony had shown me the document before showing the court, Judge Lamb had ordered that the jury be dismissed permanently. We were all horrified, not only does this mean that I will have to do it all again, which was bad enough, but she also went on to say that Tony is deeply upset he had broken down crying because Judge Lamb has held him in contempt of court and taken him off the case. She also explained that Judge Lamb would be writing personally to Tony's superior to log a formal complaint. Lorrinda just broke out into tears. Tony walked in, his face was so distressed. Gillian left us to be with Tony. "Ingrid, I am so, so sorry that this has happened. We did not discuss the document. I just wanted your permission. And now I have messed up so badly, I'm so sorry to you all." Tony broke down right in front of us. We couldn't do this without him, it was too much to bear. I didn't care that I had to give my evidence again. I just wanted Tony in the court with me, we all did. Tony's colleague Hannah would be managing our case from here on out, thank God, we had already met her before. She too was lovely. Tony's tears showed all of us just how passionate about his work he really is.

Thursday, 19th Nov 2009

I can't find the words to explain how I feel today, knowing that I have to give my evidence all over again. I genuinely don't feel as though I have the strength. I feel deflated and insecure; I'm nowhere near as confident as I was on Tuesday. With no hesitation, at 10 am we walked to courtroom number 9. Tony was sitting right outside with his head in his hands. "That's a nice face to see," I smiled as I told the court usher who was walking alongside me. Tony looked up I could clearly see that he felt dreadful for me. Seeing Tony gave me a lift. I smiled at him and said, "It's okay, Tony, honest. I'm just glad you're here." And I meant it; neither of us would be here if it wasn't for him. When everyone else slammed the door in my face, he was there. The same procedure as yesterday; I was sworn in, then came face to face with the new jury. Once again I told my story only this time, I was a lot calmer, I guess you could say I had a test run. Gillian took me through my statement, all of which lasted around one and a half hours. And then Mr Skelly took over.

Mr Skelly is Dad's Barrister. The questions he asked me were quite tame to start. It was clear to me that he didn't have much to go on; after all, his client had set him up for embarrassment. Dad told him lie after lie, it was embarrassing. Shamefully, Skelly skipped past his questions. For a moment, I must have forgotten that he was in fact the enemy so to speak. "Can I put it to you, Ingrid, that you made up all of these allegations against your father because you are indeed jealous of your father's relationship with Dionne?" he said, peering over his glasses with a stupid smug look on his face.

I laughed; now I realise he's the enemy. I laughed because it was so ridiculous. "Are you serious?" I asked him, I had to double-check that this man was for real. "What rubbish," I snapped back. My heart raced and my palms sweaty. My leg was shaking ten to a dozen. "Everyone knows why my dad was with Dionne and not my mum. My mum was an alcoholic, Dionne was a good wife," I continued.

"Am I also right in saying to you, Ingrid, that you were angry with your dad because he didn't go and beat up Carl, your mother's husband? And that you blamed Carl for your mother's death," he looked down at his papers pretending to be doing something important. What bloody crap. I couldn't believe my ears.

"First of all, I did not expect my dad to go and beat up Carl. When my mum needed us, my sister Sam went and took her from him and she came to live with me. Secondly, no I did not blame Carl for my mother's death. My mum died from cancer. What I did blame Carl for was the way that he neglected her before she died." I was furious.

Just when I thought he had given up and realised that my dad was taking him for a fool, he continued, "Isn't it true Ingrid that you did in fact make all of this up because you had seen your dad and Carl talking together at the hospital?" Once again, I laughed.

"How could I have seen them talking at the hospital when we had an injunction out on Carl? He could not come anywhere near her." I just wanted to lunge across and slap him, looking at me and judging me.

"Tell me, Ingrid, did you watch a TV show presented by Esther Rantzen back in 1982 about child abuse, and that's where you learned about the effects of child abuse, and therefore make note of it? Then used this information to make fake allegations of child abuse?"

That was it, I broke down. I screamed back, "No that is not true. How can Esther Rantzen show such explicit information about child abuse acts? And after 23 years I still use the same story, why would I?" Now it's my turn, I thought; you will listen to me. "Why would I wait 23 years to bring this all up again, why would I put myself through this when I'm quite happy with five children?" I paused for a second and took a deep breath. I grabbed my statement from in front of me and held it up to the court. "How can a child make a statement like this and no one do anything?" With that statement, I felt a release. A long gut-full sigh of pain. Tears poured down my face. For the first time, I was heard. Finally, I had told my story to the most important people who really mattered. Now there is no more I can do; just pray.

Friday, 20th Nov 2009

Tina gave her evidence. I know that halfway through she ran out of the courtroom. It wasn't easy by any means for any of us. Kathy ran after her and told her that we had all come too far and that by walking out he wins again. Tina took a short break and then returned. Tina told her story.

Monday, 23rd Nov 2009

Lorrinda gave her evidence today. Lorrinda was, as far as I knew, hard as nails. Mr Skelly's cards were marked and she had it in for him. Even with that determination, Lorrinda broke down. But she did it, and she gave Mr Skelly a rough ride, just like he had given her.

Tuesday, 24th Nov 2009

The court had called Lorrinda's nan, Beryl. D.C Weed had given Beryl a nickname; he called her the Shreddie's Nanny, of the adverts. Poor Beryl, this name will always stick with her now. Beryl did really well. Mr Skelly didn't go too hard on her as far as I know. The court also called Hannah to give Tony's evidence, she too did very well.

Wednesday, 26th Nov 2009

Lorrinda's husband, was named Ed, he had to give evidence this morning. Ed was no mug; he gave Mr Skelly all the answers he needed and no more. He defended his wife. What was strange was that neither Ed nor my dad had ever seen each other before. By lunchtime, it was Dad's turn to take the stand. The wait seemed like forever. He's very cunning and smart. Will he outwit the jury? Tina and I sat patiently in the waiting room, waiting to hear news about Dad's evidence. When Kathy, Hannah, Tony and Val returned to us they were all laughing. "What happened?" Tina and I asked them.

I sat there in my seat at the far right of the room, I felt like I was gazing in from the window. There was panic and screams of pain being released as together, Tony, and Val, all shouted, "He got TEN and a HALF years!" I just remember looking on and seeing Sammie fall into her chair and cry. Then everyone began to cry. I was numb. It was the strangest feeling. I was surprised; I was happy but also quite sad. I wished I wasn't but couldn't help it.

As the reality hit me, I could hear Val say over and over, "Inx, he's been locked up, Inx, you have done it." He was kneeling down in front of me but it was all a blur.

I stupidly laughed and said, "I know." Tony looked over at me. I felt so silly; I wanted to cry like everyone else but I couldn't. I couldn't even squeeze one tear out. Was it really over?

That was both a strange and wonderful day. When I got home, I stood in the lounge and announced to the kids what had happened. It's funny because in a mad way they almost looked blank. Like, "What's the big deal?" Little did they know, this was for them. So they know no matter who you are, you must be accountable for what you do. I had a rough night's sleep with Val on my mind. The way I feel right now, I don't even want one picture of my mum in my house. Even Dionne has disturbed me with her lack of common sense. She too has a lot to answer for. Tony called shortly after the trial had concluded. He asked me to come into his office in Chadwell Heath to discuss my big brother Val and elder sister Sam's case as they both were inspired to come forward and make a statement. Maybe this was it, maybe I just needed to make a statement in their favour, to support their allegations. I did meet with Tony shortly after the trial and agreed to do whatever I could to help Sam and Val move forward with their trials, although the thought of even being a witness for them seemed unbearable to be sat in a courtroom again and cross-examined. It didn't matter it would be worth it to see them fight and finally get closure.

Almost two years had passed since the last trial, Tony worked endlessly getting all he needed in preparation for Sam and Val's upcoming trial.

9th September 2011

Age 38. It was so nice to see Tony's friendly face again; this guy has changed my past and my future in a way that he could not possibly imagine. After catching up on how life has been treating us since the trial, Tony put on his serious face. "Right, madame," he said, gesturing for me to take a seat in his office. "Ingrid, what I am about to talk to you about, I just want you to remember that sometimes the finer details don't always change things," he said. I was so confused. What is he talking about? "Ingrid, when you gave your evidence, you said a lot more than you thought you did. You see, you told the court that on one occasion you began to bleed after your dad had abused you," he continued. I now felt completely uncomfortable, this isn't about me making a supporting statement for Val and Sam; this was about me. I began to wiggle in my seat uncomfortably. "Ingrid, do you remember telling the court about this?" he asked.

"Yes, I do," I replied, wondering where he is going with this.

"Can you tell me what happened again once you realised you were bleeding?" Tony asked while picking up his pen and hovering it above his notepad. I began to explain what had happened.

"Well, I remember I was in quite some pain the next morning when I woke up. There was only me and Sam home, my dad and Dionne had left early to go somewhere. I remember Sam teasing me because I thought I had started my period. Dionne always had a phone book by the house phone with her friend's numbers in it. Right now I can't remember where they went but I did know then. I called her and started off by telling Dionne to promise me that what I am going to tell her, she shouldn't tell my dad because I knew that if he knew I had my period, he would touch me even more. I didn't tell Dionne my reasons for saying this. Dionne promised and said I was being silly. I explained to Dionne that I thought I had started my period. She laughed and I was young for my period as I was only 10 at the time. Dionne told me to go into her bedside drawer and take out a sanitary towel. I only bled that day until the evening. I didn't actually start my period until I was 13 or 14 years old."

As I repeated what I had said in court I started to cry; I realised exactly where Tony was going with this. I broke down and said, "No, no, no. Tony, I don't want you to speak anymore."

"I'm so sorry, Ingrid, but to the court and to us here, what you have said is more like a disclosure of rape." There it was. I cried uncontrollably and Tony tried to comfort me. "Ingrid, I'm so sorry, but you have to look at it like this, it's more of a legal fact. This doesn't mean you have to change the way you have dealt with your abuse," he tried to explain but I cut him off.

"No Tony. I got by because I always told myself, at least he never had full sex with me." I felt disgusted to the core.

"Ingrid, you have always stated your dad did not penetrate you fully and maybe he truly never did, but your body was that of a child. Even a slight penetration would cause a young child to bleed, so keep telling yourself what you have done all this time so you can deal with this, that it was just abuse and not rape. In this country, any penetration in any hole, so to speak, on the human body is considered rape. Therefore, Ingrid, this takes our case to a next level. We want to charge your dad with rape. The rape of you, Sam and Valentine."

My Statement

14th September 2011

I went to see Sarah at Romford Child Protection. I gave my video evidence. I did feel quite stupid. What's so big about this? Abuse is abuse, isn't it? I not only feel vulnerable but I also feel dirty, which makes me physically sick and ashamed. I spoke to Sam and we both discovered that we both have gone through the same abuse. Rape. I really wish Tony wasn't on holiday. I need to speak to him about all of this. Am I able to go through another trial?

The second trial was set at Basildon Crown Court in 2012.

A Love Letter to a 13-Year-Old Girl

Dear Lorrinda,

Guess who?

You are wonderful and truly sweet and kind. Precious and priceless.

Stay as you are always.

This I say to you below;

WHEN STORMY NIGHTS ARE PAST

SHALL GENTLE HEART BE DISTURBED

I THINK OF YOU EVERYDAY

SLEEP I CANNOT

WITH YOU ON MY MIND

YOU ARE MY ONE AND ONLY,

MY LOVE IS ALL I HAVE; LOVE IS ALL I CAN GIVE.

There is a question here: can you find it and give me your answer?

Above is a letter that has been typed in the same layout as the original letter, which had been sent to my younger sister when she was thirteen years old from our father. We had all received one at some point in our childhood, thankfully Lorrinda kept hers and it was used as evidence. He was careful not to sign it but not careful enough as he wrote in his own handwriting.

Signs

A child or young person, who may be subjected to sexual abuse may not feel safe or feel that they are able to confide in an adult or professional person, out of fear or judgment.

These feelings of self-blame, guilt and self-loathing will have an effect internally.

Children and young people display a number of signs that they cannot understand or be able to express how they are feeling.

Children may become:

Irritable, tearful or clingy.

Have difficulty sleeping, waking up in the night.

Start bedwetting.

Bad dreams.

Young people may:

Lack confidence to try new things, or seem unable to face simple everyday challenges.

Hard to concentrate.

Problems sleeping or eating.

Angry outbursts.

Negative thoughts, like thinking bad things are going to happen.

Avoiding everyday activities i.e. going out, going to school, socialising and being around friends.

Abuse can affect the physical and mental health, of children and young people in long, and short term throughout their lives.

Children and young people demonstrate harmful behaviour as a way of coping with their feelings.

Self-harm.

Drug and alcohol misuse.

Being tearful.

Risk-taking activities or risks with their own lives.

Changes in eating and sleeping.

Self-sabotage in the following ways; Becoming withdrawn, spending a lot of time on their own. Avoiding friends and family, Low mood and lack of self-esteem or blaming themselves for what happened to themselves, outbursts of anger or risky behaviour like drinking and drugs.

They may develop eating disorders, panic attacks and feeling nervous or being on edge all the time.

www.ingramcontent.com/pod-product-compliance
Lightning Source LLC
Chambersburg PA
CBHW060501290526
45791CB00001B/211